# *Always A Servant,*
# *Never A Slave*

Rousell Thomas Jr.

ISBN 978-1-0980-7692-4 (paperback)
ISBN 978-1-0980-7693-1 (digital)

Copyright © 2021 by Rousell Thomas Jr.

All rights reserved. No part of this publication may be reproduced, distributed, or transmitted in any form or by any means, including photocopying, recording, or other electronic or mechanical methods without the prior written permission of the publisher. For permission requests, solicit the publisher via the address below.

Christian Faith Publishing, Inc.
832 Park Avenue
Meadville, PA 16335
www.christianfaithpublishing.com

Cover Illustration by Ashley Woodbury
www.3woodstudios.com

Printed in the United States of America

Dedicated to the *legacies* of the greatest African-American icons (like the late Harriet Tubman, Sojourner Truth, Frederick Douglas, etc.), who **both** *personally endured* the horrors and bitter *atrocities* of ***slavery*** in America, and still, internally *resolved* and *sacrificed their lives* to place the: *well-being, freedom and advancement of their people (race) above* their own personal safety and preservation; to the late Reverend Edward Washington Sr. born in 1887, only twenty-four years after President Abraham Lincoln's 1863 *Emancipation Proclamation*, one of the first-generation *Negroes* to live in the *deep South*, while this country struggled to implement and uphold: the Executive Order (law) to *abolish* slavery and ***free*** *ALL slaves*. As such, he (my maternal grandfather) started his life in the *hellish fire* of the darkest, most treacherous and dangerous period ever endured by any ***free*** *Negro* in the United States of America; to both underline{known} Civil Rights icons (like Thurgood Marshall, Martin Luther King Jr., Medgar Evers, Rosa Parks, etc.); and countless, ***anonymous*** heroes, who lived as *servants* and gave their lives for the cause of: *freedom and justice for all* people; to my *Lord and Savior* **Jesus Christ**, who *called* me to a life of *servanthood* **(service),** and (finally) to my **parents and grandparents**, teachers, mentors, pastors, other spiritual leaders and saints (like the late Rev. Edward Washington Sr., the late Alberta Washington, Rousell Thomas Sr., the late Virginia C. Thomas, the late Ivory Thomas Sr., the late Kate H. Hartman, the late Mrs. IdaBelle Clemmons, the late Mrs. Laura Smith, the late Mrs. Juanita Clark, the late Mr. Ivory Span, the late Mrs. Ruth Span, Mrs. Rosa Butler, the late Mrs. Annie Mae Carr, the late Mrs.

Viola Harvey; *Pastors*: the late Rev. James Otis Sr., Bishop Harry L. and Sara Williams, Rev. Ivan T. Harris, Rev. Silvia Harris, Bishop Richard L. and Lady Adele Johnson, Bishop George Searight Jr. and Lady Mary Searight, Apostle Steven W. Banks, Apostle Charlie B. Ammons, Prophet Vikki Ammons, Pastor Samuel A. and Lady Rose Thompson; my aunts and uncles, Mrs. Queen Pope and others), who have all encouraged, groomed, developed, ministered, *poured* (imparted) into, and prayed for me (over the last fifty-eight years). I **THANK GOD** *for* them (you); and THANK THEM (YOU) ALL! (Only GOD knows **ALL** of their names!)

    I (also) humbly acknowledge the pure (**genuine**) *faith, inner strength* and *perseverance* of all those men and women, who were empowered by GOD, even in the midst of personally experiencing the *horrific atrocities* of living the daily rigors of **slavery** in the United States. Yet they focused above (and beyond) their personal circumstances: to see their true *calling*, purpose, duty, and cause, that was much *greater* than themselves. Even in their *physical reality*, their belief (**FAITH**) in GOD gave them the passion, motivation, determination and *fuel* that propelled them to**: live (strive), dream, fight, climb, sacrifice, and (even *die*) to CONQUER and WIN**, not for themselves; but, to ensure the (future) *FREEDOM and security for their children*, grandchildren, and ALL *unborn* generations to come. It was this same **Supernatural Power**, greater than themselves, that (undoubtedly) had to be their *sustaining* force, through their *darkest* days and most *dire* struggles.

# CONTENTS

Foreword ..................................................................7

Preface ....................................................................9

Chapter 1: Developing a Different Spirit ...................13

Chapter 2: Model *Biblical* Servants ............................16

Chapter 3: The *Model* Servants *In My Life* .................35

Chapter 4: Always a Servant.......................................81

Chapter 5: *Whose Servant Are You?*..........................216

# FOREWORD

Over the last twenty-three years, I have had the honor and privilege of serving beside and leading with Rousell Thomas. In all of my years in ministry and leadership, I have not encountered such a vessel of serving. This servant-leader is an angel in disguise sent by God to serve His people.

This mighty man of God is an Evangelist in Restoration Christian Church of Virginia, but his leadership and influence extends to multiple ministries in the Hampton Roads Region and beyond. I have witnessed him endure hardships as a good soldier, but never has he complained about serving. Rousell Thomas is a rare gem in the Kingdom of GOD. He knows his assignment, and he is not a slave to anyone but a servant to all.

This Evangelist has not just written a book that is a good read, but he has chronicled some practical and insightful strategies that will help every reader understand that serving is a gift and a mandate from the Lord. Serving moves the believer from a selfish will to a selfless will in the order of Jesus Christ Himself.

This awe-inspiring book will provoke you to reclaim your passion and joy for serving not only in your local church, but also in your family, community, government, and social venues. Mr. Thomas is a champion for serving the elderly; therefore, it is not surprising to me that he has captured the essence of serving those who are at times lonely, isolated, absent of support or just need an empathic listener to hear them out.

In his book, *Always a Servant, Never a Slave*, this author will mesmerize some readers with his compassion for serving and provoke others to look for opportunities to be a blessing to someone else.

God has and continues to allow Mr. Thomas to serve people across multiracial, ethnic, gender, age, and social backgrounds. He is a man of integrity who practices what he preaches on a daily basis.

My love and appreciation for Rousell Thomas is second to none. Through this, his initial literary offering, you will easily see why my admiration for him and his assignment to the body of Christ is so profound.

As you read *Always a Servant, Never a Slave*, you will come in contact with the awesome vessel in whom I have come to know over the last twenty-three years in an up close and personal way; not only through ministry, but through life publicly and privately.

**Always a Servant, Never a Slave** is a practical and insightful read. The aim of this book is not to bring information, although we need it. It's not to bring counseling, although it is necessary. Its aim is to bring the reader into a closer and personal relationship with Christ in every arena of life but especially serving.

I recommend this book with my highest recommendation and I endorse this author with the highest of endorsements. Congratulations on writing this necessary and masterful book!

Charlie B. Ammons,
Apostle and General Overseer
Restoration Christian Church of Virginia

# PREFACE

As far back as we can look into the history of *civilization*, the evidence of physical *Slavery* (bondage) of men or groups of people can be seen. In the United States alone, the *import (influx), transport and enslavement* of people from **Africa** (into this country) was a reality between 1619 and 1863. During this timeframe, *a race of people* (segment of humanity) was systematically stripped of its: freedom, identity, rights, culture, families, *way of life* and (even) their *physical* lives. These people were bought and sold like cattle, chattel or any other property, to be owned, controlled, oppressed, victimized and even murdered by men, who purchased (*owned?*) them. Those enslaved prior to 1863 had **no** *choice* in the matter! Some **negroes** (people) of African origin in the **Deep South** and other southern states (states of *Alabama, Florida, Mississippi, Louisiana, Texas, Georgia, South Carolina, Arkansas,* North Carolina, Tennessee, and Virginia) did not know (discover) that they were already *officially freed* until June 19, 1865, which was roughly two years after President Abraham Lincoln had already signed and delivered the **Emancipation Proclamation** (abolishing slavery) in 1863—*freeing all slaves.* Still (**today**) in 2018, more than 155 years after the fact, we can still see the *deep rooted*, negative (*evil*) and *debilitating* effects (prejudices, injustices, *racial profiling, devaluing,* false imprisonment, murdering, etc...) still lingering, in our society, since the 1960s *Civil Rights* Movement and before.

The second form and 2018 version of *servitude* that exists in our country's **Democracy**, both <u>requires</u> and <u>allows</u> individuals and groups of people to be *elected* (voted) into official positions of *author-*

*ity* (*offices* of government) by the same citizens **(people)**, whom those officials are elected to *represent* and ***serve.***

> *Even the son of man (JESUS) did <u>not</u> come to be served; but, to **serve others** and **to give his life** (a ransom) for many.* (**MARK 10:45 NIV/KJV**)

The **objective** of this book is to inspire, provoke and empower readers, of both this current and future generations, to realize, embrace, and demonstrate (*walk in* and *live out*) true FREEDOM! This book has been written, in an attempt to accomplish that objective, as I address and shed some light upon the premise of whether (or not) a person can experience ***Freedom (While) In Servitude***? TODAY, a person's ability to realize true *Freedom*, in every area (arena) of his/her life, is absolutely within one's grasp, if and when that individual can: develop, demonstrate and epitomize that *true **servant's spirit* (attitude)**. YOU can go through your *individual* life: (***serving***) as a *servant*; or you can decide to merely ***exist***—by serving as a ***slave***! *It's your **choice**!*

What made (both) those historic *icons* (famous) and the *anonymous* servants **Great**, whom I dedicated this book to, was the fact that they ***chose*** to **live** their daily lives, as willing ***Servants (of GOD),*** instead of mere **"*slaves*"** to men! It was never just about themselves; regardless of: where they were physically located; what they did not *have*; or what they were not **allowed** to *do*. Their *singular* perspective was **not**: maybe (one day), after I *get to freedom* or when I *strike it rich* (then) maybe I'll help someone else. **NO!** Instead, it was always about**:** what could they do ***now*** (right ***then*** and ***there***) to *serve GOD*, by encouraging, helping, strengthening and uplifting others, around them. (Even, while they (themselves) were in physical *bondage* (slavery), oppressed, poor, uneducated, etc.)

Their *greatness* was their Spirit! The **Spirit** of GOD (within them) was their <u>greatness</u>!

Their greatness was: in their <u>giving</u>, in their <u>sacrificing</u>, in their <u>helping</u> others, and in their <u>serving</u> (Him). It was in their daily *living*. They lived (greatly) each day, as if it were their last; until (eventually), it actually was their **last** (physical) day on this earth. To describe this *greatness* that they possessed, Pastor Henry Wynn (of Kampala, Uganda, in Africa) would tell you that:

> *"They were (\*like) The* **<u>Wind</u>**! *No one could tell from where (which way) they had come or where they were going to (next)."* (Scripture Reference: **JOHN 3:8 NIV/KJV**)

Therein lies the secret to why the *slave catchers* were <u>not</u> able to *capture* them; nor, could any *opposition* or earthly government hinder them (or stop their movement/cause).

So even after they (themselves) had *escaped* and gained physical **Freedom**, they constantly and continuously were compelled (had to) ***go back*** or **march, etc**. (into the *hostile* environments) to ***free* others**! (<u>Note</u>: Even at the risk of being killed or recaptured themselves.)

Most people—who were *observers or contemporaries* (in their lifetime) or you (\**Now*) reading or looking back (in 2018–2020 *hindsight*)—would focus on those elements of *risk* or *danger* involved, and question their choice(s) to ***do*** it, under those conditions. However, ***Wisdom*** says to us (*now*), that it was their very <u>willingness</u> **to serve** and ***DO*** (under those conditions) that really **transcended** them—from simply *risking* their lives—to actually *living* (fulfilling) their lives! Those known and *unnamed*, great **servants** were *always **free***; and they had been chosen and sent to share (impart) their **Freedom** with (into) **others**, in this world.

**HARRIET TUBMAN**
born a *slave, as: Araminta Ross, on March 6, 1822 in Dorchester County, MD.

**FREDERICK DOUGLASS**
born *into slavery as: Frederick Augustus Washington Bailey in February 1818, in Talbot County, MD.

CHAPTER 1

# Developing a Different Spirit

On Sunday, August 21, 2016, Pastor Wilburforce Bezudde, who is originally from Uganda and *pastor* of his church in Stockholm, Sweden, visited and preached to our ministry in Newport News, Virginia. During his sermon, Pastor Wilburforce made the statement that GOD, in scripture, sometimes identifies Himself with an *Eagle* and the *Lion* (i.e., the *LION of The Tribe of Judah*). Pastor Wilburforce (then) ask two questions: What makes the *lion*: the *King of The Jungle*? And what makes an eagle: the King over all other birds?

Although the Lion is **not** the *fastest, biggest, smartest*, nor *strongest* animal (in the jungle), all other animals there, and even humans, recognize the Lion, as the *King*. The lion possesses a ***spirit* (attitude)** of *ferociousness* that no other animal can match. Therefore, its power and authority to reign (identity and recognition as *King*) stems from his superior and dominant **spirit**. Likewise, the Eagle possesses the most phenomenal vision, power and strength of any flying creature, which allows it to fly both through and above fierce storms (*hurricanes*). Eagles also have the capacity to *see* a rodent (on the ground), from a height of five miles up in the sky; thus, an eagle has the ability to *view* things from the ***highest (possible) perspective***.

Lastly, **GOD** (himself) described a man (*Caleb*) as: "my servant Caleb, because he had *another **(different)** spirit* within him, and hath *followed me fully* (**whole-heartedly**)." (**Reference both of these**

**Bible scriptures: NUMBERS 13:25-33 and NUMBERS 14:20-24 KJV/NIV)**

When you study people in the Bible, who had a *different spirit* like (Joshua, Joseph, David and JESUS), your focus and attention will be drawn to how they: *think*, *talk*, *live*, *pray*, and *fight*. So what does it mean for a man or woman to **have a *different spirit*** (from GOD's perspective/viewpoint)? It means to**:** have the Spirit of GOD; walking and operating under the power, influence and focus of GOD; following *whole-heartedly* after GOD; to make every decision based on GOD's *(Higher) perspective***;** to *fight* from a higher perspective**;** to *fight* (to defeat or destroy) the evil, wicked and negative spirit (*operating within* or behind the man), while **not** *destroying* the man (or person). This *different* **spirit** must be developed, within an individual (over time), as he or she consistently faces, lives through and overcomes the issues/injustices, struggles, challenges, and *storms* of life.

Now at fifty-eight years of age, I am—and have always been—a *Servant*; but I have never been a *Slave*! So what is (or makes) the *difference* between a true *servant* vs. a *slave*? The same *Different Spirit*/ (Attitude) that distinguishes the lion and eagle from other animals, also distinguishes and epitomizes the difference between a willing *servant* and a *slave*. Clearly, these two are NOT the same. We must recognize, identify and understand this irrefutable *difference*, in order to *expound* upon the concept or question of whether *Freedom (can or does exist, while) in servitude*, or whether a person can *be free*, while *serving*. The word *servitude* denotes or indicates a state or condition of:

(1) slavery (*bondage*)—where someone *owns* you or another person(s) or someone *belongs* to someone (as they would own land, animals or property); a *dark, bitter, oppressive and dehumanizing, hopeless* state of being; or (2) being required to perform certain *duties* of a *servant,* maybe *menial* task or some other tasks (like an *elected* position or *hired official*: such as President, Governor, Mayor, or police officer). Unequivocally, I say: *YES*; there can be and absolutely already (now) is: <u>*FREEDOM in the midst of Servitude,*</u> when and if, the individual (person) in that condition (position) of servitude has the *right* **spirit** (attitude).

A true ***servant*** has this ***different spirit*** that (first) makes him or her <u>*willing*</u>; then, that same ***willingness*** (to serve) segues or leads (secondly) into being: <u>***obedient***</u>. His/her *willingness to <u>serve</u>* is based upon and stems from one's commitment, loyalty, love and/or faithfulness to the person/people whom he/she is *serving*; to the duty/ responsibilities of the position (job); or simply, to one's *Spiritual <u>relationship</u>* with GOD.

And the Bible scripture clearly states that, "If ye be (**<u>both</u>**) *willing* and *obedient*, you shall eat the good of the land" (ISAIAH 1:19 KJV).

In contrast, a ***slave*** is ***beaten*** into ***doing*** what he/she does. The *spirit* (and/or ***will***) of the *slave* has been crushed (broken) by his/her *oppressors*, until the slave (eventually) succumbs to living a *broken*, *futile*, *defeated* and *hopeless* life**;** and, if he/she gets the opportunity to run—they're gone! Ironically, the next closest *kin* (similarity) to being a slave, would be a ***free*** person who has been <u>elected</u> into a position and/or <u>*hired*</u> (*paid*) to fulfill a job; however, that individual ***does not***: care about, nor has any genuine regard, concern, nor loyalty to the people that he/she is responsible to *serve*, or the duty/honor for the position he/she holds, nor the oath he/she has taken. This person (a *hierling*) is**:** *just in it for* the money or whatever *perks* they can get, while the *gig* lasts. Therefore, he or she **will <u>never</u>** (*personally*) <u>*sacrifice*</u> anything of their own; have **no** dedication or <u>*commitment*</u>, nor have any *<u>intention</u>* of faithfully fulfilling the duties/responsibilities of the position (job), which he or she holds.

In conclusion these two, the ***Servant*** and the ***Slave***, are <u>NOT</u> the same; because, they possess ***two*** **different** *spirits* (*attitudes*): mind-sets, perspectives, motivations, *experiences*… **<u>REALITIES</u>**!

# CHAPTER 2

# Model *Biblical* Servants

As I researched the *Bible* scriptures to find people, who **served GOD** with a *different* **spirit,** these individuals stood out. I refer to them as <u>model</u> (or ideal) ***servants***. GOD has created every (<u>each</u>) one of us for a *particular* ***Purpose*** (which HE has ordained for us); with a *specific* (Objective) ***Mission***; and a *predetermined* ***Process***, consisting of a life-long series of ***assignments***. Each (every) individual <u>assignment</u> represents a ***defining*** moment in our (*spiritual*) **growth and maturation**, within that process. And while there are obviously thousands of (*individuals*) persons detailed throughout the Bible, I have highlighted a <u>selected</u> (small) group, who (*in the scriptures*) consistently <u>epitomized</u> the characteristics that are (both) required of and desired in all great and loyal ***servants***.

> *"Moreover, it is required in stewards, that a man be found faithful."* (**1 CORINTHIANS 4:1-2 KJV**)

> *"Now, it is required that those who have been given a trust must prove faithful."* (**1 CORINTHIANS 4:1-2 NIV**)

I have selected the following **seven** *servants*, as some of those, who**:** (1) ***remained faithful to GOD and His calling***, <u>above</u> *every-*

*one* and *everything* else; (2) **embraced** and **remained true to** his/her (*GOD-given*) **identity** versus (vs.) the rejections/opinions of men, issues/*pressures* of life or natural desires; (3) **clung to (completed)** his/her (*GOD-ordained*) **process** vs. *aborting* their process(es), despite associated hardship, tribulations, perils, threats of death, etc.; (4) **never (ever)** falsely *accused, walked away from* or **rebelled** *(turned) against* **GOD;** and (5) ***fulfilled*** their (*GOD-ordained*) **Purpose** and ***accomplished*** their **Missions**, while *completing* their *assignments (which defined them)* versus *settling* for bribes, *worldly* pleasure of *lusts, promised* rewards or praises of men, etc.

The first *ideal **servant***, that I want to highlight, is **Joseph** (the younger son of Jacob, the father whom GOD later re-named *Israel*). Joseph's life can be clearly seen in the last thirteen chapters **(chapters 37 and 39–50)** of the Book of **Genesis**, the *very first* of sixty-six books in the Bible. From the very beginning, Israel (Joseph's father) loved Joseph dearly; because he was a special son (chosen of GOD) and born in his father's *old age*. **GOD's** special *gift (anointing)* was upon and ***His presence*** was with Joseph, as a young boy. Joseph recognized that he was *gifted*, through the ***dreams (visions)*** that GOD showed him; although, he did not fully understand (his *purpose, calling, or mission*) yet. Israel could already see, that Joseph was more reliable and trustworthy than his other (*older*) sons. Joseph's father made (gave) him a special coat, so the older brothers perceived that their father loved Joseph more than them. Joseph's anointing was a **_blessing_** that gained him immediate (early) *favor* and *trust* of his father. At the same time, it ***appeared*** to be a *curse*, that caused his older brothers to: be jealous (envious), despise and even **hate** him (their younger brother); because, the brothers did **not** recognize, understand, nor appreciate Joseph's **gift**.

At the age of **seventeen years old**, Joseph's brothers threw him in a pit and discussed killing (*murdering*) him; however, they finally decided to sell him (to foreign *merchantmen/slave traders*), who were passing by, and deceived their father into believing that an animal had killed Joseph (his favorite son). These *traders* were bound for Egypt; and when they arrived in Egypt, they sold Joseph (again), to Potiphar (an officer of Pharaoh's Army and *captain of the guards* (of the King's prison and Palace). As Joseph faithfully and whole-heartedly **served** in this *earthly master's* house, Potiphar quickly *saw* (recognized/realized) that **the LORD was with Joseph**, causing **everything** *that Joseph did* to **prosper** in his hands. Thus, Joseph found *grace* and *favor* in the master's (Potiphar's) sight; and he made Joseph **overseer** over his house, and **entrusted** (**everything**) *that he owned into Joseph's hand* (placed under Joseph's *care* or *charge*).

With Joseph in charge, Potiphar did not have to personally concern himself with anything, except to eat the food that was served to him.

Over time, Potiphar's wife also recognized how prosperous Joseph was. She became *infatuated* with (and **lusted** continuously) for Joseph. At every turn (opportunity), she manipulated situations and excuses to order others slaves, to leave the house, so that she could attempt to seduce (entice) and *rape* Joseph; however, Joseph consistently and continuously rejected her advances. *Joseph's sincere loyalty and dedication to GOD, enabled him to maintain his character, integrity and right standing With GOD.* Therefore, he *refused* to *sin against GOD* (*with* another man's wife); no matter how *persistently* she pressured, pursued, and tried to *entrap* him for about ten years. (Ironically.) In response to Joseph's final *rejection* (of her), Potiphar's wife ***falsely accused*** Joseph *of **attempting to rape** her*

As a result of her *charge* against Joseph, her husband (Potiphar)—in a state of *blind* **rage**—had Joseph thrown into the Pharaoh's (King's) palace **prison**.

> "And we know that **all things work together for good** to them that Love GOD, to them who are the called according to his purpose." (**ROMANS 8:28 KJV**)

> "And we know that **in all things GOD works for the good** of those who Love him, who have been called according to his purpose." (**ROMANS 8:28 NIV**)

Therefore, even *while in prison*, **GOD** was <u>with</u> *Joseph*. And Joseph remained true to form; proved himself to be faithful to GOD and **GOD's *process*** for his life. Although, Joseph was clearly innocent (of the charge), he **<u>refused</u>** *to play **the victim** (card)*. The *Captain of the guards* (**jailer**), after recognizing his *anointing* and integrity, placed Joseph *in charge* of **<u>all</u>** the *other prisoners*. So even there, Joseph gained the *favor, trust* and grace of everyone, no matter <u>where</u> he was (physically located). He always maintained the ***freedom to BE himself*** and to ***DO the right thing, in every situation*** (opportunity). His *personal **gift,*** of experiencing **dreams (*visions*)** and ***interpretation*** (*divine* **revelation** of the <u>meaning</u>) of ***others'*** dreams, was later <u>**needed**</u>, recognized, appreciated and remembered (by other prisons). This same ***gift*** would, eventually, gain him access—(**at thirty years old**)—into the Pharaoh's (King's) palace.

**GOD's *process*** (for Joseph's life) used <u>unfair</u> treatments of (*personal*) *hatred/rejections of brothers (family)/men, slavery, false accusations and imprisonment,* which (also) took Joseph through <u>undesirable</u> duty assignments (*steps along the way*) from**:** *the pit*; being sold into *bondage* (as a ***transport*** mechanism); a second, long-term tour (ten years) of *slavery* in Potiphar's house (in Egypt); being ***falsely accused*** of *attempted rape*; which additionally, resulted in *three years in prison*. He was required (by GOD) to face and endure **ALL** of these **hardships** (*personal **wilderness tests***), along with having the (daily) relationship with his father *stripped away from him*, by his own brothers, before he could (eventually) be *elevated* to that <u>*ultimate*</u> position and assignment (as Governor over all of Egypt), eventually fulfilling his (*GOD-ordained*) **PURPOSE** and **MISSION**. The scriptures (*in* **Genesis *chapters 41–50*****),** clearly *disclose* that GOD's plan, *calling* and intent (for Joseph) was to***:** transplant* him into Egypt and to ***elevate*** Joseph to the position of *second in command* (or second most powerful man in all of Egypt), for the purpose of ***saving*** (*not only*) his family (*Israelites*); but, he was responsibility ***for the survival of countless families throughout Egypt and the Middle East Region*** (from the famine), while relocating the *Israelites*.

Joseph's *example* compels us to realize that, even when the steps of one's (life) **process** do **not** (appear to) *line-up* or *make sense*, our (*Faithful*) GOD is still: willing and ABLE!

(Note: For additional **Revelation** and **perspective** on JOSEPH and the **keys** to his *life of servitude*, please refer to my sermon, entitled: **FREEDOM IN SERVITUDE**, in chapter 4 of this book.)

The next *ideal* (biblical) servant, that I want to highlight is: Joshua. His life can be clearly seen in the entire twenty-four chapters of the *Old Testament* book of **Joshua** (named in his honor). The name *Joshua* was taken from the Hebrew word *yehoshua*, meaning *GOD's salvation*. After the death of Moses, Joshua represented the presence of GOD within the midst of the Hebrew people, assuring their victory as they crossed over the Jordan River into Canaan (The *Promised* Land). The book of Joshua tells the story of how GOD's chosen people answered the challenge *to be free* as they followed Joshua, the new *deliverer chosen* and *sent* by GOD, as Moses's successor, to go into and **possess** the land. In possessing or *taking possession* of the land, GOD used Joshua to manifest (secure) the salvation and deliverance for His people (**JOSHUA 1:1-11 KJV**).

Joshua and Caleb were the only two adults (men) delivered from Egyptian bondage that were permitted to enter the *Promised Land*, because they remained *faithful servants*, who fully obeyed and wholeheartedly followed **GOD**. All of the other (prior) adult men (who had left Egypt) were destroyed (consumed) in the wilderness, because they did **not** *obey* the voice of *GOD*. (Note: They were also the *only* two, of the twelve men originally sent by Moses to *spy out* (recon) the land, that returned with a ***good report***.)

During their **conquests** throughout the Land of Canaan, Joshua demonstrated his *strategic leadership* skills, etching the battle of Jericho into the memory of peoples all over the world.

In the *process*, Joshua had the responsibility to lead the masses, through a *divided* (*parted*) Jordan River in their initial *crossing over* (into Canaan), followed by constant **wars** against *opposing* nations (inhabitants); keeping the people focused to meditate on GOD's laws/instructions and teaching the children to know their history, as well as, dealing with the *sin* and **rebellion** of the people. So from

Joshua's youth, through his elevation as the new **leader** of the Nation of Israel and all of his *conquests*, up until he waxed old and stricken in age, even when the odds seemed to be overwhelmingly *stacked against* him, his people were divided (some *rebelled*) or conditions were *unfavorable*, Joshua remained ***faithful*** and ***obedient*** to **GOD,** while remaining strong and courageous!

**Ruth** is another ***ideal*** (biblical) servant, who is not as often spoken of or referenced in today's discussions. Her story can be seen in one of the smallest books of the Old Testament scriptures. This book, named for (or after) her, is only seven pages long, consisting of four chapters. The name *Ruth* in Hebrew means *a female friend*; in essence, she was a Friend *of GOD*!

The story, of this pagan girl from Moab, takes place during the turbulent period of **the Judges**. Ruth had to face and endure: the death of her husband (a *foreigner of Bethlehem-Judah*) after ten years of marriage, leaving her *widowed* at a very young age; homelessness; loss of her own country and identity; entrusting herself and *wholeheartedly* committing her very life unto her mother-in-law (Naomi; also *widowed* and without substance); acceptance of her mother-in-law's lifestyle, culture and *GOD* (**all** as her own); her submission to all of the counsel and instructions of Naomi. Ruth absolutely believed that the GOD (of Abraham, Isaac, and Jacob) was ***the one and only GOD***. Naomi's own husband (Elimelech) died first, followed ten years later, by the sudden deaths of both of her two sons (Mahlon and Chilion). This resulted in Naomi pleading with and begging both of her daughters-in-law (Orpah and Ruth) to leave her and return to their own families' in Moab, because they were in a ***hopeless*** situation (all widows) with **no** man left to take care of them. However, when Orpah agreed to *turn back* (left or abandoned) Naomi, Ruth clave to and vowed to never leave Naomi's side (**RUTH 1:11-19 NIV**).

Because of Ruth's perfect devotion to ***doing*** *what was* ***right***, she was blessed to be married again, after her first husband was dead. Her second or subsequent marriage was to Boaz, a close relative of Naomi (Ruth's mother-in-law) in Bethlehem. Through Ruth's faithfulness and devotion, she also brought restoration, renewed life (vitality) and long-term prosperity (back) unto her (first) mother-in-law. Being from Moab, Ruth was a great testimony to the fact that **redemption** is ***by the spirit*** and **not** *by the flesh*!

The marriage of Boaz and Ruth led to the birth of their son (Obed), who himself fathered Jesse (the father of the eventual *King David*). This means that great-grandparents of David (and ancestors in the lineage of JESUS) were descendants both of *Israel* (Hebrews) and pagans (*unbelievers*). This was Ruth's *crowning glory* and *GOD-ordained* purpose, that through the mysterious *power of GOD*, she was used in the establishment of the *royal prophetic lineage* of JESUS CHRIST!

The next *ideal* (biblical) servant, that I want to highlight is: Samuel. His story can be found in the first twenty-five chapters (1–25) of the *Old Testament* book of 1 Samuel.

*Samuel* in Hebrew means: *one who represents the Power of GOD*, a *remarkably gifted* individual. This Book of Samuel is a record of *true dedication* to the *Word* and *Will* of GOD.

As a wife, who had been unable to conceive a child, Hannah was bitterly and relentlessly vexed by another woman. Therefore, she made a vow to the LORD (GOD) that if he would (*bless*) give her a son, Hannah would present him back to serve GOD all the days of the child's life (1 SAMUEL 1:1-28 KJV). True to her promise, Samuel's mother delivered him to the temple, immediately after he had been *weaned* (from breastfeeding), to present Samuel to the LORD, leaving him there to abide and serve.

As a *gift*, from GOD, to his *barren* mother (Hannah), Samuel was destined to become one of the greatest leaders, judges, prophets, and priests in the Old Testament. As a very young boy, Samuel ministered unto the LORD, initially, *by serving* Eli (the priest). As Eli began to lose his eyesight and the time of his death neared, GOD *called* Samuel and began to speak *directly* to the boy, at about twelve years old. Thus Samuel grew as a prophet, and the LORD was (from that time) always with him; and GOD caused *every word that Samuel spoke to come to past* (manifest/happen). Therefore, all of Israel from Dan to Beersheba knew that Samuel was established to be a prophet of the LORD (1 SAMUEL 3:19-20 KJV). Years later, Samuel also became a _wise_ and _fair_ judge in Israel. Samuel even established schools to train (teach) prophets how to guide Israel.

GOD used and allowed Samuel to assist in _unifying_ Israel into _one_ kingdom; and then, GOD instructed him to anoint Saul as the _first_ King of Israel. Saul's reign lasted for Forty (40) years. Eventually Saul became _disobedient_ and stood in the way of (_hindered_) Israel's salvation and the _truth,_ forsaking GOD's counsel that was given by Samuel. After GOD rejected Saul from being king and _rent_ (tore) the kingdom of Israel from him, Samuel went no more to see Saul, until the day of Saul's death. Finally Saul was destroyed, because of his own disobedience and defiance, which made it necessary for GOD to send Samuel to anoint David, as the _next_ King of Israel. Through everything from his early childhood through his death in old age, Samuel remained faithfully dedicated and obedient to GOD. Samuel fulfilled his mother's promise: he served GOD _all the days of his life_. Therefore, in return, GOD <u>blessed</u> Samuel _all the days of his life!_

This leads us directly to the next _ideal_ (biblical) servant, that I want to highlight: **David.** His life can be clearly seen in the <u>last</u> fifteen chapters (16–31) of the _Old Testament_ book of **1 Samuel,** the <u>entire</u> twenty-four chapters (1–24) of the _Old Testament_ book of **2 Samuel,** concluding in the <u>first</u> two chapters (1–2) of the _Old Testament_ book of **1 Kings.**

The name _David_ means _beloved._ Other descriptions and personal references of this man (David) included: the **apple of GOD's eye**; the **man after GOD's own heart**; and, the _one whom GOD was bound to hear, because of his (David's) unchanging heart_. In choosing David to be the next king over all of Israel, GOD chose the <u>ruddy</u> and <u>youngest</u> of Jesse's eight sons. David was only a boy, who tended (kept) his father's sheep: a mere _shepherd boy_ (in the eyes of his older brothers and _unknown_ to the people, throughout the nation and kingdom).

> "The LORD does not look at the things man looks at. Man looks at the outward appearance, but the LORD looks at the heart." (**1 SAMUEL 16:7 NIV**)

As a young boy, David was called (in) from the field, so that Samuel (*The Seer* or Prophet) could pour oil on David to *officially* **anoint** him (as GOD's <u>chosen</u> one to be the next king over all of Israel). David was thus anointed in the presence of all his brothers, to their dismay and anger; and, *the Spirit of the LORD* came upon David (***was with him***) from that day forward. Still, David returned to the field to tend his father's sheep, during which time, he was being prepared, trained and matured for his future assignments.

David's preparation and testing (development and *proving*) occurred over the next fifteen years or more. First, he had to learn to be **<u>alone</u>** *with GOD*. In the *isolation* of the fields, David learned to experience the presence and protection of the LORD (operate <u>without</u> fear); to *hear*, trust, and worship GOD (playing his harp, singing and dancing). However, he also learned to *fight* with the *sling* (weapon) that GOD provided to him, when he conquered (killed) both a *lion* and a *bear*, that attempted to take a lamb out of his father's sheep herd. It was this same training *experience* and David's trust in the presence and spirit of the LORD (with him), that enabled him to defeat (***slew***) the Philistine *giant* (***Goliath***), who was a champion *warrior* and professional soldier, standing ten and a half feet tall. David accepted this challenge with only his sling and stones (*<u>without</u>* a sword, spear or body armor), while King Saul and all the soldiers of the army of Israel, were afraid to fight this giant (face-to-face or *one-on-one*).

When David slew the giant and, afterward, cut off the giant's head with the giant's own sword, it caused the enemy army to flee and triggered a complete *routing* of the Philistine army (**1 SAMUEL 17 KJV**).

David's demonstration of bravery (boldness) and skill caught the king's eye and gained him respect and fame throughout the army and the kingdom of Israel. Initially, King Saul loved him and requested his continued service in his palace and army. And David went out wherever King Saul sent him, and behaved himself wisely. Therefore Saul set David over the men of war; and, David was genuinely accepted in the sight of all the people and all Saul's servants. The more victories (conquests) David led the army through, the more the soldiers and the people loved him (even more than King Saul). However, the more *popular* and <u>*beloved*</u> David grew (in the eyes and hearts of all the people), the more King Saul began to **envy, hate and fear** him. The *evil* spirit in Saul began to plot against and attempted to kill David on multiple occasions.

David refused to marry Saul's elder daughter (Merah), as a means for Saul to bribe and control (with the intent to betray) David, using the enemy army (in battle). Later, Saul's younger daughter fell in love with David. So King Saul offered her (Michal) to be David's wife (with the same previous intent). David initially refused to be the king's son-in-law but subsequently, married Michal. Michal's genuine love (for David) caused Saul to fear David, even **more**.

Once Saul realized the Philistine army would never be able to kill David in battle, because of the presence of the LORD's spirit with him, Saul tried to persuade his son Jonathan and all his servants to kill David. However, the soul of Jonathan was knitted with the soul of David, and Jonathan loved David as his own soul. As a result, Jonathan warned David that Saul sought to kill him. Upon David's return from his latest conquest (a victorious *slaughter*), as the women and people began to flock from all the cities of the kingdom to dance and sing praises to David's greatness, Saul attempted to kill him with a javelin (spear) inside the palace. But David eluded the spear and escaped out of the palace. Therefore, David became a ***fugitive*** (*running for his life*) from King Saul; although, he was an *innocent* man, who had done nothing wrong and only *served* his enraged King, in the most *faithfully* and *loyal* manner possible.

David has gone from his father's field (tending sheep), to the king's palace (service), to *hiding* in various mountain areas, into the *cave* of **Adullam**. Still, David's **anointing** for *leadership*, coupled with his faithfulness and the presence of GOD's spirit, was so obvious (even as a *fugitive*), that four hundred men (from across the kingdom) were genuinely *drawn to* (sought out) David, even in the caves. All of these men were in: *distress*, *debt*, and *despair*. The pure **desperation** of their situations and their need for *hope*, caused them to be drawn to the **spirit of GOD** (*within* David). In David's (current) *unwarranted and undeserved* state, he has been betrayed (by King Saul) and is *most* **vulnerable.** As reassurance to David, GOD gives (sends) him the fore-mentioned men, which later increased to six hundred men, to run with him, that David (eventually) *trains*, leads and transforms into **warriors** (mighty *men of valor*).

While King Saul and his army pursued/*hunted* (David) with all his heart and might. David had two opportunities, in which GOD delivered King Saul into his hand. However, on both occasions, when he could have ***slew*** King Saul, David refused to stretch forth his hand against GOD's anointed (the king). Instead, David resolved to yield Saul over unto the LORD, that GOD himself would determine how and when Saul would die (**1 SAMUEL 24:1-12, 1 SAMUEL 26 KJV**).

From that time, David and his men continued to move throughout the land of the Philistines, as they fought and cleared the land of its original inhabitants for another year plus additional months.

It was during this time that David, his men and their families suffered their greatest grief and loss at **Ziglag**. So when David and his men returned to their habitation, after a three days *exploit*, they found that the ***Amalekite*s** had burned their city to the ground and taken away all of their wives and children (families), as *captives*. As David and his men were initially overwhelmed in *grief* for their families, the men *turned on* David and thought to *stone* him (their leader). However, David's family was also taken captives; but David encouraged himself in the LORD his GOD. Therefore, after consulting the LORD (GOD), David (eventually) was able to calm the men. Then GOD told David to pursue the enemy and *guaranteed* that they would overtake their enemy and ***recover all*** (rescue and re-gain) their families, without fail (**1 SAMUEL 30:1-26 KJV**).

This great experience taught David and his men how to endure, walk with (and trust GOD) through their deepest grief/*sorrow*, while also preparing them for the subsequent *praise* to GOD.

Three days later, after David's men and their families were reunited in Ziglag (from defeating the Amalekites), a messenger came to give a report to David. Then, David was told that King Saul and his sons had been killed in battle, as the army of Israel had been routed in a battle. David mourned and *fasted* for King Saul, his beloved friend Jonathan, and the people and house of Israel. Shortly thereafter, David went to the city of Judah, where the men of Judah poured *oil* on David and anointed him to be their King over Judah. David reigned over Judah for seven and a half years. Following those years, all of the elders of ***the twelve tribes*** of Israel gathered at **Hebron**, where David was finally *anointed with oil* and officially became the **King over all of Israel** (GOD's original intent and promise for his life), which was announced in the presence of his father (Jesse) and his brothers, when Samuel previously anointed him, as a young shepherd boy. King David was thirty years old when he began to reign; and he reigned for forty years (until the age of seventy years old). This included the seven and a half years that he reigned (in Hebron) over Judah; and an additional thirty-three and a half years, that he reigned over all of Israel (in Jerusalem).

King David never denied that GOD was the source of his wisdom and strength, despite his many transgressions and punishments. King David always confessed and reconciled himself with his Maker (Creator). He was still consistent in following (obeying) the instructions of GOD. This principle was paramount in establishing the Nation of Israel, after Saul's failure in Godly righteousness. In the end, it was prophesied that the Messiah would come from the line of David. It is important to remember that King David's moral failures did not abrogate (abolish or put aside or end) the covenant given to his lineage through Abraham. GOD promised David and his descendants an ever-lasting Kingdom (**2 SAMUEL 7:12-13 KJV**).

The next *ideal* (biblical) servant, that I want to highlight is: <u>**Paul.**</u> His *personal* story (life and ministry) can be found in **chapters 9–28** of the New Testament Book of **ACTS** (or *The ACTS of the Apostles*). Paul was the man of GOD, who emerged from the <u>converted</u> (previous) Saul of Tarsus, after he had regained his *physical* sight and been filled with the Holy Spirit (**ACTS 9:10-21 KJV**).

Paul, eventually, became one of the greatest Apostles in the New Testament; although, he was **<u>not</u>** one of the original twelve disciples. It is also doubtful that he (even) ever, personally, saw Jesus Christ *in the flesh*.

*Prior* to *Saul's conversion and transformation to believing The LORD*, to the point of *serving the LORD, with his whole heart*, Saul (initially) persecuted the Church with a great *zeal* (*passion*). He was the most out-spoken and radical *persecutor* of the early church. Saul made *havoc* of the church, entering into every house, and haling (also beating) men and women, whom he threw into prison. And Saul, yet breathing out threatening(s) and slaughter against the disciples (followers) of the LORD, acquired letters from the high priest that gave him special authority and permission to persecute, beat, arrest and cast them into prison. Saul's (personal) encounter with the LORD JESUS, left him blind for three days, during which Saul did not *see*, *eat* nor *drink* (ACTS 7, 8:1-4, 9:1-9 KJV/NIV).

*Upon Saul's conversion,* the LORD spoke to Ananias, concerning Saul, as GOD sent (used) Ananias to go and lay hands on Saul, that he would receive his sight (sight was *restored*) and he received the Holy Ghost (Spirit).

> *"Go thy way: for he is a chosen vessel unto me, to bear my name before the Gentiles, and kings, and the children of Israel. For I will show him great things he must suffer for my name's sake."* (ACTS 9:15-16 KJV/NIV)

Despite Saul's past/prior sin, guilt and opposition against the LORD and the Gospel of JESUS (Christ), Saul's <u>conversion</u> was *certainly* sure; and his *acceptance* of and *commitment* to it were *genuine* and *whole-hearted*. So his original *zeal* (fiery passion) immediately drove him, as Saul began to serve GOD (went *to work spreading the Gospel of the LORD* (JESUS CHRIST). In accordance with the LORD statement (above) to Ananias, Saul's *trials* and *sufferings* (for the Gospel and the LORD's sake), also, began *immediately*! Just as *surely*, *persistently* (*doggedly*), and *zealously* (or *passionately*), as Saul had (formerly) *persecuted*, *targeted* and *attacked* Jesus's disciples, likewise, Saul (himself) experienced the opposition (buffeting), resentment and attacks, from <u>both</u> sides. The original *Disciples* (*Apostles*), as well as most subsequent disciples, shunned (*eschewed*) and resented Saul (now called or renamed *PAUL*), because they did <u>not</u> trust, but, only <u>*feared*</u> him. On the other hand, *Saul's* own (former) <u>allies</u> (the Jewish leaders), along with the *mobs* of *persecutors* and *bounty-hunters* plotted against, targeted and *sought to kill* him (now *Paul*) (ACTS 9:18-26, 29 KJV/NIV).

Although, Paul had to *suffer* many things, even to *reap* much of what he (himself) had previously *sown* (against Jesus's original disciples), the Spirit of the LORD caused Barnabas (the *encourager*) to embrace, welcome and walk with (support) Paul, as his ministry was being established (proven). During this time (*infancy season* of Paul's ministry), when the Jews saw that multitudes were gathering to hear (listen to) Paul's preaching, they were filled with envy (jealousy and rage), calling Paul's messages contradicting and blaspheming. Therefore, the Jews *stirred up* (instigated and enraged) both devout and honorable women, as well as, the chief men of the city (Jerusalem) to arouse *persecution* against Paul and Barnabas; and, expelled them out of their city/coasts.

Next, Paul and Barnabas moved onto Iconium (ancient city in *present-day* Turkey), where they preached in the synagogue. And although a great multitude of both Jews, and also, Greeks came to believe (the Gospel). However, the *unbelieving* Jews stirred up the Gentiles; and, made their minds *evil affected* against the brethren. When there was an assault made both of Gentiles, and also of the Jews, along with the rulers, to use them despitefully (wickedly) to stone Paul and Barnabas. The Holy Ghost warned Paul and Barnabas, making them aware of this plot. Later in Lycaonia, after Paul had performed a miracle, healing a lame man, who had been lamed from birth and never before walked, certain Jews (who had followed them from Antioch and Iconium) persuaded the people to stone Paul, supposing that he was dead. However, after they had carried Paul out of that city, and crowded around his body, Paul rose (stood up) and went on to Derbe, with Barnabas the next day, to continue preaching (ACTS 14:11-20 KJV/NIV).

The Apostle Paul faithfully, persistently, and *passionately* preached the Gospel, to both Jews and Gentiles, in various cities throughout the regions. While *unbelievers* of both groups constantly and publicly *persecuted* Paul, still great numbers (eventually) believed upon the LORD JESUS and were saved! And GOD wrought special signs and miracles by the hands of Paul. Even to the point of *raising from the dead*, a certain man (named Eutychus), who had fallen from a third loft (balcony) window, during one of Paul's late night sermons (ACTS 19:11-20, 20:7-12 KJV/NIV).

The Apostle Paul would, later, continue on to be beaten (smitten) on many occasions, imprisoned, shipwrecked, etc., etc., etc…

During Paul lifetime, he was successful in *spreading the Gospel* of Jesus Christ (and delivering the Kingdom of GOD) to the Gentiles (and Jews alike). He persuaded and led thousands to accept Salvation, through faith in the LORD JESUS; planted many churches; mentored sons (like Timothy) and other follow *servants of GOD* (both men and women). All of this, while remaining faithful and firmly *standing his ground* in the face of opposition and the most extreme trials, sufferings, and persecution (compared to any of the other Apostles or Christian leaders of his day or any era). From the day of his *conversion*, until his physical death, the Apostle Paul never ever looked or turned back; while, he remained steadfast and obedient (*only*) to Christ. By the end of his lifetime (absolutely), *no one* could question or doubt the Apostle Paul's: *commitment* to the LORD (JESUS) and his gospel; *faith* in GOD; *passion* for reaching the *lost* souls; nor, his *courage* and *boldness* in the face of persecution, hostile opposition or the threat of *death*. It is reported that Nero (the Roman Emperor), eventually, condemned the Apostle Paul to *death* by *beheading* (decapitation).

The *Epistle* is an ecclesiastical letter generally written by one with church *authority* to admonish, praise, instruct, or inform a religious congregation of believers of the early Christian Church (during the first century). The Epistle was a popular means to reaching the Christian Church, since most of the churches were unofficially accepted by the Roman government. Paul, one of the greatest Apostles of the New Testament, commonly used this method of communication with the newly-formed churches (congregations) because he was *regularly* either *imprisoned* or *stranded* in *far away* places. Paul wrote to different ethnic communities and congregations, throughout the Mediterranean and African-Asiatic regions. In the New Testament writings, there are twenty-one epistles, of which, fourteen are attributed to Paul. (That is *twice* (or *double*), as many as, *all* of the original twelve apostles—*combined*!)

However, of all the individuals ever mentioned or named throughout the Scriptures, the only *ONE* that we are <u>*specifically*</u> instructed, directed, and *required to emulate* is <u>*JESUS*</u>. For there is *no other* name, given in heaven or on the earth, by which (or through whom), men can be *saved*. As the only begotten *Son of GOD*, it is *He* that was *given* (*sent*), as the *pure* and *perfect* sacrifice to**:** die on the cross (in the place of sinful men), for man's *transgressions*; *redeem* mankind (or *take away* the sins of the world); and provide salvation (or give us *eternal* or everlasting *Life*), by HIS *Resurrection* from the dead and return to (*GOD the FATHER*). He is both the atonement and the *propitiation* for our sins. HE is *the Word* (of GOD) that was made *flesh* and dwelt among men.

In the Old Testament, He was prophesied about in the Book of *Isaiah* (chapter 53), a foreshadowing of his impending (*eventual*) sacrifice. Then, *Isaiah* (chapter 61) declares his earthly *mission* with its associated *assignments*, which JESUS (himself) *reiterated* in His initial sermon (in the New Testament, **LUKE 4:16-18 KJV/NIV**).

JESUS's full earthly life and ministry (spanning thirty-three years), can be clearly seen and studied in the first four books (***MATTHEW, MARK, LUKE***, and ***JOHN***), referred to as **The Gospels** of The New Testament. The *Gospels* thoroughly reflects everything <u>*relevant*</u> about JESUS's life, ministry and purpose; beginning with his *Immaculate* Conception and imminent **birth**, throughout his earthly existence (developmental *process*) and ministry, to include his **Crucifixion** (death on the cross), temporary burial/ **Resurrection** and His **Ascension** (back unto the **FATHER)** into Heaven.

JESUS came as our one <u>pure</u> *example*, the *living* personification (embodiment) of GOD's righteous expectation of man's existence. He **demonstrated** for us (mankind): how to live this life *in the flesh*, while remaining focus on *pleasing* and being *obedient* to GOD. He proved that we could (daily) ***choose* NOT** to sin (against GOD). He <u>taught</u> his initial disciples, and ***still reveals or shows*** us (His subsequent followers), how to *walk in*, share and give GOD's true (agape) **love** one to another, by loving GOD <u>***first***</u> (with our whole being);

and, loving our neighbors as ourselves. Everything that JESUS did was predicated upon and motivated from LOVE. He always placed the *needs* and *concerns* (burdens) of others, above his own. And he responded to them with **compassion** and ***forgiveness***! He taught the disciples, by his example, **to pray** (*daily*), interceding for the conditions of others. He demonstrated how to *let our lights shine* before men; so that they can **see** our *good works* and **glorify** Our Father (in Heaven).

He taught and showed us, how to ***affect*** the *world* around him (in which he lived), by being the ***salt*** and ***light***, that made people and environments around him better, to the Glory of GOD. He *called*, taught and trained, *poured into* and empowered His disciples, making them *Fishers of Men*; then, He *sent* them out to prepare and prove them to do *greater works*, upon his pending departure. Eventually, he fulfilled **every** single assignment, objective and mission that GOD had ordained for him to accomplish. He spent all of his adult life and ministry *doing good*, *healing* all manner of diseases—to include *leprosy* (skin) and issues of chronic bleeding (blood), and *freeing* those who were in bondage (physical and *spiritual* bondage). JESUS gave **sight** to the blind; caused the lame to **walk**; unstopped deaf ears to **hear**; loosed the tongue of the *mute* (dumb), enabling them to **talk**. JESUS performed all kinds of supernatural *miracles*. He **raised** (**resurrected**) people from the dead. He **exercised authority over** (rebuked and *cast out*) *unclean* (evil and demonic) spirits. He opposed the hypocrisy and unrighteous authorities, who placed burdens on and oppressed the people. He always *related* to the people with **compassion**, ***forgiveness***, empathy and ***love***.

As a reward (from sinful men) for all the ***good*** that he bestowed upon others, JESUS was rejected, betrayed, despised, persecuted, beaten, *tortured*, and crucified! Yet JESUS (himself) was without sin and no *guile* was found in his mouth. Even after going to the cross (Jesus's crucifixion) and *laying down his life* (for not only his friends), but for all men (mankind), the Jewish (religious) leaders and Roman officials ridiculed and dishonored JESUS; and they subsequently paid *false witnesses* to try to discredit him. However, we understand that the Word of GOD is true; and, JESUS is (indeed) the Way, the

Truth and the Light! And our access to the FATHER is only available (possible) through him (his sacrifice).

However, JESUS embraced and remained <u>faithful</u> to the ***process***, for which he was predestined. He constantly and consistently declared in scriptures that he would only *say* and *do* what he had heard and seen from the Father. He **never** (***ever***) did anything out of selfish ambition or vain conceit. Regardless of the constant **plots** of wicked King, politicians (government officials) and *religious* rulers to **murde**r (*kill*) him and the **attempts** of enemy forces to *discredit* him, JESUS remained obedient unto GOD (The FATHER) in all situations/circumstances, even unto *death on the cross!* (The punishment of *Crucifixion* was to be *cursed on a tree*!) His demonstrated ***humility*** and submission to the *will of the Father* were openly rewarded by the FATHER, who has highly exalted him and given him the one name that is **above every name:** on the earth, in heaven and under the earth. That at the name of ***JESUS***, <u>every</u> knee must bow and <u>every</u> tongue must confess that: JESUS CHRIST IS LORD! **(EPHESIANS 2:9-11 KJV/NIV)**.

Now, he has *predestined* and <u>*requires*</u> us to be the ***salt*** of the earth and the ***light*** of this world, in which we currently live. Therefore, as (***His***) *21st Century* ***disciples*** (or *followers*) in 2018 and beyond, we can <u>best</u> *honor* and ***emulate*** him (the Lord **JESUS CHRIST**), by <u>following</u> his example and <u>embodying</u> his ***character***, as described in the paragraph above, and demonstrated in the following scripture reference **(EPHESIANS 2:1-8 KJV/NIV)**.

The fact that all seven of these servants came from such ***<u>diverse</u>*** and ***<u>obscure</u>*** backgrounds is absolutely AMAZING! **None** (*not one*) of the first six servants, that we have reviewed, were considered (by human society or *man's standards*) to be**:** *favorable* or from choice pedigree; highly *educated*; rich or famous; *popular* or of any notable reputation. Additionally, **<u>none</u>** (**not** *one*) of those same six servants were *living* a comfortable or carefree life; nor, were any enjoying a desirable, *charmed* career or *dream* lifestyle, at the time that GOD chose or *called* them in to service. Furthermore, *only* JESUS (the *seventh* servant reviewed) *knew* what it was truly like to *give up absolutely Everything*. However, the <u>origin</u> of his thirty-three years (*life* on earth) and the *process* leading up to his final three years' ministry (and that *tour of service*) <u>epitomized</u> personal *poverty* and *obscurity*, beginning with his *immaculate conception* and *birth* in a manger (inside of an animal stable). This same origin (*immaculate conception*) was, then, and still is *impossible*, from a *scientific* and *intellectual* standpoint. JESUS was the *only* (one) servant that *lived* a *sinless* life (on earth) and *best represented* and served GOD (The FATHER); while, showing compassion for, forgiving, and loving people in every situation. Still, even he faced (encountered) and endured all of the: hardships, ridicule, rejection, hatred and abuse, etc., in his earthly lifetime.

So it is *ridiculous* that today (in 2017 and beyond), society has such a profound struggle or problem embracing the *genuine diversities* in people (global diversity of human society).

In conclusion, there was *one* critical characteristic or *attribute* that <u>ALL</u> seven of those servants had *in common*. At some point, they all came to acknowledge, accept (embrace) and whole-heartedly trusted (had faith in) GOD. Only JESUS (initially) had this attribute, from the very beginning; however, the other six servants did get it (also), at various points and ages, along the development *processes* of their lives. Yet in the end, they all demonstrated, through their attitudes and decisions—that they were *ALL willing Servants* of GOD; instead of (or *not*) *slaves*, who had been *forced* (beaten) or coerced into serving Him.

CHAPTER 3

## The *Model* Servants *In My Life*

"I have *always* been a *Servant*; but, I have never been a *Slave*"!
—Rousell Thomas Jr.

"For I know the thoughts that I think toward you," saith the LORD, "thoughts of peace, and not of evil, to give you an expected end."
—**JEREMIAH 29:11 (KJV)**

"For I know the plans that I have for you," declares the LORD, "plans to prosper you and not to harm you, plans to give you hope and a future."
—**JEREMIAH 29:11 (NIV)**

"Before I formed you in the womb, I knew you, before you were born I set you apart; I appointed you as a prophet to the nations."
—**JEREMIAH 1:4-8 (KJV/NIV)**

Even in today's **technological** age with the Internet (our ***information super highway***) and medical advances, the *Centenarians Club* (group of **people one hundred years old or older**) is still an exclusive, very minuscule group of individuals. So very few children (youth) or even adults, in our society/communities, can say that they have personally *met* or talked to someone who was or is one hundred years or older. An even more minuscule group of children can say that they personally know and/or has ever had the privilege to closely and regularly interact with one of these **centenarians** (***one hundred years*** old people, ***vessels*** *of walking* wisdom).

These individuals, who should be *treasured*; however, more often than not, these same individuals *pine away* (*deteriorate*) in a state of: isolation, seclusion, loneliness, depression and/or as victims of Alzheimer's disease or dementia. Therefore, the *vast* treasures of their **wisdom** is *untapped*, being wasted, **not** passed on and *interred with their bones (buried or goes into the grave* with *them*)! (Note: This fact reminds me of the statement that Marcus Antonius (aka: Marc Antony) made in his speech at Gaius Julius Caesar's (a.k.a., Julius Caesar's) funeral, following the emperor's assassination on March 15, 44 BC).

> *"The evil (men does) lives after them, the good is oft interred with their bones. So let it be with Caesar."* (**Marcus Antonius, 83 BC-30 BC**)

Finding a child in 2017–2018, who actually (intimately) knew or personally knows his or her own *great* grandparent or *great–great–*grandparent, of any age is ***abnormal***, in today's society. Whereas, finding that same level of relationships, with those beyond ninety-years old, is as **rare** as *finding a **pearl** in a single boat-load of oysters*. I **don't** just mean *hearing* or learning a name, which someone told them or they were able to find in an internet (database) search or from a piece of paper (your parent's birth certificate) or other document. I mean actually spending (real) *personal **time*** with that relative or ancestor.

I thank GOD that I was blessed to have been an exception to that fore-mentioned analogy. In my lifetime, I was blessed to have been able to both personally know and interact (on a daily or weekly basis) with four different **centenarians**, all from my hometown. Amazingly, three of the four were my *biological* relatives. There was Mr. Hosea *Hosie* Triggs (102 years and 11 months old), a deacon in our church, that everyone affectionately called *Poppa Hosie*. He had been born February 22, 1872, and died on January 2, 1975. Although, he was not a close relative, there was a period of time that I got to see, hear, shake hands with and receive from his wisdom each week, at our church services and *prayer meetings*. Those other three *Centenarians* in my childhood or lifetime, who were **not** just <u>names</u> written in a tablet or book, nor <u>*pictures*</u> on a wall; but, *live* relatives that I was blessed to interact with. They were: the late Ms. Louella Robinson, my <u>*great*</u> grandmother (102 or 103 years old); her son, the late Ivory Thomas Sr., my paternal grandfather (101 years old); and the late Reverend Edward Washington Sr., my maternal grandfather (one hundred years and eight months *young*).

True to GOD's **plan, intent** and ***word*** for my life, He has set me in the *specific* family and surrounded me, from the very day of my birth, with **pillars** *of Faith* (model *servants*) to <u>mentor</u> and <u>prepare</u> me, for those *assignments* (*work* that GOD had planned for me to do).

There have been a whole myriad of these significant individuals, who were actually ***divine connections***, through whom GOD would guide, bless and propel me through life, from birth to now, at the age of fifty-eight.

The <u>*first*</u> of these (model *servants*/***pillars*** in my life), there from *birth* through my formative adulthood years, was **Reverend Edward Washington Sr.** He was my grandfather; and, my mother's biological father. He lived in the same house (home) in which I was born and reared; although, he had been born in January 1887, in Louisiana. So he turned seventy-five years *young*, when I was only sixteen <u>*days*</u> of age. Besides my parents, he was the only **mentor** with me *from the very beginning*; and, who: remained with, *pour into* and *covered* me for the longest period of time (throughout my childhood and *formative* years of my life, including the initial years of my adulthood). He was also the one, who had the most profound and greatest impact upon me; because, his age and unique experiences (with GOD) provided a **depth of Faith and Wisdom**, that none of the others (since) have been able to match.

From the time I was in kindergarten, *Head Start* and first grade (four to six years old), I've always been *in awe* of the energy, vitality, physical strength and wisdom of my grandfather. This was especially true because of his age and ability, at the time. Here was a gentleman who was always seventy-five years older than I was. (He had turned seventy-five years, exactly *sixteen days* after I was born.) So the routine things, that he did, were not the normal *daily* activities or feats that one could *reasonably* expect from any eighty-year-old man. He actually possessed the physical strength, endurance, and stamina to work harder, longer and (under the most extreme heat conditions) than any eighty-year-old man, since the Emancipation Proclamation had freed *slaves*.

As I grew older, while watching him work and listening to his *philosophy on life* (based upon GOD's Word), I discovered and came to both understand and appreciate what *fueled*, inspired and motivated him to be able to do *hard labor*, as efficiently and faithfully as the average man, who was less than half his age. Everything about his life was based on and revolved around his **faith in GOD**. How he thought, what he believed, and all the things that he said and did were hinged on *FAITH* and his determination to be *productive* (useful) *every* day of his life. His quotes, in subsequent paragraphs, *epitomize* (reflect) his wisdom, personal *work ethic* and philosophy on life, which were all founded on biblical principles (GOD's Word).

The most profound thing (prophetic fact) I ever heard him say was: **"GOD has promised me that I'm going to live to be one hundred years of age."** As far back as I can remember, right up until I was a twenty-five-year-old officer (2nd Lieutenant) in the US Army, I saw and heard how he ***clung to*** and **believed** this promise from GOD (to him).

And through all of his *hardships*, tribulations and *curves* (changes) that life threw at him, he believed this promise with all his heart and with all the faith (assurance) of Abram/Abraham (in **Genesis**, Old Testament of the Bible). I really don't think that anyone has ever believed (or been more persuaded of) anything, more than my grandfather (*genuinely*) believed that he would eventually live to the *ripe* age of one hundred years. <u>Why did he believe this? Simply,</u> **just because: GOD told him, that he would!**

Now, ***remember***: <u>when</u> he was born, the *cruel times* (era) that he lived in (through), the contagious terminal illness that his mother had (as he tried to assist and care for her) when he was only eight, etc. In addition to all of that, he (himself) lived with *hypertension* (disease of high blood pressure) and worked *like a mule*, performing *hard labor* in extreme heat conditions of southern Louisiana, to include working in the sugar cane fields and digging *graves* at the age of eighty-seven years. He did this type of harsh physical labor for nearly thirty years beyond the legal *retirement age*; thus, he worked, at this *senior* stage of his life, longer and harder than most men work their entire lives. But to his credit, like Abraham, he also **believed** GOD. Therefore, I believe that GOD imputed (counted) this as *righteousness* unto my grandfather.

> *"Abraham believed GOD, and it was imputed (credited) unto him for righteousness."* **(JAMES 2:23)**

YES, my grandfather (also) was *fully persuaded*. His faith (trust) was **in GOD** to fulfill (**honor** or bring to pass) that promise, which GOD had personally made to him. Therefore, he believed and stood firmly on his belief that: If GOD said (promised) something, GOD would certainly do it.

> *"GOD is not a man that HE should lie, nor the son of a man, that HE should repent. Hath HE said, and shall he not do it? or hath HE spoken, and shall he not make it good?"* **(NUMBERS 23:19)**

> *"In GOD, I have put my trust; I will not be afraid."* **(PSALM 56:11)**

Another *motivating factor* or *source of inspiration* for my grandfather's life was the fact that he said, *"I have never, ever seen anything in the Bible about a man retiring from GOD's service, purpose, or work."* Therefore, he said: *"I intend to continue to work (serve) faithfully, until I can't do it, no more."* He was determined with all his heart and might to do this, until he could no longer continue, regardless (or *in spite*) of his age. My grandfather believed and often said, *"the race is not given to the swift (fastest), nor the battle to the strong (strongest), but to him that endures and proves faithful to the end."*

> *"Be thou faithful unto death, and I shall give thee a "crown of (eternal) life."* **(REVELATION 2:10)**

He believed that his obligation (responsibility) was to be productive (*fruitful*) in his service to GOD, so that GOD would be glorified (receive *glory*). As long as GOD gave him the *physical* strength and strengthened him with might *in the inner man* (soul and spirit), he maintained the *will power* to continue to *work*/serve (do GOD's will).

> *"Be steadfast, unmovable, always abounding in the work of the Lord, for as much as ye know, that your labor shall not be "in vain."* **(1 CORINTHIANS 15:58)**

Based upon his *own* purpose (and its *requisite* for productivity and fruitfulness), he refused to merely just *exist* (be idle) or occupy space. So he always said, *"when I get so that I can't do any more, then it will be time to ask the Lord to take me home."* He said he never wanted to have to depend on anyone to do routine things for him: feed him, bathe him, physically carry him around, etc. From my grandfather's perspective, it was absolutely imperative that he maintain his physical capability, strength, activity of his limbs (mobility).

> *"Make it your ambition to lead a quiet life, to mind your own business and work with your hands; just as we told you, so that your daily life may win respect of outsiders and so that you will not be dependent on anybody."* **(1 THESSALONIANS 4:11)**

He lived his life, simply and solely to serve GOD and did everything within his ability to help others; while he remained determined never to become a *burden* on anyone.

This, too, would later prove to be prophetic, before his death.

Another one of his *key motivations* was his *favorite* scripture: **Psalms 1**.

I always knew that this was his favorite scripture, long before he ever told me.

As I was being reared in the same houses (through my childhood) with my grandfather, he and us (four boys) shared the same bedroom, and sometimes the same bed. Before my grandmother (his wife) died, we lived in that same big *shotgun house*, that I previously described, before that *catastrophic* fire (in chapter 1 of my other book, entitled: **Emerged From Fires and Storms.**) My grandmother passed away three years later, when I was seven years old and in the second grade. After my grandmother's death, the two subsequent homes, in which we lived, were single-family homes; each had three bedrooms: one room for my parents, one room for the guys (grandfather and the boys), and one bedroom for the girls (my three sisters). This, coupled with the fact that I spent more time alone with my grandfather, as he worked in his garden or in the cemetery (as the elder grandson), ensured that my relationship with him was *closer* than most kids get to enjoy with their grandparents.

I can still remember lying awake in my bed (morning and night) and listening to my grandfather (when he knelt down to pray); he would always recite the scriptures from **Psalms 1,** as the *lead in* to his prayers. Before very long, I was quoting it (softly or *under my breath*) along with him; although, he probably didn't hear me any of those times. Needless to say, this was the very first scripture that I, consequently, memorized and learned, as a very young boy. Throughout his life, he *lived* (epitomized) that scripture. In him, I *saw* that strong, fruitful (productive) vessel, that *tree planted by the rivers of water*, the **Blessed Man**), that this scripture describes. And he *faithfully* **lived** (walked) in accordance with those conditions and prerequisites of GOD's Word. This means that he did **NOT**: *walk in the counsel of the ungodly* (seek advice from or conspire with ungodly men); nor, <u>*stand* in *the way of sinners*</u> (didn't block or hinder people from seeing, coming to and experiencing GOD's grace); nor, <u>*sit in the seat of the scornful*</u> (didn't seize every opportunity to *judge* or ruin the reputation of others). Instead, he took great delight (joy) in **meditating on** (pondering) the word of GOD, and practiced *doing* and *living* in obedience to it. Through my adult life (still Today), this is my favorite scripture and *a motivation* for me *in life*, as well.

Throughout my (initial) twenty-five years, while he was alive and *standing on* GOD's promise for his life, <u>he never, ever referred to himself as old.</u> He always used the term *young* when referring to his own age. He always said things like, **"I'm ninety years *young*; I'm ninety-five years *young*; etc."** His whole attitude, outlook and mind-set were focused on *living* a productive (*fruitful*) life, while *serving* GOD and *giving* to the needs of others, regardless of *how long* he had to do it or *how little* (*materially*) he got, in return for his efforts.

My grandfather saw **every** single day as <u>one more opportunity</u> to serve (glorify) GOD and help others, <u>not</u> time to be complacent or rest (retire) on yesterday's service (work). He used even his most menial *daily* tasks to honor and serve GOD, if not through its actual magnitude (impact), at least, in the *manner* in which he did them or the effort that he invested (*poured into*) them. He believed that, in order to be acceptable to GOD, his *work* had to be worthwhile (purposeful and challenging), and done honestly, sincerely (and *willingly*). So he *always* approached it that very same way!) For my grandfather, being **in his prime** just meant being physically capable, mentally sound and emotionally willing to work or *to do* physical labor. Therefore, for *over* ninety years of his life, that is exactly **where he remained** (and what he **DID**)!

He never tried to deny, hide or cover up his age. In fact, he was just the *opposite*. I can still see his little grin (smile) on his face and hear his words, as he'd often proudly announce his age to people in church or walking down the street. Whenever someone would *drive up* next to him, as he walked along the road and say, "Hey Reverend Washington; would you like a ride?" He'd reply, "*No, dawling (darling); I'm alright. You know, I'm* **ninety-two** *years* **young***, and I feel pretty good, too!*"

*Reverend Edward Washington Sr.*
*(My maternal Grandfather) in 1940s*

In fact, the title of one of his favorite *spiritual* songs or hymns was: <u>A Land Where We'll **Never** Grow **Old.**</u>

Through my grandpa's life, I witnessed a *life-long demonstration* of faith, wisdom and the *essence of life*. In him, I saw (firsthand) a man, who lived a simple (but honest) Christian *lifestyle*; *willingly* worked (physically) hard; and a *servant* of GOD, who knew his place (function) *within the Body of Christ*. His goals in life were **to help any and everybody that he could and to serve GOD** *faithfully.* He would give (away) the *very last dollar* in his pouch (wallet) to someone *in need*, that he passed on the street. Often, I watched him do exactly that.

During my army career, I've traveled to numerous countries all over the world, and personally, walked on *holy sites* like **Mt. Nebo** (where Moses died) and through the streets of ancient Jerusalem, along the **Via Dolorosa** (the *road of Sorrow* or Jesus Christ's route to his *crucifixion* on Golgotha Hill); still, my grandpa is the most honest man that I would or could ever meet. He **always** went *out of his way*, went *that extra mile* or sacrificed whatever was necessary to fulfill a *vow* or *honor* (keep) a promise that he had made to **GOD,** *even if or when the recipient did not realize it.*

For example, while *over eighty-five years* of age, he still walked seven miles (*one way* to the next town) in ninety-plus degree temperatures with 100 percent humidity weather conditions, on occasions, just to visit an *ill* (sick) person, in order to keep his word. Then, after his visit (of one to two hours), he'd walk (seven miles) back home, in those same weather conditions. His **determination to prove *faithful* in his service (stewardship)** ensured that extreme heat; threatening thunderstorms; hypertension (high blood pressure); a headache or leg cramp; nor the **lack** *of: money, volunteers (help) or other resources* did *NOT* prevent him from fulfilling his duties/responsibilities (as he ministered to the church and *chaired* (led) society/community organizations). For decades, my grandfather *simultaneously* served as *Assistant Pastor* of our church (**New Salem Baptist Church**), *President* of the **Home Industrial Society**, *President* of the **Shield Benevolent Society** and *President* of the **Willing Workers Association**. Through more **than one hundred years** of the world's *tribulations* and *hardships*, he **persevered** and remained faithful to GOD, no matter what the *world* threw at him!

> *"I have fought the "good fight; I have finished the race; I have kept the faith; Henceforth, there is "in store" for me the "crown of righteousness," which the Lord, the righteous judge, will award to me on that day."* **(2 TIMOTHY 4:7-8 KJV/NIV)**

In honor of my grandfather's faithful service to GOD and his church (New Salem Baptist Church), our church had implemented, *carried out* and upheld a tradition (from 1960 through 1987), that all services conducted on **every *fifth*** Sunday of any month (during his lifetime) were dedicated to him (Rev. Edward Washington). My grandfather lived an extraordinary (yet simple) life; and accordingly, GOD blessed him with one extraordinary privilege. A **servant** normally does NOT get the opportunity to sit **alive** (in the midst of) and witness his/her own *Home-going* Celebration (or *funeral*) service. However, this is, in essence (*in a sense*), exactly what he was allowed to do. On Sunday (January 29, 1987), for his **one hundred**th **birthday celebration and dedication service,** my grandfather had the unique privilege to *smell his flowers,* while he was still ***alive***. He personally *saw and heard (first-hand)* the results of his labors and what a significant impact he had made on the lives of the people in his community, as well as, the ***legacy*** that he left. Basically, he was allowed to hear his own eulogy preached, in advance (just over eight months before his death). What he already knew, based upon the Word of GOD, was visibly confirmed to him in this *Dedication* Service. The ***fruits*** *of his labor* were clearly evident, and this was GOD's way of confirming to him and everyone else that his life had **not** been lived *in vain.*

As I look back (in *retrospect*) at <u>*what*</u> *made my grandfather (mentor) tick***:**

I can recall **his *blessed* (*assurance*)** that he would live to be one hundred years of age. He **believed** GOD's promise to him. He ***purposed*** *in his heart* (resolved within himself) <u>***never***</u> **to *retire*** from his service to GOD or *daily **work***. He saw his daily *productivity* as a component of *his service* (to GOD).

When he could no longer **be *productive***, he would rather ask GOD to take him home, than continue to just <u>*exist*</u>, as a *useless* vessel. All of his decisions and daily practices were based on his commitment to be faithful to GOD**,** as he lived a simple, honest life based upon GOD's Word.

In short, just like Jesus Christ, he <u>only</u> wanted to *faithfully **DO*** what GOD wanted him to do and help others in the process, for ***as long as*** GOD *allowed* him to do that! (**Note:** If I can do *that*: *follow his example,* I will have lived a successful and *fulfilled* life too!)

YES, my grandfather (mentor) taught and demonstrated, to me, the meaning of *work* and the essence and PURPOSE of *life.* And while I did <u>NOT</u> always recognize or understand what was happening (while I was *in the classroom* of the situations or events), I still managed to successfully *glean,* learn and to absorb wisdom from this *old **schoolmaster***. His inspiration, along with my *faith* in GOD, and the other role models and provisions that GOD surrounded me with (together) have all powered (or propelled) me through and lifted me above ALL the *challenges* and *tribulations* that I had conquered, before we laid him to rest in September 1987. But as I stood (there) **at his *graveside*** (*a recently promoted **1st Lieutenant***) wearing my Army Class A (*Dress Green* uniform) and saluted him *that day*, ***I knew what time it was.***

**NOW, his mantle or baton** (of GOD's faithful *servant*) was <u>passed to ME</u>!

From that day forward (and throughout the remainder of my life), my grandfather's *charge* to me could have easily been summed up in the following two instructions (biblical scriptures):

> *"Those things which ye have both learned and received, and heard and seen in me: do; and the Peace of GOD shall be with you."* **(PHILIPPIANS 4:9)**

> *"Endure hardship with us like a "good soldier of Jesus Christ."* **(2 TIMOTHY 2:3)**

*My maternal grandfather upon his death, at over one hundred years (September 3, 1987)*

## Mr. Ivory "Hooker" Thomas Sr.
(Mar. 11, 1909-Apr. 3, 2010, age **101 years**)

    This was my paternal grandfather (my father's dad), who was another model citizen and *pillar* in our community. He had previously served in World War II; and upon returning to his hometown, he was always highly respected by both children and adults (alike). He was a big man, with a towering physical frame (stature), about six feet, four inches tall and weighing about 240–250 lbs. As he walked down the streets, his confident gait (strut), as well as, his starched and *spit polished* appearance captured everyone's (men. women and children's) attention, whether those people were black or white (Negros or Caucasians). Initially, after the war, the primary or majority of work opportunities, afforded to him and other Negro men (in Louisiana), were in the areas of: field laborers, janitors, road construction, fishing/shrimp boats or (offshore) oil drilling rigs in the Gulf of Mexico. Despite the status quo, (eventually) my grandfather's character, integrity, physical strength, stamina, and work ethic propelled him into other *public service* job positions, within our town (community). Ironically, he once told me, that it was a white *boss man* on one of his job in the sugar cane fields that gave him the nickname *the Hooker*; because, he was the best and only man that could ride on top of the cane transport trailer, while leaning over with a huge metal hook, and single-handedly lifted (pulled up) those huge bundles of sugar cane (up) onto the trailer. He also had that same knack or ability to later pull nets onto the fishing boats. So that nickname <u>stuck</u> with (followed) him throughout the decades of his adult life. Therefore, he was always known as and called *Mr. Hooker* Thomas, or just simply *Hook* to his close friends and peers.

    I can remember, as a young boy, when he worked as the primary operator (engineer or facilitator) at our town's (Patterson's) official Water *Treatment* Plant. And although I never knew him to own an automobile (of his own), he <u>proudly</u> *strutted* (walked) to work every morning, dressed in his (normal attire): *starched* white shirt, starched and *creased* khaki pants, and *spit-shined* black shoes. My cousins and other children would stand by the roadside and watch him, passing by, as if he were a soldier *marching off* to war (with his chest poked out, head up, and eyes to the front). And even though, he would always speak, his head and eyes never turned to the left or right, and his focus remained straight ahead, as he marched on. His appearance, as well as, his job performance always commanded and provoked the respect of all the people around him, whether they were: children, adults, family, *friends or enemies (opposition)*, black or white! His greatest (signature or personal) qualities were that he was always: the best and hardest *worker*, arrived with the neatest appearance; ready early and the <u>*first*</u> one to *show up* (arrive); well organized; and *meant* what he said (*his word was his bond*)!

Some of his favorite hobbies and *past time* events included baseball, softball, enjoying family (holiday and summer) social gatherings, and taking *road trips* to the Houston Astrodome (for Astros vs. Dodgers) baseball games, although his favorite player was Hank Aaron (so his favorite team was the Atlanta Braves). Even in his later years (while over ninety years old), you only had to mention (once) or propose *going to a baseball game*; and he was immediately *up to the challenge*. Therefore, my grandpa would ask: "*When; and what time do I have to be ready for you to pick (me) up?*"

During my adult years (as an active duty Army Officer), and even after I had retired from the military (in November 2005), I can attest to the fact that my grandpa was still demonstrating all of his signature qualities. Whenever I visited my hometown, *on leaves* (temporary visits) throughout my twenty years career, he would be quite excited to see me on every first day that I'd visit his home.

During those *initial* visits, he would always ask when I was *leaving town* again; then, he would ask me to come and drive him around town on one particular day (if I was home on the third or fourth day of the month) to *run his errands and pay his bills.*

That was a great way for us to spend some quality time together, during any of my (military *leave*) visits. No matter which days (of those weeks) we agreed upon, <u>every</u> time that I arrived to *pick-up* my grandpa, he was always ready (early) and *pacing back and forth* (outside) across his front porch, with his normal neat and starched appearance (impeccable dress code). When he got into my vehicle, he always had all of his bill envelopes in the chest pocket of his shirt or coat. Those envelopes would each contained the *specific amount of money* (*exact* change or to the *near-*

*est* dollar) required to pay each particular bill; and those envelopes were always arranged in the *sequence* (order) of the locations that we would be driving to (for example: *Patterson Town Hall* (for water and gas), *Cleco* (electric) company, then *Cox* (tv cable) company, etc.) This was a direct testament to his meticulous planning, sound mind and organizational prowess, even when he was eighty to ninety-six years of age.

*Mr. Ivory "Hooker" Thomas Sr. (my paternal grandfather)*

After the death of his second wife in November 1998, my grandpa lived and functioned (to include cooking meals) <u>*alone*</u> for seven additional years, through his ninety-sixth birthday.

Unfortunately (in the winter of 2005), my grandpa suffered a horrible *fall* in his home, which resulted in him breaking a rib, that also punctured a lung. Eventually after an initial *hospital stay*, he was relocated (moved) into a local nursing home, to complete an extensive *rehabilitation* period. Tragically, he suffered another catastrophe (inside the nursing home), when an employee of that facility *rolled over* his toes (foot), with a huge *metal* (mobile) *meal or medicine* cart (cabinet). This injury, eventually, resulted in a catastrophic *infection* and permanent pain and mobility issues, which kept him confined to the nursing home for the final five years of his life (from the ages of 96–101 years old).

When I visited him there in the nursing home, from the time of his ninety-seventh birthday and beyond, he always *yearned* (longed) to *go back home* to live (independently) in his own house (again). However, his days of *independent living* were gone (permanently lost). He would (then) say to me: "*Rou, I had no idea that I would live to be this old!*"

My dad visited his father (my grandpa *Hook*) every single day, either on his way to and/or from work, as a part of his daily routine. He also received regular visits from his other two children (my Aunt Hattie and Uncle Matthew) and many of his grandchildren, who lived there in the town and surrounding areas. During my grandpa's final two years, the only other thing that he could *count on* was GOD's *Faithfulness* (toward him). In the end (on my final visits), my grandpa's mind and memory were still very *keen* (sharp); however, there were days when the pain in his toes (foot) was so great that I heard him pray, for GOD to just allow him to die and *escape* his physical agony.

The final *yearning* of a *true servant* (and child of GOD) is simply: to go to *be with Him* (GOD), which is also to be free *from the pain and cares* of this world (earthly existence).

I eventually went back home to Louisiana, from Virginia, for that final *farewell* (homegoing celebration) for my grandpa *Hook* in 2010, which was just over thirty days past his 101st birthday. That was nearly twenty-three years after my other grandfather (Rev. Edward Washington Sr.) had already been gone. Although, one always knew (GOD had promised him) that he would live to reach one hundred years of age, and the other *had no idea* that he would live to be so old, they both eventually lived beyond that one hundred years (*Centenarians*) milestone. They were both greatly blessed; and, left great legacies for myself, siblings and countless others to follow!

The next of these (model *servants/pillars* in My Life), there from *birth* and into my early adulthood years (*and beyond*), were my parents: Rousell Thomas Sr. and the late Virginia C. (Washington) Thomas. From the time that we (siblings) were old enough to walk, talk, and remember, two things were ever present in our lives: spiritual guidance and our parents' discipline.

My grandfather was an old Baptist preacher, my father a church deacon and choir member, and my mother was an usher. So the fact that we'd be taken to church and Sunday school, was understood (*nonnegotiable*) and as automatic as—school opening in August, my grandfather and parents going to work (their jobs) on Monday morning, or *Christmas* and *winter* in December. However, I never felt (in reference to going to church or worshipping GOD) that I was being forced to do something that I did not *want* to do or didn't enjoy. In fact, I had a need to go and a *sensing* that there were some things that I wanted (*needed*) to do and enjoyed doing, once I got there. Like singing in the kids (junior) choir or paying attention to answer questions in Sunday school. The same *motivation* and sense of purpose, that drove my efforts in public elementary school, also carried over into church and Sunday school or vice versa.

The first *lessons of life* that my daddy stressed (taught) to us were: the *fear of God* and *respect for authority*. In terms of respect for authority, he ensured that we understood: at home, our parents *called the shots*; in Sunday school or public school, the teachers were *in charge*, etc., etc., etc. In other words, we (as children) would always respect whoever the responsible adult was in the particular *position of authority*, in every situation (at all times).

I can *vividly* remember (as far back as kindergarten) hearing him say, "*Nothing burns me up (vexes me) more than seeing a kid trying to have his/her way (with an adult)*." And when I heard him say it, I knew that he meant it. His actions confirmed or reinforced his sentiments. And his perspective (TODAY) has not changed on that issue. I can clearly remember, as a young child, hearing my daddy tell school teachers, other adults at my church, and even neighbors (in my presence): "*If you see him or any one of mine "getting out of line" (unruly), you just put a belt on his butt (behind). And if he gives you any trouble (resistance) or you feel that you can't handle the situation, then just call me; and, I'll leave from my job to come (there) and take care of him!*" (Note: *There* simply meant wherever I [or that sibling] would have been at that particular time, and it really did NOT matter *where* that was.) My mother, also, was never *shy* or reluctant when it was time for *discipline*. She very easily got enough arm exercise, while *swinging a belt* (during our childhood), to ensure that she would never develop stiffness and arthritis in her arm, during our lifetime.

Our parents made sure that we understood: what the *rules* were, what behavior (conduct) was expected and acceptable, as well as, what the *consequences* were. I (and my siblings) *came* when we were called; asked permission to go anywhere or leave out of the house or yard; said: "Yes, ma'am" and "No, sir" to adults (elders); and we were never allowed to back talk or sass (respond negatively to) any adult. Not only did we (siblings) understand and respect my daddy's sentiments of discipline, but all of the cousins and neighborhood kids (who hung around our house) did, as well. If other children were at or in his house, then they followed the (same) rules too, no questions asked! In fact, whenever it became necessary (while my Aunt Hattie was gone to work at her job), for my dad to go over to her house to discipline one of her children, all it took was a phone call (request).

Upon receiving that request, from her or one of her older children, *my dad* would be out the door, like a *bolt—(not Usain)—of lightning*; and immediately (without challenge) *martial law* was established at that house.

Another significant *life lesson*, that my parents taught us, was that of *having and handling individual responsibilities* (*at an early age*). Of course, all of us (children) were responsible for our own *homework* from school. But we (siblings) also all had additional assigned (*chores*), that we were responsible for doing at home, from about seven years old and above. Our *chores* included things like making our beds and cleaning our rooms; sweeping floors and/or vacuuming carpets; dusting furniture; washing dishes; doing laundry (washing, hanging, folding, and putting away or re-distributing the clothes); etc… And of course, a parent would always check to ensure that the tasks had been correctly or satisfactorily completed. If we or a friend asked our parents if we could go outside to play, their response was based mostly on whether or not I (or a sibling) had finished taking care of my (our) responsibilities: chores and school work, *first*! If my (our) work was not done or not done to parents' satisfaction, we could forget about going outside or *playing*. Certainly, I wanted to have the opportunity to go and play. At home, just as at school or in Sunday school, I wanted to **prove** what I could do. Therefore, my goal was always to do a *great* job. That meant that I had to do the required task both *quickly* and **well** (or in an **excellent** manner).

Both of my parents, like my grandparents, were always very *hard working* people. My father's first (*initial*) job was working at the previously *segregated* school (Hattie A. Watts). His second or next job was for the huge *Halliburton* Service Corporations, which were actually owned by former Vice-President Dick Cheney. But this one job (alone) didn't pay enough for my dad to support our large family.

However, he very soon began to work an additional (second) job, as one of the <u>two</u> very first *negro* police officers, under the leadership of the first ever-elected *negro Chief of Police* in our town's history. That chief's name was Mr. Jesse Paul (or **Chief**), a retired Navy veteran with thirty-eight years of active military service. My daddy, along with Mr. Junius Levy were his first two *negro* police officers, during the Chief's *inaugural* term. Initially, my dad did this *part-time*, as a *night shift* **dispatcher**. Later, he became a full time *police officer* (patrolman), while also serving as a *volunteer* firefighter for our town's (Patterson) *Volunteer* Fire Department. He also held some self-employment contractor jobs (*cleaning* for banks, restaurants, etc. at night only on certain evening). Sometimes, my mother and/or I would go to assist or filled-in for him, on some of these night-time *gigs*. I can remember times, during my childhood, when my dad actually worked (held) three jobs, at the same time.

*Patterson Police Department: 1970 (Louisiana)*

**Note:** Rousell Thomas Sr. (*My Dad*) is depicted by the red arrow, left side on the second row, in the photo above.

His daily routine, then, consisted of long hours at one job, come home to eat and bathe, sometimes get a short *nap*, then go to another job. I observed, over the years, his **consistent *sense of responsibility* to fulfill his obligations and his obsession for being *on time.*** No matter how tired he was or how he felt, when he returned from the first job, he always met his obligation/duties in going to the next (night) job. And he was persistent that he not be *slowed down or made late* for his scheduled shift time (work) or arrival for church services. While my father was never in the military, his father (my *other* grandfather) was; so, my father always wanted to be at his appointed place of duty on time; and show up with a neat, *sharp* uniform. (That's what we later referred to, in the military, as a ***strack*** appearance.) I've always respected the fact that he consistently worked extremely hard, just to build his *reputation* as an honest, faithful worker and to gain the *common respect* (in the community) that is reasonably due to every (upstanding) man, even if he is a *negro* or viewed as a *colored* or black man). And this *respect*, obviously, did **NOT** come quickly or easily (for any of those) from the vast majority of *Caucasian or white citizens*, in that old, *segregated* (prejudiced) environment.

*"A good name is rather to be chosen than great riches."* **(PROVERBS 22:1)**

My father worked for **Halliburton Services Corporation**. (in their warehouse's *Shipping and Receiving* Dept.) continuously for about fourteen years of my childhood and adolescent years, before a huge *downsizing* caused he and thousands of other employees to be *laid-off* (released). He also had a few other jobs.

However, when I reviewed the totality of his adulthood's *work* vs. ***living***, it was transparently clear to me that he had simultaneously and continuously lived a *life of **Service*** throughout his entire adulthood, which has spanned more than fifty-eight years already, through the age of seventy-eight.

Although, he started out as a *custodian* (or janitor and *crossing guard*) at our old segregated school, everything within him caused him to pursue and *flow* into (operate in) positions of (*public safety* and *community*) **service.** My daddy was a policeman, *patrolling* the streets, from the time I was a third (third) grader and into my early adulthood (and <u>beyond</u> my college years), easily totaling thirty years. During the early years of my military career, he was still *actively serving,* as a police officer. My father took great pride in the fact that he always sought to enforce the law consistently and equally, regardless of whether the citizens involved were *black* or *white*. And his approach was always the same, to attempt to approach everyone with respect; but, pushing or taking him *left* (<u>off</u>) of that initial posture could turn out to be a *big ****mistake***! At the same time, he attained and functioned as a leader (officer) in the town's Volunteer Fire Department. I can still remember awakening to the fire station's *official* radio (*base station* box) **blasting** or **blaring** out fire **alarms,** in the middle of the night or *wee* hours of the morning (2:00 or 3:00 a.m.), which sent all of the volunteer firemen *scurrying* to and from the Fire Station and/or the scene of the *fire*.

During the latter years of his police career, as his street *patrolling* shifts decreased, my father became one of the department's primary (**police**) *security officers* at all of the High School's home games/sporting events. He was also the *official escort* policeman, who traveled on the school bus with the High School teams to all *road* games. When he finally retired from the police department, he transitioned back into working full-time at the high school, which allowed him to serve as an *active* **mentor** and **role model** for all students; where he continued *working,* until the <u>last</u> of all of *his* (local) *biological* (grandchildren) had graduated. At that point, he retired from the St. Mary Parish school system; and began a new level of *semi-retired* employment at the Patterson Civics Center. My dad *served* faithfully in this final position from 1993 through 2019, to remain actively involved in the community, while also keeping himself busy, after my mother's death in 2004.

As far back as anyone in town can remember (since his childhood), Rousell Thomas Sr. (my father) had always been a *leader*, positive *role model*, *peace-maker* and mentor. Based upon his reputation and the testimonies of people who have lived their entire lives in Patterson, these same *traits* and his character have remained consistent (throughout his life), while a youth in school; young man/citizen in the community; *deacon* (leader) and Sunday school teacher in the church, *player-**manager*** of his league softball teams, police officer, *Lieutenant* (fireman) of the fire department or civil servant elsewhere (students' mentor/role model or *confidant* for coaches/staff), and his roles in other organizations. I can remember, even when I was a youth/teenager, church members, other key leaders and older citizens were always requesting and *coaxing* (advising and encouraging) my dad to run for *Chief of Police* or *Mayor* of our town. For decades, he had a number of influential people, who prodded, encouraged and supported him to consider seeking one of these official offices (positions); however, he (*personally*) had **no desire** to be involved in *politics*, etc. And for him, it was NEVER about position, recognition, popularity or awards. It was simply about his *call* and **passion** (heart to *help* people and **serve GOD,** despite any associated *suffering*)! So if you're wondering, what did I *receive* (inherit) from my dad, besides his name and a love for certain sports?

I know for a fact, that I have the exact same**:** propensity for **leadership** (gift to *lead*), **passion** (*zeal* or inner *drive*) and **aversion** (disaffection or dislike) for personal praise and *fanfare,* as a result of our (genuine) service.

To illustrate my father's disposition toward *fanfare* and (receiving) personal praise, I will share our 2011 *Surprise* (**Retirement**) Banquet, which we (siblings) held in his honor, in conjunction with his *Retirement* from the St. Mary Parish School System. We all knew that he would never *agree* to us doing this event (*for* him); therefore, it absolutely had to be coordinated and executed as the *strictest, stealthiest,* **ultimate***:* **SURPRISE**! Otherwise, it never would have happened, because my dad would've *pulled the plug* (turned off) the event. Therefore, we decided (agreed amongst ourselves) that we had to *just **do** it* (**first**); and ask for forgiveness (afterward)!

My siblings and I understood that we would only get ONE **shot** at (or *opportunity*) to successful *pull off* this event (in **honor** of our father), without him anticipating and ***de-railing*** (or sabotaging) it. So we carefully coordinated and planned it *long distance*, over about **eight** weeks, **twelve hundred** (1,200) miles and **cell** phones. However, it had to be done with all of the <u>secrecy</u> (on a *Need to Know only* basis), precision, and *stealth* as any critical military operation; or our dad would have commanded us to *scrub* (kill or abort) our mission (event).

    To make a *long* story—***short*** (after all of the preliminary coordination with my siblings in Louisiana), we drove (traveled together), my family from Virginia and my sister's (Angela's) family from North Carolina, to Louisiana on Tuesday and Wednesday (November 1 and 2, 2011). As part of our *(camouflage)* ***concealment*** plan, to ensure that my dad had no *clue* of our <u>imminent</u> arrival, I called and spoke to him from my vehicle, as we drove through Georgia. Through our fifteen minutes conversation, I gave him the impression that we were just relaxing in Virginia. Near the end of our conversation, I specifically asked him, "*when was the last time that <u>you</u> spoke to Angela? I need to call her, myself, in the next couple of days.*" About five hours later, Angela (my sister) directly called my dad (from the very same vehicle), on <u>her</u> cell phone, while we were driving through Alabama. After we were sure that our dad had no *inkling* (or hint) that we were **coming to town** or <u>what</u> was about to happen, Angela and I proceeded to contact (via internet and cell phone) a few *special* co-workers (like Mr. Steve Bierhurst, the *former* Fire Chief of the Patterson Volunteer Fire Dept. and others) to invite them to share their *personal* reflections/memories in my dad's ***honor*** at the (Surprise) Celebration Banquet. Everyone that we contacted, from my dad's past career/jobs of Civil Service (as far as 38 years prior), were genuinely willing and thoroughly excited to both attend and to speak on his behalf. Once we arrived into our immediate hometown area, I was (even) able to collect some special (old) photos of my dad from all of his previous jobs and civic organizations; from which, I produced a computer *slideshow* presentation. Kathy, my older sister, had already successfully *reserved* the **Patterson Civic Center** (my dad's current *semi-retirement* employer) as our event's site; and (of course), it was reserved under some <u>phony</u> name and (fictitious) event. After **all *this*:** the ***undercover*** coordination;

(strategic) *ruse* tactics; our *covert* (secret) **arrival** into the area and two or three days of **concealed** (*out-of-sight* or *under the radar*) **lodging** in a neighboring town, we were still facing the single most *prominent* hurdle (obstacle) to overcome. That single, most prominent hurdle **was:** HOW do we get him to definitely *show up* at the designated place and time of an event (*in his honor*), without him knowing that he was going (there) to attend his own (***Surprise***) celebration?

For this final ***clincher***, my sister (Kathy) got my dad's boss (Mr. Jerry Boyles) and one of his co-workers (Ms. Andrea Jones) to ensure that they would ensure that my dad ***would be present*** at the appointed place and time of the event. In order to accomplish that desired **end**, Mr. Jerry (the facility manager) called my dad, the day before the event, requesting that he come in to ***work*** (as the site's *host-facilitator* for our event, under the *ruse* (disguise) of some *personal* **emergency** situation. Because they (also) knew his disposition under the circumstances, they agreed to help us; while, we were all *banking* (***relying***) on his *heart* and willingness to help others (in distress)!

Finally, on the day of my father's (*Surprise*) *Retirement* Banquet, all things worked together, as if *orchestrated* by the very **Hand of GOD**! The facility's parking lot and event's venue was packed with (both) local *participants* and others from afar. Certain vehicles, those with license plates that might prematurely *catch his attention* or cause him to be suspicious, etc., like ours from Virginia, North Carolina or my sister Anita's from Zachary/Baton Rouge, LA, were parked (out-of-sight) on the opposite side of the building. As he arrived (about thirty minutes before his *designated* shift (***start***) time, Ms. Andrea Jones (the initial ***decoy*** *distressed* co-worker), met him outside of the building's main entrance and thanked him for *coming in* and pretended to go out to her vehicle. After she told my dad that the *guest* banquet ***group*** were already gathering *inside* the *reserved* Banquet area of the facility, he proceeded inside the building. He was dressed in his normal work attire of khaki pants, a button-up or pull-over polo shirt and a baseball (style) cap.

Finally, after having been alerted that my dad **had** (actually) arrived, we got everyone ready to *greet* (or salute) him, as *customary* for this type of *Surprise* event. When he (<u>*unsuspectingly*</u>) opened the door to enter the banquet room, everyone yelled: "**SURPRISE!**"

He was *stunned* by the **shock and awe** of the **thunderous** impact of that moment; his mouth dropped open; and, he *initially* <u>stepped</u> <u>back</u>, as if to say: I **don't** belong or should <u>*not*</u> be here! In our obvious *anticipation* of his reaction, my family (from Virginia) and Angela's (my sister's family that traveled from North Carolina) were positioned closest to the door, where he entered. So we immediately caught his attention and moved quickly to greet and embrace him. As the initial **shock** *subsided*, all of his questions came flooding out: *what are you all doing here*; *when did you all get into town*; <u>**what**</u> is going on or **have** you all gotten me <u>into</u>**?** Then, his attention turned to his clothes (attire). All we could do was **apologize** and **pull him** <u>*into the moment*</u>! There was **no other** way to *do* it!

Ms. Andrea Jones (his *on duty* co-worker) came back into the building/office (to **work**); and, my father's role, reluctantly **shifted** from his job position, *unexpectedly* for him, to the *official* **person of honor** at <u>his</u> (own) *surprise* banquet. It turned out to be just as **Grand** and **impactful** as it should have been; because, he had earned and <u>deserved</u> it. And we know that it was definitely the most humbling and gratifying experience of his life, which had ever been done <u>solely</u> to **honor** (salute) and **thank** him, as a result of his *life of Service*.

All of his family (siblings, children, etc.) and extended family, local friends and others from as far away as Houston, TX, current Church leaders and members, City officials, former co-workers, students/mentees, and citizens *gathered* to honor him. Those attendees, ranging from school-aged children to senior citizens (up to ninety years old), were all *there* just to **honor** him, for <u>five</u> <u>decades</u> of civic and community service. Mayor Rodney Grogan officially presented the *Keys To the City* to my father. Special friends and co-workers, from as far back as his earliest jobs, were there to share their reflections, sentiments, and memories of *serving* (working) with him. It was a great celebration and a monumental event.

As we left town and drove back to North Carolina and Virginia (between November 9 and 10, 2011), we were grateful that we had taken the opportunity to do this; although, he would <u>not</u> have <u>*ever*</u>

*agreed* or ***chosen*** to have this done (for himself). The ***justice*** (in this situation) was the fact (that): while he did <u>*not*</u> get what he would have chosen (or *wanted*), still, he got *exactly* what he had earned and ***deserved***. Additionally, it happened, while he was still *alive*; and, he *personally* **saw** and **felt** the *love* and ***appreciation*** (of his family, friends, neighbors, as well as, official representatives of our town, civic organizations, and citizens from across St. Mary *Parish* (or county equivalent)! The only primary person ***missing*** from (or <u>**not**</u> in attendance), at that ***grand Surprise*** Celebration for my dad in 2011, was my mother (the late **Virginia C. Thomas**).

As I reflect back upon my mother, as an ideal *role model* from my birth until her (untimely or unexpected) death in 2004, she was (both) an *angelic* being and a *spiritual **giant***, wrapped up in this *small* physical frame (or package). And it was clearly evident to me that she, too, *lived* her entire life (<u>**not**</u> for herself); but, she always lived to ***bless*** **others**. Over her entire lifetime, she ***faithfully*** *served*, gave and *sacrificed* so much; while, she was being empowered to *faithfully* **do** *so much for* **so many people** (especially the elderly and disabled ones in (both) our church and community/neighborhoods). She *tirelessly* served for more than fifty (50) years in the same church as: an usher and greeter, Vice-President and (later) President of the Usher Board, *Chair-person* on Committees, held District *leadership* positions in the Union Sixth District Missionary Baptist Association's Annual Conventions, as well as, other auxiliaries and associations, etc.

Additionally, she traveled, throughout the area and state, to actively participate in ministry and spiritual events, programs and community services.

My mother the primary (volunteer) transporter of widows, elderly and disabled members to and from *weekly* church services. She would visit elderly people in their homes, in nursing homes or hospitals, whether they were members of our, another or **no** church. She would always willingly take them to their appointments or she'd go run errands for them. Some of those that I can specifically remember were**:** Mrs. Eva Watson, Ms. Alberta Tate, Mrs. Viola Bracelet (*Ma Vie*), Mrs. Alberta McFall, great Aunt Elnora Sterling (*Nannan*), Mrs. Mary Wright (*Miss Shine*), Mrs. Bell, etc. All of these women were **widows**, except Mrs. Mary Wright (*Ms. Shine*). These people (individuals) and assigned tasks represented the heart of her personal ministry and *spiritual* **calling**.

As a very small boy (from three to seven years old), I can remember my mother walking to her job, where she did *day work* for a Caucasian woman (named Mrs. Dotson) and her family. That job consisted of cooking their food, cleaning their house, doing their laundry, etc., and taking care of their small children, who were <u>not</u> in school (yet). (**Note**: For anyone reading this book (now), who may be (personally) *unfamiliar* with the *day work* system, just think about that popular theater <u>movie</u> entitled: *The Help*, if you have seen it. I would recommend that you just **rent** that movie (if you have not already seen it)!)

Years later (while I was in junior high, high school and college), my mother worked as a <u>*cashier*</u> in our town's primary local grocery supermarket (*Roy's Supermarket*). In subsequent years, she eventually became the primary bus driver for the children of our church's (Children's) *Day Care* and *Head-Start* (Pre-School) Programs.

**Virginia C. Thomas** (my mother) was the ultimate ***Ambassador For Christ***; because, she *genuinely* **loved** <u>**all**</u> people! During my twenty-plus years <u>*active*</u> *duty* Army career, she visited (came to) every permanent duty station (or *long-term* assignment) location, where I had ever lived,<u> except</u> Saudi Arabia. Those assignment locations included Germany, while touring Paris, France, etc. (with us).

No matter**:** the situation; the state, country, or continent; the *culture*, language, race or (color of people); nor their age or size, my mother's normal smile, gentle demeanor and genuine *loving* compassion <u>*attracted*</u> and <u>*endeared*</u> <u>*everyone*</u> (to herself and to her GOD); and, she *embraced* Everybody! She never met anyone that she considered to be an alien or a <u>*stranger*</u>. And I can honestly say that she *welcomed* them *all*; *treated* (gave to) them all the same; and she left them all feeling that they were *loved* and *respected* (by her and by GOD), regardless of whether she met them in a church, on a street, on a bus/plane, in a store or in a park. She made each individual feel both acknowledged (noticed) and significant. <u>*Every*</u> time (no matter where, without *fail*), whenever my mother departed from one of my duty stations, numerous people—who had met and interacted with her (at every location), verbally expressed to me: how *loving* she had been to them; how *special* she made them feel; and, what a *remarkable spirit* they believed (recognized or *discerned*) that she had. Now, that's the way to *represent* CHRIST!

In terms of what my mother contributed or poured into me, I believe that GOD either specifically told her or showed her in a dream (or *vision*) <u>what</u> my spiritual gifts were and/or <u>how</u> He intended to use me. (At some point and time, GOD revealed (to her) those areas of my ministry <u>*calling*</u>; and, the specific assignments eventually manifested. EVERYTHING—that I am *doing* (now) in my *five-fold* Ministry Office of an *Evangelist*, as well as, my new *passion <u>to</u> <u>write</u>* these books, that GOD had already developed within me (over the years) and is (now) manifesting—all point back to the things that she required of me in my formative years. She always required me to: *shadow* my grandfather, as well as, to aide (or assist) her to transport the elderly, widows and disabled members of our church and community.

However, even more remarkably, she always (<u>first</u>) planned her programs (around my military *leave* or *visiting* schedule) and (<u>secondly</u>) required me to *speak publicly* on every one of her church and other programs. She would call me and say, "*Pete, what dates are you coming home (to visit from the Army)?*" After I would check the calendar and give her some dates, then she would say, "*Ok. I am planning a program on this specific date and I'm putting you on the program; so, you know that you need to be ready to speak.*" That's the way that she did it to me, every time! Her <u>*intent*</u> (*Objective*), all those years ago, was always simply to give me a *platform* for my voice to be heard (*publicly*). It did <u>not</u> matter (to her) whether twenty, fifty, one hundred or one thousand people would be there (present) to hear what I had to say; she just wanted me to <u>have</u> <u>the</u> <u>platform</u> to speak (both to and for The Kingdom of GOD). So, (Today) in this book, I'm saying: THANKS, MOM!

Now, I have actually embraced *writing books*, as my new <u>platform</u>! So (now) here I am sitting and typing this book, more that fifteen years after her death and realizing, WOW, she must have actually known (*something*) about this day! That's why, when I told her back in 2002, that I was (*seriously*) going to write a book, she *immediately* (without any hesitation) *approvingly* said to me, *"I KNOW!"* Ironically, that *first* (initial) book, that I referenced to her and had already half-written, was not this same book.

You see, my intent and purpose for that first book—(*Emerged From Fires and Storms*)—was simply to produce a personal *gift* to give to my mother, at my *official* Retirement Ceremony, in conjunction with *leaving* the Army in 2005. My plan was to present the very *First autographed* copy, as a *surprise*, at that ceremony. After I began writing that book, I had already decided that I'd never let her see it, before the grand ceremony. I felt *adamant* about that decision, for two reasons. First, I truly wanted the book to be a personal *gift* solely for her. Secondly, upon *initially* receiving the published book, I wanted to see her *initial* (acceptance) reaction of: *genuine* (*pure*), *raw* (*unscripted*) and *priceless* JOY!

(Note: Therefore, I never (ever) even gave her any *indication* (or *clue*) of when she could expect to see that book.) In summary, although it was an *admirable* gesture, I had actually (selfishly) planned to give her this *personal* gift (book); although, my mother was NEVER a *selfish* person. Therefore, GOD obviously *intended* (*desired*) for the book to be an *inspirational* (global *activation*) *gift* to the *Body of Christ* (the *Church's multitudes of millions* of people around the world).

Remember, when I said (earlier), that my mother did not live life *for herself*, but she always lived *for* others? As the true *Ambassador of Christ* that she was, GOD knew that her personal heart's desire would have been to share (her *personal gift* from me) with everyone that she possibly could. However, that still would have resulted in a *miniscule* impact, instead of the global reach and impact, which GOD (Himself) had desired and intended! Ultimately, GOD's thoughts, wisdom and desires are always *exceedingly and abundantly greater (or far above) anything* that you or I can (*ever*) even ask, think or imagine!

With my official *Retirement* approaching (pending) in 2005. Here's when and how GOD began to *alter* or *adjust* my previous plan and position (mindset)! In June 2004, my mother visited my family, during my last year of *active duty* service in New Jersey. We knew that she came for a <u>two-week</u> *visit* to spend time with my family and to attend my oldest daughter's (Aleisha's) High School Graduation; however (*unbeknown to us* at that time), those surface reasons were only a <u>part</u> (fraction) of GOD's (overall) *Plan*.

My mother spent the <u>first</u> week, established a normal *routine*; while, doing all of those <u>desirable</u> (and pleasant) things like spending and enjoying *time* at the local park and playground with our two youngest children (Joshua and Bethany), at that time. She also got to spend some quality time with my wife (Georgette), during the day, when the three girls were at school. Yes; she had the pleasure of *personally* attending my oldest daughter's HS Graduation in New Jersey; although, my parents lived in Louisiana. Additionally, I got to do a couple of things with her (alone) like going for a *walk* (around a pond) or a *drive* around my job location or surrounding town(s). Consequently, while <u>only</u> GOD *knew* it (then), this would be the *very* last *weeks, days* (*times*) that any of us would ever have <u>with</u> <u>her</u> (my mother) *alive*.

During the *second* (*final*) week, after I came home from work (about 5:30 p.m.) one day, the *Holy Spirit* (*Spirit of GOD*) said to me: "*Go get that book and give it to her.*" I started walking up the stairs. But about three stair steps up, I thought (within myself): "*No! I don't want her to see it like that; it's <u>not</u> a finished book, yet.*" I continued to walk up, while arguing (within) and wrestling (*in my spirit*). I didn't know why I was being led to give it to her (<u>now</u>); and, everything in my flesh and soul (mind) was screaming: "*No, not <u>yet</u>; not yet*!" However, the *command* (order) from the Spirit of GOD to my spirit was so clear, that I felt *compelled* to obey (GOD's *voice*). After about two minutes, I came *somberly* down the stairs and (*reluctantly*) gave the <u>manuscript</u> (*unfinished* book *draft*) to my mother.

As I handed it (over) to her, I said, "*I know we have talked about me writing this book. But it is not finished, yet. I still have a lot to add. However, when you look at this, you can see where I am in the process (development) and what it's all about. Tell me what you think. Remember, it's not finished—yet!*" She immediately smiled and said: "*Ok!*" Then, she sat it down next to her, on the lamp table and continued to play with my son (Joshua) and my youngest daughter (Bethany), in the living room.

I kept glancing at her, throughout that evening to see, when she would open it up. However, she continued her normal *routine* of playing with the two young ones, before we sat down to eat *dinner* or *supper* (depending upon what section of the country you live in or came from).

While eating and (afterward), when the two youngest children had already taken their baths and been tucked into bed, my mother's attention shifted to talking to the older girls (Aleisha (the senior) and Karen (a freshman) in high school) and watching TV. When the older girls went to bed about 9:45–10:00 p.m., we (adults) continued to watch the TV movie, until my wife (Georgette) went up for bed, about 10:45–11:00. My mom and I are both *late night* folks (*night owls*); so, I kept her company until midnight. Up to this point, my mother had not *opened* the manuscript, at all (yet). About that time, I kissed her <u>good night</u> and went up for bed; because I had to get up at 4:30–5:00 a.m. to report-in for *physical training* (which military folks refer to as: *PT*).

The next day, I arrived at home from *work* (again), about 5:30 p.m. I noticed that the manuscript was sitting in the same spot, on the lamp table, as the previous night. My mother was in her usual spot (in her favorite *arm-chair* or *sitting on the floor* (carpet), playing with the kids. Throughout the evening, she continued with her (and now our) <u>normal</u> *routine*. She never gave me any hint or *clue* (at all), that she had started reading the manuscript (yet). This night, like the night before, I had never seen her <u>open</u> up the manuscript. Finally (about 11:15 p.m.), when it was just the two of us left downstairs, I asked my mom, "*So you didn't get a chance to check out the book (yet); or, was it just too boring?*" (<u>Note</u>: It was as if she had been personally *bottled up* in a genie bottle; while, I was being *strung along* and waiting for her *reaction* and *feedback*.) As soon as I asked her that question, it was as though the cork popped off and she immediately *erupted* (literally *exploded)* with all the <u>genuine</u> and innocent *excitement* of a little *toddler* (kid) in a toy or candy store. She could no longer contain herself, as she *beamed* (*glowed*) *from ear-to-ear* and said, "Oh, that book…it was *GREAT!* It was so awesome and exciting that, once I started to read it, I could <u>not</u> put it down (to go to bed). So I just read the whole thing from *cover-to-cover*, before I went to bed (about 4:30 a.m. this morning)." Then, she sounded like she might hyperventilate, as she said, "*now, remember when your Aunt Lillie Mae…; and, don't forget about…*" To which I calmly responded, "*I know. Remember, I told you: I'm not finished, yet*!" Her reaction (honestly) was, as close as possible to, the pure and raw reaction that I could have ever envisioned seeing from her, in the public forum of my Retirement *Ceremony* (a year later in 2005), after the *real deal* (*finalized* book) would have actually been completed, published, autographed and *personally* presented to her. As the manuscript currently was (on that night), it gave her great joy! The only other times I can remember my mother being that excited (for or with me) were: when she held our *first* baby (oldest daughter) for the *very first* time in 1986; as well as, with each of my three other children (later in 1989, 1996, and 2001); when she traveled (with us) in Paris and Germany; when she *flew* on an airplane for the very *first* time. As she *soared*, through those miraculous *mazes* of fluffy, *amazingly artistic shapes* of *cotton-ball* (textured) clouds, all she kept saying (in the airplane) was: "*Wheeee! Wheeeee!*"

(Note: That's the same innocent reaction and *raw* gestures that one might reasonably expect from a g*enuinely* excited kid, while riding on a giant *roller coaster* over *Busch Gardens* or *Six Flags Over Texas*, etc. PRICELESS!)

A few days later, my wife and children hugged and kissed my mother, *Good-bye*, just before I drove her to Edison, NJ (near the *HQs, 78th Division (TS)*, which was my job location at that time). Once in Edison, NJ, we parked my SUV and caught the train up to the Newark Int'l Airport in Newark, NJ. That train transported my mother and I right up to the *air-rail* elevators, and up into the Airport's *Departures* Terminal. My mother and I (then) literally took our final *walk together* into that terminal along two primary corridors, leading to the security screening area, which was as far as I could go—*with* her. We *talked* and *laughed* all the way through the corridors to the security screening *check-point*. That's where I gave her one last *Good-bye* hug and kiss, before she walked through the security scanner. As she left me standing there, she had the biggest, most joyful, jubilant, care-free and peaceful smile on her face (beaming from ear-to-ear), <u>without</u> a care in this world. She had the kind of *smile* that I would expect an *Angel* (whose <u>relaxing up *in Heaven*</u>) to have. However, I did <u>not</u> *move* (at all) from that spot, for about five minutes; because, I *knew* my mother! So I already knew that once she finally *cleared* through that *security **access*** gate, she would *look back* to smile and wave, at me (again and again), about every six or seven steps, until she finally turned a corner and was completely out of sight. That's what I expected her to do; and, that's exactly what she did! Therefore, she had to have turned back around and repeated that *routine* a total of six or more times. And every single time she did, I was still standing (<u>posted</u> *stationary*) there to return those same sentiments (gestures) back to her. Finally, after she was totally *out-of-sight,* then, I turned away, smiled (to myself) and walked out of the airport.

*Mrs. Virginia Catherine Thomas (my mother)*

When I returned back home that June evening (in 2004), after transporting my mother to the airport (for her return flight back to Louisiana), I was very grateful having had her there with us for those two weeks and the graduation. Grateful, more, that we had made her feel so *special* and *loved*, during her visit. I still did not understand (yet) or know <u>*why*</u> I had been led (by the Holy Spirit) to give her the manuscript; which allowed her to see that *unfinished* draft, before it was a *real* book. However, <u>*something*</u> (a *piece* of this puzzle) was still *missing* (for me); and, I could <u>*not*</u> *put my finger on* (or pinpoint) exactly <u>*what*</u> that was.

 Eventually (on November 12, 2004), five months later, I finally got a warning or *clue* to that *missing* (puzzle) *piece* of information. It was a Friday evening and I had just arrived home (from work), about 5:30 p.m. EST. Once I went into the house, I took off and hung-up my military uniform's BDU shirt, loosened the laces of my boots, and went downstairs to lay on the carpeted floor, to relax for a while (in the living room). Approximately forty minutes after I got home, I could hear my daughter (Karen, the fourteen years old, freshman) talking, on the telephone, to her cousin/my niece (Kalon) in Louisiana. After a few minutes, I could hear their conversation <u>*shift*</u> (change) to a tone of anxiety, fear and dread, to the point that they both began to cry (during the conversation). Then my daughter said that my niece had just told her that, while my mother and other family members were driving to a high school football (playoff) game, something *tragic* occurred in my mother's *physical condition* that required them to rush her immediately to a hospital emergency room. After <u>finally</u> reaching my father and older sister, who were traveling with my mother, I had to wait another hour, before they would have *detailed* information from the emergency room medical staff. (*Initially*), they could only tell me that there was no automobile accident; but, my mother had suffered some sort of *life-threatening* medical emergency condition, that caused her to lose consciousness, with <u>*no*</u> *oxygen* (supplied) to her brain. This was indicated by the *foaming* from her mouth, after she had lost consciousness (for a certain period of time). ALL that we could do (in both Louisiana and New Jersey), for the next two hours, was *pray* and *wait*! Finally, we got an accurate *update* in New Jersey, via telephone.

The doctors confirmed that my mother had suffered from *congestive heart failure* (CHF).

And although she had suffered from a *loss* of oxygen to her brain, doctors were able to *revive* and *stabilize* her; now, she was in *critical* condition in the Intensive Care Unit (ICU). GOD, this was a *blind side* shot that I never saw coming, like a *sucker punch* to the nose (from left field), without provocation or warning! Besides our *Prayers*, doctors were keeping her under <u>observation</u> and running periodic *tests* to measure any levels of *brain activity*.

On Monday (*Nov. 15, 2004*), after three full days of being hooked-up to an artificial respirator or Life Support system, <u>without</u> any measurable *brain activity* (eventually) the doctors *officially* pronounced my mother *brain dead*, on that day. Just like that, she was suddenly <u>gone</u>! So five months after my mother left our house in New Jersey, I (subsequently) knew <u>why</u> I had to let her see the *unfinished* manuscript (earlier) in June; because, GOD knew that there would *never* be any other opportunity for her to *see* (<u>nor</u> *receive*) it. My family would never get another opportunity to <u>see</u> or <u>hug</u> her (again) in this earth realm.

As I look back (now in 2018), my mother's *transition* (from earth to Glory) and her *departure* from this <u>physical</u> life (as we know it), marked several things (to include): (1) the <u>termination</u> of my own *plan*; (2) the <u>loss</u> or *disappearance* of any (previous) sense of *urgency* or *excitement*, that I once had, to finish that initial book; (3) a *fourteen* years *delay* in *publishing* that *inaugural* book, to fulfill GOD's intent and plan for presenting that book, as a *gift* to the Body of Christ (The Kingdom), and (4) a thirteen years *delay* in my launching (or *activation*) of this GOD-ordained (*writing*) platform, which *He* had previously chosen as the *vehicle* (*wings*), upon which my ministry *messages* can *travel* in both current and subsequent *seasons* of my life, even <u>beyond</u> my own *lifetime*. In reality, that fore-mentioned *thirteen years* **delay,** in the actual **publishing** of that particular book, was eventually extended to sixteen years, until the Summer of 2021.

In life, my mother continuously provided an *initial* platform, for the *voice* (of my ministry and anointing) to be cultivated and developed, through my gift of public speaking. However, GOD chose to (*exponentially*) **expand** my **global reach** and my assignments' *audience* to include *multitudes*, some of whom, I will <u>never</u> have direct (*face-to-face*) access to, through traditional *public speaking* venues. In her final years and through her death (*transition* to Glory), GOD used my mother to **inspire** (*push* or **propel**) me, into the *activation* of my *required* (next and higher level) **writing** platform. Although my mother was (*personally*) **blessed**, to **see** a **glimpse** of the *gift* of my writing; she realized that it was <u>***never***</u> meant to be just**:** to or for **her** (alone).

Ultimately, my mother's **joy** was made ***complete***, in fulfilling that **final** *assignment* <u>with</u> (and to) me. In doing so, she has already been (and shall *forever* be) a great **BLESSING** to both me and ***countless*** other (*current*) individuals and **future multitudes** or generations to come (within the Body of CHRIST), around the globe.

We can all recall and name some famous *National* and *Global leaders,* who were great servant-*leaders* and *role models***,** like Dr. Martin Luther King Jr., President Nelson Mandela, Mother Teresa, Rev. Billy Graham and others. Three of these four named individuals were *Nobel Peace Prize* recipients (Dr. MLK Jr., in 1964; Mother Teresa (born Agnes Gonxha Bojaxhiu), in 1979; and President Nelson Mandela, in 1993). After all, Dr. King's monumental personal contributions to, as well as his universal recognition as *the Leader of,* The *Civil Rights* Movement benefited masses of humanity (globally). However, the vast majority of all the significant **daily** *role models* (in my personal life and within our communities), consisted primarily of the ***village*** of**:** teachers; hard-working, adult neighbors; parents and grandparents; church leaders; youth coaches, etc. (Together) they all collectively guided, mentored, disciplined and *poured into* the children within their neighborhoods, churches and schools. I specifically <u>*named*</u> (in the **Preface** of this book), a number of those individuals, who both directly impacted me and some are still impacting their local *hometown* neighborhoods/communities, and our (global) *world* **today**.

Because I grew up in the *Deep South* (Louisiana) and attended public school, during the final years of ***segregation*** and the *implementation* and initial (*trial*) years of ***integration***, I have <u>vivid</u> (*personal*) memories of those times and experiences. These *deep rooted* memories stem from (me) personally *living in* and navigating through those environments (*walking* that terrain), **not** from watching some **media—manipulated** (propaganda *censored* or politically *spun*) movie.

Here, I will **not** go into what *the daily grind of those days* entailed (consisted of) for young African-American children, in this book. (Note: I do that quite vividly in my next book: **Emerged From Fires and Storms**!) Since *this* chapter, of this book, is dedicated to highlighting some of the specific (*personal*) Role Models and (*local*) **heroes** from my childhood and life, suffice it to say that I can still remember all of my regular teachers from Kindergarten and *Head-Start* through High School (Graduation). I can vividly remember **those** teachers: who were dedicated and conscientious; those who were prejudiced (bigots); those who truly loved children (cared for their students); those who were incompetent or were only there for a paycheck; etc.

In terms of teachers, I remember the original version of *The Good, The Bad, And The Ugly*: the good (**best**) ones, the bad (*mediocre*) ones, and the ugly (*worst*) ones. I can clearly remember my Kindergarten teacher (Mrs. Idabelle Clemmons), who lived *diagonally across the street,* from my family's initial house. I can (still) remember my very first elementary (first grade) teacher (Mrs. Laura C. Smith), who I adored as a teacher; but, her child-birth and *maternity leave* caused her to be *replaced* by Ms. Small (for about four months or most of the Spring Semester) of that year. I can still remember the Principal (Mr. Joseph *Professor* Ball), the Librarian (Mrs. Henderson), and those *tenured teachers* (Mrs. Portia Jackson, Mrs. Maggie Wren, Mrs. Emma O'Gwen, Mrs. Jenkins and Mr. Allen "Doc" Williams, these were all dedicated, *long-term* teachers from the old **segregated** and not equal school system. Some of whom had also (previously) taught our parents, aunts and uncles. I can still remember Ms. Tillman (who later married, and became Mrs. Alexander), who had the reputation as the absolute, *hands-down*, **meanest** teacher, in terms of *disciplining* students, at that school.

I never (personally) had an African-American **male** teacher, until after *integration*, when I had Mr. Morgan, as my *Homeroom* and Social Studies teacher. Some of my (other) absolute favorite teachers were: Mrs. Claire Bourg (fifth grade); Mrs. Juanita Clark (seventh grade);

Coach Jerry Simmons (eighth and ninth grades, History); Mrs. Lena Bernard (tenth grade, Home Economics); Mr. Allen "Doc" Williams (eleventh grade, Geography), who was both *old school* and only my second African-American *male* teacher; Mrs. Rosemary Ayers (ninth through eleventh grades: English I, II, and IV classes); Coach Carey Mac Staples (Algebra); Ms. JoAnne Landry (eleventh grade, Business Math) and Mrs. Calamari (tenth and eleventh grades, Chemistry). My two (personal) favorite football coaches were Head Coach Jack Andre and Coach *Hollywood* Cooper (*Defensive Backs* Coach).

 As I was sitting and writing this book, I began to ponder the schools, teachers, administrators and staffs, that I had personally encountered, from both the **segregated** and **integrated** school systems. I was compelled to reflect upon the differences (*disparities* in the funding $$$; size and maintenance conditions of schools' buildings, supplies/books, benefits/treatment and pay) between the two from 1935–1973. Additionally, I began to think about how *under-appreciated* and *under-paid* teachers feel in 2018, despite all of the current technological advances in equipment and aides (computers, electronic tablets, calculators, and online *distance learning* system capabilities). Those *thought-provoking* reflections (**now**) made two exceptionally **special** teachers (Mrs. Portia Jackson and Mrs. Claire Bourg) **stand out**, in my mind. So I must highlight them (now) in this book. The most accurate and revelatory **truth** about these two teachers, from my personal perspective, is simply to say, "*[**Outwardly**], they were like **night and day**, yet [**inwardly**], they were **identical** or exactly the **same**!*"

 I had already previously known Mrs. Portia Jackson from our neighborhood, as she lived around the corner from two of my childhood residences (homes) and directly across the street from our old segregated (negro) school: **Hattie A. Watt School**. My primary (*personal observations*) recollections, interactions with and/or knowledge of *both* of these women, specifically as *teachers,* goes back to 1972–73. When my original fifth grade teacher (Ms. Cooper) left in the Fall of 1972, due to an illness, Mrs. Claire Bourg became my *new* fifth grade **teacher**, for the remainder of the school year. On the (skin) *surface*, they were like day and night! One (Mrs. Claire Bourg) was a Caucasian woman, with solid white (gray) hair, facial wrinkles and *age spots*, who had grown and advanced (prior) in her teaching profession, through the old *Jim Crow, segregated* schools for **whites** only. Conversely, Mrs. Portia Jackson was an educator of *African* and Native-American ancestry, with shiny black hair and a wrinkle-free, flawless facial complexion, who had risen and advanced in her teaching profession, through the opposite, *segregated and unequal* schools for **negroes** only. Additionally, they both had been born and reared in that (same) local area; while, they lived two opposite (opposing) realities of the same *Jim Crow, segregated* system of racism and bigotry (which comprised and engulfed both of their professional, social and personal lives).

However, these two women were *more alike* (or the same) than they were: *different*.

Both of these teachers (Mrs. Claire Bourg and Mrs. Portia Jackson) had the same *servant* **Spirit**. They both had the same ***conscientious*** *dedication, commitment, loyalty* and *character*, in carrying out their responsibilities as *educators*. They both proved to have: the same **genuine care and concern** for all their students (equally), as well as, the same **love** for their profession. This fact was clearly evident to me (even as a fifth grade student in 1973); and, it was absolutely and *undeniably* true. How else could anyone (otherwise) explain how and why both of these fifth grade school teachers were already the **longest tenured** teachers in our town's schools, as well as, throughout *St. Mary* Parish and possibly the entire State of Louisiana, in 1973. In that year, Mrs. Claire Bourg had already been teaching for forty-one years; while, Mrs. Portia Jackson had already been teaching for thirty-eight years. That's exactly why I referred to that particular period of 1935–1973; because 1935 was the first year that both women were *working* in the education profession, although Mrs. Claire Bourg's teaching career began in 1932 (three years earlier). By 1973, Both of these women had already made the same *life-long* commitment to **teaching**, in the *worst* region and at the *worst* time, while that profession was **_NOT_**: comfortable, popular, financially lucrative; nor, easily navigated, based upon the *built-in* **turmoil**, associated with the *dismantling* of the old *Jim Crow*, segregated school system and the *hate-laden* implementation of public schools' **Integration**. Additionally, both were already beyond the required age for **Retirement** (pension) *eligibility*. Finally, these two teachers had both made the <u>same</u> choice (decision) to *rise above* the ***bigotry and hatred*** that their society's system, as well as, profession authorities, close family, friends/acquaintances and/or neighbors may have attempted to *force* upon them.

I originally realized (in 1973) that Mrs. Claire L. Bourg was definitely *old*, for a fifth grade teacher; but, I honestly did not know exactly how old she was, until I researched her on the Internet in November 2017. When I came across her name in Census Data (between 1900–1910), I learned that this <u>***beloved***</u> teacher was born on July 20, 1903, and died on December 24, 1995, **at ninety-two years** of age. Which also meant that she was already **seventy years old**, as my fifth grade teacher in 1972–1973. Similarly, Mrs. Portia Jackson was already **sixty-five years old**, as a fifth grade teacher in that same year. Wow! It is absolutely remarkable, even *mind-boggling* that these two elderly women were both able to *teach* <u>daily</u>, for so many decades, and accomplish such extraordinary feats (in helping to dismantle *segregation* and usher in *integration*); while *working* in such a *tumultuous*, *hateful*, and *stress-filled* environment of (*daily*) ***overt*** and ***accepted*** **terrorism**!

In March 2018, I found Mrs. Portia Nerissa (Humphrey) Jackson's obituary, which revealed that she was born on June 9, 1908; however, she just recently died on November 22, 2016, at the age of **108 years** old. What a glorious testament to the *life-long **legacy*** of *Education* that both of these exceptional ***servants*** left in St. Mary Parish (Louisiana). Today, there is <u>**no**</u> possible way for us to ever really know exactly how many children were educated, impacted, nurtured, protected and changed by these two women and others like them (that I have named in this book). In the end, these two educators (Mrs. Bourg and Mrs. Jackson) had poured ***knowledge*** and ***love*** into generations of children and families, as they each individually and actively taught for more than forty years (eighty-plus years combined), during their careers in both the <u>*segregated*</u> and <u>*integrated*</u> school systems in Louisiana. While I believe that all the other fore-mentioned teachers, that I named had similar (or equal) love *for* and dedication *to* their *Calling* and students, clearly no teachers displayed it more (over time) than those two.

*Ms. Portia Nerissa (Humphrey) Jackson*
*(June 9, 1908__November 22, 2016)*

    While in high school, I had a genuine respect, and even developed a special *admiration*, for several of my teachers and coaches (like Mr. Allen "Doc" Williams, Mrs. Lena Bernard, Mrs. Rosemary Carlino Ayres, Coach Jerry Simmons, Coach Jack Andre and a few others). Remember, my parents guidance/expectations and my father's ever-persistent, unrelenting requirement: that we (children) always respect all adults and those in authority. So we always **did**; because, my dad had very strict disciplinary measures, which would result in some very harsh consequences, if we did not. I always started with a level of *common respect* for (toward) all teachers. However, as I began to know the individual teacher's or administrator's personality, heart (attitude and intentions toward me) and *character* or <u>*lack*</u> thereof, through interacting with him or her over a period of time, I found that my *respect* sometimes shifted from the individual (himself/herself) to their official <u>*position*</u> only. In some cases and situations, individual people's **attitudes** and **character** (even those in positions of authority), do **not** warrant or deserve my respect or the respect of others, whom they are assigned to serve or supervise. *That* fact has been consistently **true** throughout school, my career and my life!

Notably, those teachers and others in authority, who personally *deserve,* not only my genuine respect, but also provoke (or inspire) a true admiration to develop within me—are really both ***special*** and great people! The character and ability of any individual, who can do that, goes far beyond one's job position or title. Those who possessed such special qualities, not only demonstrated (revealed) what they *possessed inside*; but, they also ***discerned*** and ***appreciated*** (*recognized* and *valued*) what I and other students, also, *possessed* inside of us. All of those teachers and coaches, that I mentioned above, did that to me. And they tried to *pull it out* of me, as well as their other students, in order to make us grow and flourish. Their ultimate objective was only to see us develop and grow into productive and outstanding citizens. However, each of them did that in their own uniquely different ways.

**Mrs. Rosemary Carlino Ayres** was another one of those extraordinary teachers, who had ***risen above*** the bigotry and hatred that she had obviously seen, been affiliated with and exposed to (and probably even encourage to embrace); however, she chose to possess a different spirit and embrace the opposite mind-set. That fact spoke volumes to my heart! She was my English teacher throughout high school (for all my class levels of English I, III, and IV). In my third year of high school, which was also my final year, I was in her English IV class. One of the things, that she required us to do, was to *memorize* pieces of literature (poems, etc. such as**:** *Annabelle Lee*, one of Edgar Allen Poe's poems in honor of his *deceased* wife; and, Marc Antony's speech rendered at Julius Cesar's funeral (in the theatre play *Julius Cesar***,** written by William Shakespeare), etc.). Each time that she would assign one of these literary selections for our class to memorize, she'd allow us about three weeks to learn it. Afterward, she would randomly and without warning, select various moments, during class sessions to *individually call-up* (select) four to six different students per class session, to (*individually*) recite the literature for an impromptu oral presentation grade. Whenever she called your name, you had to be ready; because, you only got one opportunity.

The ***more*** (of the poem) that you could memorize (recite) and the ***better*** you could present (*orally* deliver) it, the higher your final grade was. This process was repeated session after session (for about seven or eight sessions), until everyone had been tested and graded. Finally, after the entire class had gone through both of the fore-mentioned literary works (the poem *Annabelle Lee* and Marc Antony speech from Julius Cesar's funeral), some of the students asked Mrs. Ayres one day, "*why do we have to do all this (reciting poems), we won't need to know this or will never ever use this stuff again, in our future job careers?*" Mrs. Ayres replied, "*maybe you will never need to use these again, but I can guarantee you one thing*: *if you ever* really **learn** *them, you will never ever forget them!*"

And I can attest to the fact that Mrs. Ayres was absolutely correct; because more than forty years has already passed, since I was in her classes, yet I have always been able to randomly recite those two pieces (verbatim) over all these years. In fact, my cousin Donnette, for the first twenty-five years (through college and while I was on *active duty* in the Army), whenever I went back home to visit, would always test me to see if I could still remember and recite those poems (upon request).

While I was in Mrs. Ayres's English IV class in 1978–'79, I was simultaneously on of the **senior** *Captains* for our football team, on a regular basis that year. As such, two of us (Team Captains) would be selected each week to represent the team at the podium to give an impromptu speech at our weekly (Friday morning) *Pep Rally*, leading up to that week's football game. Each time that I went up to the podium, with another Captain, the other guys would always want me to give the speech. The *gift* (and art) of public speaking came *easily* (naturally) for me; and, I could really capture and inspire the *student body* population. Sometimes, if I tried to get the other guy(s), at the podium with me, to give the speech, or if I was not even one of the guys up at the podium that week, a few of the students (in the bleacher seats) would demonstratively or provocatively begin to stump their feet, while chanting: "*we want Rousell; we want Rousell; we want Rousell…!*" This chant would grow, swell and magnify, throughout the entire student body, until they were in a frenzy!

Eventually, I would speak, if I was one of the guys at the podium; or (if I was not up at the podium), one of the administrators or coaches would have to *quiet down* the student population, so that other guys at the podium could get the (courtesy) opportunity to speak.

One Friday morning, after one of these long, demonstrative *crowd stirring* chants, for me to give the Pep Rally speech, I walked into Mrs. Ayres's classroom about two hours later. As I approached the room, she was standing outside of the doorway, as her students were walking in. When I got to her (outside her classroom door), she just began to shake her head (up and down), whiling smiling at me. Then, she said, "*Now, what office are you going to run for?*" I immediately smiled back and nodded (to acknowledge her question) and said, "Good morning!" However, I truly had **no** intention of running for any public offices; so, I did not directly address that question. However, I heard (*acknowledged*) and *appreciated* it! To me that day, that was Mrs. Ayres's way of saying **to me:** I hear your speeches; I see you; and, I can appreciate and *value* what's inside of you! Mrs. Ayres, like Mrs. Rosie Butler (my childhood Youth Choir Director at Church) and my late mother, before her, all recognized and openly appreciated my ***gift*** (and passion) in public speaking.

It was because of my clear recollections of Mrs. Ayres's sentiment and actions (proving to *value* and *treat* all of her students, equally and fairly), as I was writing this book forty years later, that I felt compelled to include and acknowledge her. More importantly, I sincerely desired to contact her and let her know (how much I appreciated her), if and while, she was still *alive*. To that end, on that Monday night (November 13, 2017), I did an inquiry of (looked up) Mrs. Ayres on the internet. The information that I found told me that she and her husband had moved away from my hometown and state. I could see that there were two other resident locations that she had, after leaving my hometown; however, there was **no** obvious way to get a phone number for her. At that point, I reached out to one of her daughters (Anna) that I remembered from school. We had spent some years (together) in the school's Marching Band. With the help of the internet, I (telephonically) contacted Anna, who was now married and living in a nearby town (about eight miles from our hometown). After a pleasant and *reflective* conversation with Anna, I learned that her parents (specifically her mother and my former teacher: Mrs. Rosemary Ayres) would be moving back to our hometown early in 2018. I would have loved to personally say "*Thank You*" (face-to face). Unfortunately, both Mrs. Ayres and Coach Jerry Simmons have both passed away in my hometown, since then.

I would be selfishly *remiss or negligent* if I did **not** share (with you), the most profound and fascinating **revelation**, that GOD gave (showed) me, while writing this chapter of the book. The revelation was the spiritual answer to a personal question that I had: <u>why</u> was there such a *drastic* difference in their physical aging process over time? One seemed to be slowed down while the other appeared to have been accelerated (sped up), as the years passed. Therefore, I was compelled to ponder and meditated on this question for a few weeks. I had to go a lot deeper than their skin color!

GOD eventually gave me this revelation (*spiritual truth* or answer) to my question in 2018, a few weeks after I had thoroughly compared Mrs. Portia Jackson (the African-Native American teacher at sixty-five years old) and Mrs. Claire Bourg (the Caucasian teacher at seventy years old). The key or underlying truth was that (spiritually) a person can never allow **bitterness** to enter his/her *heart* (spirit or core essence of one's being) because eventually it will accelerate the decline in health and wellness of the physical body.

Although both of those teachers had lived through and endured the same era (periods and conditions of the Old Jim Crow system of racism, discrimination, and injustices) albeit from two different (opposing) sides of the system. And it had impacted (affected) them both, differently. Nevertheless, their commitment and dedication to their *calling* (to teach) and their genuine love and compassion for all of their students were exactly the same!

Mrs. Portia Jackson's genuine love (while the *oppressed* target of that system) allowed her to *humbly* **confront** the racism and bigotry with: her own self-respect, dignity, forgiveness, and freedom from retaliation (never becoming like her oppressors). This allowed her to age *gracefully* in GOD's care! Mrs. Claire Bourg's genuine love __ (as an innocent observer from the oppressors side) __ compelled her to both reject (abhor and resent) the ugly evil of that system and to recognize and embrace the guilt, shame, and responsibility of the racism and bigotry of her family members/friends, White American culture and ancestors. She would have immediately **righted** this wrong, if it were in her individual and personal authority to do so. However, because this was not within her power to correct this and her **anguish** was so *great,* she eventually *internalized* (embodied and took on) the *burden and weight* of the guilt, shame, and responsibility for the grave sin that she saw and felt incapable to reverse or undo. It was the negative effect of carrying this internal burden of bitterness toward this system and obviously some of her own relatives (people) that eventually began to appear visibly while deteriorating the health and wellness of her physical body. Therein was the underlying cause of the **acceleration** in her (personal) *physical aging* process! I knew that I needed to share this revelation with you all now before leaving this chapter because it will impact me and I hope that it impacts you for the rest of our lives.

# CHAPTER 4

# Always a Servant

*"I have <u>always</u> been a **servant**; but, I have never been a **slave**!"* (Rousell Thomas Jr.)

On Friday afternoon, November 30, 2011, I was driving home from a local *Walmart* store. Suddenly, it was (as if) a *scroll* opened before me and I began to see and recall all of the places that I had been throughout my life. As I reflected upon all these places, where I had traveled or lived, and the opportunities that I had to *serve* and/or minister to other people, the Spirit of *GOD* said to me: "See; I have given you <u>*millions*</u> *of opportunities*!" Because GOD requires us to <u>*serve*</u> and help other people, he has to give us those opportunities to do so. He (then) revealed to me that these opportunities were/are actually *portals* (like doors and windows); through which, we (the *servants* of GOD) gain access in order to *positively influence* the lives of people and *impact* the world's systems—for the *Kingdom of GOD*. As I reflect back over my life (now), I can see how GOD enabled me to be molded and prepared for the plans and purpose that He has *called* (and *predestined*) me to fulfill in 2017 and beyond. So let's look back at my *molding and preparation* process.

I had been born, Rousell Thomas Jr., on January 13, 1962. I was the second child, but the first son, of seven children that would eventually be born to my parents. I had already been *called forth* (by GOD), and delivered by a veteran (seasoned) Negro *mid-wife* in a local home (outside of the confines of a public hospital). That fact was the *normal* situation and *routine* practice for *Negro* births (deliveries), during that time of segregation in that region of the country. Eventually, there would be four boys (Gerald, George, Edward and myself) and three girls (Kathy, Angela, and Anita). My parents, Rousell Thomas Sr. and Virginia (Washington) Thomas, were a *hard working*, *God-fearing*, young couple, living in the *Deep South* in a little town called Patterson, Louisiana. (To find it on the map, you'd have to go all the way down to the *sole of the Boot*, a fraction of an inch from the water's edge of the *Gulf of Mexico*.) And although ninety-nine years had already elapsed since the *Emancipation Proclamation* officially ended slavery in this country, *Jim Crow* (the *Unwritten Laws* of the *deep South's racism, bigotry, discrimination and segregation*) were still *alive*, *prevalent* and a part of our (*daily*) lives.

My grandfather on my mother's side (*her* biological father), Reverend Edward Washington Sr., had been born on January 29, 1887, so he turned seventy-five years *young*, exactly *sixteen days* after my birth. (Note: He never referred to, or called himself: *old*.)

I was reared in a home with two *working* parents, who both **served** GOD; and, a grandfather, who was an old Baptist preacher. My father served as a deacon in our church and had multiple jobs, during my childhood years. There were times when he simultaneously held two or three jobs at the same time. One of his jobs was serving as a *police officer*, under the *first* **negro** (*African-American*) **Chief of Police** (Chief Jesse Paul), in our town's history.

(Note: I believe that the key factor, in this accomplishment, was the fact that he had also reached the rank of *Chief* in the US Navy, during a thirty-eight-year career.) Without additional pay, my dad and some of the other men (also) served as *volunteer* firemen. My mother served as an usher and greeter in the church; while working her jobs in domestic housework and (later) cashier in a local grocery store. And my grandfather (her dad) was a Baptist preacher and the Assistant Pastor in our church. So we (children) were always exposed to constant structure, respect, and responsibility (*chores*). As one of the two oldest children, my older sister (Kathy) and I had to assist with the younger siblings' diapers, in addition to: doing laundry (hanging clothes *on the line*, taking down (in) and folding clothes); cooking rice and washing dishes; sweeping floors (and later) vacuuming carpets; dusting furniture; walking to the neighborhood store; etc. (**Note:** We are talking about *washing*, the old white cloth diapers, *by hand* on a *scrubbing board*, inside of an old metal tub or sometimes in a plastic bucket; because, society's modern (*disposable*) **Pampers** or their equivalents did **not** exist back then.)

Although lions and eagles are always *born* **free**; people were (are), in some times and places, *born* **slaves** (designated or *labeled*, as such, **at birth**). However, like racists and bigots, who are NOT born as such, ALL (of the above) must have their distinct *spirits (attitudes) developed over time*, in accordance with the manner, environments and systems in which they are*: taught* and/or *trained*. Lions teach and train their cubs; while, parents/families, communities and cultures teach and train their children (in developing them), through their established processes. Therefore, *the sooner or (earlier)* our children are taught, trained and focused toward (willingly) *serving* others (their elders and communities, etc.)—*the Better*! When/if our *youth* are allowed to exist, without having *this* spirit (attitude) established and developed within them—the greater the probability that they may never get it. It never (ever) just happens (by chance)!

The *Call on my life* (requirement) to *serve* others, began (for me) at the age of six years old, that's when I was *baptized* and gave my life to GOD. This was the start of my life of real *servanthood*. My first significant role (mission at six years old) was to **shadow** and serve as the *unofficial* (1968–1970s, **pre**-*Tech* version of) a *Life Alert* System for my grandfather (at the age of eighty-three years), whenever he had to dig a grave in the *segregated* cemetery. Here's how that original *manual* system worked. If it was a *Saturday* or *Summer* day (**no** school), and a **negro** (or an *African-American*) resident had *passed away* (died) in our town, my grandfather (alone) would dig the grave *from scratch* (start to finish) with a shovel. In this situation, my mother always required me to get up and go (just before dawn) with him to the cemetery, to *observe* (monitor), as a safety precaution. And although I was *not* big enough or old enough to help actually **dig**, my job was to *run and get some help*, if he fainted, had a *heat-related* injury, heart attack, or stroke. Therefore, I was his *personal* **Life Alert** System (from 1969–1974), <u>before</u> our **modern** (2018 and beyond) *technology* even existed. This was extremely significant on summer days (back then), when the temperatures were 98–103 degrees, along with humidity of 100 percent; while, my grandfather was already eighty-one to eighty-seven years (***young***), during that period. Therefore, this system was also implemented (activated), when my grandfather did any **strenuous** work like cutting grass on his large property or working in his extensive garden. (I was able to actually help him a lot more, when doing these tasks.)

I've always been an *excellent* student, well-known and highly-respected in my neighborhood/community and church. So my parents extended a higher level of responsibilities to me, at nine years old. These *new* responsibilities included walking **alone** (across our town) to get mail from the Post Office box; pay the rent to Mr. Piccou (Housing Authority Office); and assisting my grandfather, even more. This led to other seniors/(*elderly*) people, in our church and community, requesting me to run errands and do tasks for them, some of which required me to handle their money, also.

I can vividly remember accompanying my mother on Sundays, to pick-up some of the *elderly mothers/widows* of the church (called *deaconesses or stewardesses*) like: Mother Eva Watson, my *great grandma* Louella Robinson, and Mrs. Mary Wright. Therefore, as the eldest son, my role was to physically assist them in getting up and down the steps (from their porches, into and out of the car) and finally into and out of the church. These women were not only elderly (between *seventy* to *one hundred years* old); they also walked on canes or had some other form of disabilities. Grandma Louella Robinson was actually my <u>grea</u>t grandmother, my <u>father's</u> biological grandmother, who actually died at the age of 103 or 104 years old. Because she was born, during a period when **negroes** were not admitted (served or *treated*) in public hospitals and <u>no</u> official *birth certificates* were provided, there was a question as to which year she had been born. At the time of her death, she was easily the oldest person in the family, the church and the town, during a very short period of my life. [Note: Vital information about *births*, *baptisms*, *marriages* and *deaths* were normally recorded (in their Bibles, if at all, or only <u>*verbally*</u> passed from older to younger generations.] *Mother* Eva Watson, on the other hand, was the eldest **mother** of our little church for most of my childhood and into my college years. She lived alone, as a widow well into her nineties. At ninety-two years of age, I remember that she was physically strong and walked (up and down steps/stairs) very well; but, her eyesight was *fading,* which seriously impaired her vision, in her last years. However, her *mind* was <u>always</u> sound (mentally *sharp*); while, her ***faith*** in GOD and the ***determination***, with which she lived, *never* (ever) wavered. Mrs. Mary Wright (known to everyone as ***Miss Shine***), had a serious problem with one leg, that was *twisted* (canted) to one side. So she had always walked with a cane, while dragging her *clubbed foot.* I am not sure if this original condition had resulted from an earlier accident or disease. But I do know that she did (later) suffer a *stroke*, which affected one side of her body (entirely) to include her face/mouth, as well as, her motor skills. Mrs. Mary Wright was still (absolutely) the <u>second</u> *most outspoken* and (verbally) ***fiery*** elderly woman,<u> "runner-up"</u> to my paternal grandmother *only*, in all of my travels around the world. She and her husband (Mr. David) lived across town. Finally, as the *President* of our church's Usher Board, *Miss Shine* knew that my mother (the Vice-President of her Usher Board) and I would arrive to transport her to services every Sunday morning. After she suffered the stroke, she could not get around, as well, any more. However, she <u>always</u> freely *spoke* her mind; and, she would not hesitate to *give anyone a piece of her mind*! During the last two years of *Miss Shine's* life, my mother had to fulfill a lot of her *President's* responsibilities/duties. My mother succeeded Miss Shine, as President of our church's Usher Board, upon *Miss Shine's* death, and for the rest of my mother's life.

There were several other elderly people in my neighborhoods (community) and church that I can remember cheerfully *serving*, by running errands or cutting their grass/lawns, etc., like Mrs. Alberta McFall; Aunt Josephine Richards (both my *great aunt* and Godmother, who had *christened* me); Mrs. Annie Mae Carr and others. At church, I *served*: Mr. Ivory Span (our superintendent of Sunday school), as well as, Mrs. Rosie Butler and Mrs. Ruth Span (my Junior

Choir Directors); while, I fulfilled the duties of a Sunday school teacher and *Master of Ceremonies* for most (Monthly) Youth and Junior Choir Programs. All of those were in addition to my *paternal* grandparents (Mr. Ivory Thomas Sr. and Kate Hartman Thomas) on my father's side. I, often, had to walk alone to take lunch to this grandfather, at his job site (our town's Water Treatment Plant), cut his lawn/grass, etc.

There were certain school teachers that began to place great **trust** in and *unofficial* responsibility upon me. For example, my <u>fourth</u> grade teacher, Ms. Dorothy Smith had a serious problem with *heartburn/acid indigestion*. I can remember several occasions, when she would call me up to her desk, actually pass me money and send me to the store (*down the street*), to get her some *Rolaids*. That was a huge thing; because: I was only in the fourth grade; and students were **<u>NOT</u>** allowed to leave the school campus (alone) at that time. So, this clearly showed the **trust** that she placed in me each time, to go *quietly* there and come straight back (<u>without:</u> drawing *attention* to myself, getting into *mischief* nor *deviating* from the mission). Her job was on-the-line! Her entire career would've easily been *jeopardized* or **lost**, if I had made one false (or suspicious) step along the way. Additionally, on test or exam days, whenever I finished the test/exam (*first*, of all the students), Ms. Smith and a few other teachers (Mr. Morgan, Ms. Carr and Ms. Juanita Clark), between fourth to seventh grade, would *immediately* grade my test. I'd go back to my desk quietly and put my head down, while the rest of my classmates continued to take their tests (exams). Upon grading (scoring) my exam, those teachers would (then) have all the other students turn their exams in to me (as they finished); and, I graded them during the remaining class period, thus relieving those teachers from having to grade those exams (as their *homework*). Although, I knew these were obviously **<u>not</u>** my duties (responsibilities) as a *student;* but, I never complained. I understood that this proved that they honestly saw positive qualities in me, which caused them to place a higher level of *expectancy* on and *trust* in me (at a very early age). There, I was <u>unofficially</u> *serving* those teachers.

Additionally, when I was a sixth grade student (eleven years old), my aunt and cousins, who had previously shared the same house with my grandmother, moved across town, into a separate house. Since my grandmother was now suddenly living alone, I assisted her in the transition of that new living arrangement. For much of that school year, I slept over at my grandmother's house, so that I would be there, in case, she needed assistance or any help during the night. I went to school in the mornings, then, to my parents' house after school. After spending about three to four hours there (after school), I went back over to my grandmother's house just before *dark*. On Saturdays and Sundays, I spent most of the *day* at my parents' house or at various events (church, etc.), then (just before *dark*), I went back over to my grandmother's house—to spend the *nights*.

Finally, there was Mr. Joe Elliot Williams. After my maternal grandfather (Reverend Edward Washington Sr.), this individual represented one of my most unique *assignments*, during my childhood. Everyone seemed to pronounce his name as *Joe L-yut*. He was my dad's cousin. He had a disability, as a result of a stroke and/or some other previous injury. He had a *partially withered* hand and dragged one *crippled* leg. Therefore, he limped, while walking with a cane.

This gentleman seemed to talk, from deep (down) within his throat, in a low (*hushed*), but very distinctive and *raspy* voice. When I was very young (ages three to eight years old), Joe Elliot lived in the same home with my father's great aunt (Mrs. Florence or "Florella" Johnson), who we all called *Aunt Hunt* (or "A-Hunt"). Later, after she passed away, Joe Elliot remained living (alone) in that same house, even with his disabilities. So he developed (both) a great trust in and dependency upon me (over the years), to run errands: going to the store, for him; cutting his grass/lawn, etc. He would call me (for some form of assistance) at least three days a week; and, he'd say: "*Hey Rou (**cuz**), can you come and go to the store, for me?*" I can still remember his usual (*long* version) shopping list, which he verbally dictated to me (in his distinctive *hushed and raspy* voice), consisting of: a loaf of bread, a pack of *ox tails* or chicken legs/gizzards, or some other type of meat, a pack of (them) vanilla creme (*creamy*) cookies, a Pepsi cola, and a pack (roll) of *five-fla-*

vor Lifesavers (candy). The short list was sometimes only: a pack of cigarettes, ginger cake, a soda and a pack of Lifesavers candy (the *5-flavors*), **cuz**. And I also remember how he always spoke with a calm and very pleasant demeanor, as he smiled.

    My unique *assignment* to **serve** Joe Elliot extended from about ages ten to eighteen years old. Anytime that he called my parents' house, while I was away playing baseball in the park or in my friend's (Robert's) backyard, then, my mother would tell him to call Robert's parents' house. At that point, Robert's mother (Mrs. Estherina Riles) would yell out to us: "Rousell and Robert, Joe L-yut want y'all to go to the store, for him." We would, then, stop (*suspend*) our ball game and proceed to Mr. Joe's house to assist with his needs (or concerns). Sometimes, we just ran an errand (or two), then, immediately returned to our baseball game. Other times, we would actually sit and talk with Mr. Joe Elliot, to keep him *company* (bonding) for a while. These occasions proved to be extremely valuable (for him) and significant *bonding* sessions with us; because, he spent so much time alone (in isolation). As I demonstrated my faithfulness and trustworthiness in this assignment to Joe Elliot, with Robert coming along, we were actually establishing (developing) him, as my subsequent *successor* or replacement. When I (eventually) left town to *go away* to college in 1980, Mr. Joe Elliot began to call Robert; and, he officially became that faithful *go to* guy, so that my departure left **no** <u>void</u>. My previous assignment (*temporarily*) passed to Robert, until I returned each *summer*; and, he faithfully accepted it. From 1980 and beyond, it was *increasingly* becoming **<u>his</u>** (Robert's) <u>personal</u> assignment! However, I continued to visit and run errands for *cuz* (Joe Elliot), sometimes alone and other times with my girlfriend (Georgette), during those summers; and, before we got married and *moved away* (in September 1985), to start my career in the US Army.

    It was through GOD's process of using those fore-mentioned experiences, that GOD actually *prepared and shaped* me, as a boy; while developing the *passion* and *character* (within me) <u>required</u> to **serve** his people (Him) now. It was an honor and gave me great joy to serve those loved ones and pillars in my community (town), who had done and endured so much in life. They were, also, people that I had known all of my life.

I have learned over my lifetime, as a *servant* of GOD, that GOD has *not* changed. His character never changes! In the course of fulfilling my duties (in service to Him), sometimes, GOD has **sent** (and still **sends**) me to other people, primarily *elderly* seniors, *widows* or the disabled. And at other times, He has **sent** (and still **sends**) other people to me—for the purpose of me—Blessing and ***serving*** them!

(Just as GOD did with the Prophet Elijah, He **sent** him to the widow at Zarephath in the Bible, reference the Book of **1 KINGS 17:8-24 KJV/NIV.**) Now, I am sure that **most** people would welcome having divine blessings to come to them; while, they would consider it to be quite appealing and desirable for themselves to be visited and have their lives *touched by an Angel!* However, how many of you would rather *seek* **to *Be*** that ***Angel***, through whom GOD ***touches*** other peoples' lives?

GOD does **not** (and will not) allow you to *pick and choose*: ***whom*** you will serve, nor the circumstances (conditions) under or in which you will serve (Him). GOD commands us to serve: total *strangers* and/or other people who seem incompatible or foreign (to us), or who may be considered *undesirable*/outcasts (to others). Still, GOD requires His servants to receive each opportunity (to treat every individual) with the *same* genuine *passion*, *character* and *love*, when serving such *strangers*, as I previously demonstrated, while serving relatives and acquaintances (in my *preparation* process in my hometown). Treating each subsequent person (opportunity) with that exact same level of honor, willingness and joy, that brings (Him) Glory. That's *what* GOD has expected of me all of these years (and now also expects of *you*). That's the *servant's (Character) Test!*

> "Let brotherly love continue. Be not forgetful to entertain strangers: for thereby (doing), some have entertained **angels** unawares." **(HEBREWS 13:1-2 KJV/NIV)**

With that same ***attitude*** and ***perspective*** in mind, let me share (with you) some of those personal (*special*) assignments, from the **Touched By An Angel** *episodes* of my **own** life.

## Dr. Annie Lee (Shaw) Barnes, PhD
(1932-present)

In mid-May 1994, I had already driven (**1,377** miles) from my current military assignment in Storrs, CT to Fort Leavenworth, KS in order to fulfill a temporary duty (TDY) assignment, while attending the U. S. Army's *Combined Arms Staff Service School* (CAS3). This was one of those official, mandatory **Officers' Professional Development** courses that <u>**all**</u> active duty Army Officers (in the rank of *Captain*) were required to complete, before attaining the *rank* of **Major**. My temporary duty status (there at Fort Leavenworth) lasted about three months; so, this is exactly where I was located <u>during</u>**:** the *murders* of Nicole Simpson and Ronald Goldman; the infamous (turtle-speed *trailing*) *Bronco chase* of O. J. Simpson and Al Cowlings; and the complete murder investigation, which eventually led to the subsequent trial of O. J. Simpson (for those *murders*). GOD used this same TDY assignment, in the Summer of 1994, as my (*Divine Appointment*) opportunity to meet Dr. Annie Barnes. **GOD** uses some very unique and **sovereign** ways to place his servants in special *predestined* <u>locations</u> and in situations, at <u>times</u> of His choosing, so that our good works will bring glory and honor to Him (GOD).

> *"For it is GOD (GOD's Spirit) who works in us (you) both to will and do (act) in order to fulfill his good purposes (pleasure)."*
> **(PHILIPIANS 2:13 KJV/NIV)**

Therefore, to that very end and for His purposes, here is how GOD orchestrated my connection with Dr. Annie Barnes (or Dr. Annie Shaw-Barnes). It was a very sunny, summer day in July, about 4:00 p.m. I had just finished *physical training* (or *PT*): *running* about three miles around Fort Leavenworth. As I stop running and continued to *walk* for a short distance to *cool down* and slow my heart rate, I noticed (across the highway or major roadway) that a car had stopped. I could see, from where I was walking, that the driver was a very short, African-American woman. She appeared to be slightly older than (or about ten years senior to) my own mother's age. Immediately, I knew that she appeared to be *lost*, because she was standing outside of the driver's side door and alternated glancing down at a roadmap (atlas) and then at this particular house across on her side of the highway. I could clearly see (discern) that she was contemplating (debating within herself) whether she could walk up to that house and ask for directions or assistance; however, there was a huge *Confederate* Flag flying from the screen porch of that house.

She had never looked over in my direction, as I approached from a distance (on the opposite side of the roadway. She did **not** see me (yet); nor had she asked me for any help. Therefore, I *clearly* had the opportunity to casually pass her by (on opposite side of the highway), <u>without</u> her even seeing me or **without** even speaking to her. **Most** or the vast majority of people (in this situation) with a stranger, would have done just <u>that</u>: ***nothing***!

Another very small group (or **minority** *percentage* of individuals) may have just spoken or called over to ask if she needed some driving *directions* (if anything): doing (*only*) the obvious ***bare minimum*** deed! Finally, a very **miniscule** (**faithful few**), would have gone out of their way or actually commit to willingly go that extra mile to ensure all of this stranger's needs were met (like the *Good Samaritan* in the Scriptures) **(LUKE 10:29-37 KJV/NIV)**.

<u>Who</u> was this ***stranger***, anyway? Who were her parents or relatives (her *lineage*); <u>where</u> did she come from; was she a person of status (high position), reputation or wealth? Under the present circumstances, NONE of that mattered to me. All I knew, at that moment, was that this woman had a legitimate *dilemma* (real situation) that required *help* and (now) GOD has caused *our paths to cross* (placed me in her path), sent me to this very spot (her location) at this ***defining*** *moment*. If GOD did <u>not</u> intent for me to *aid* her, I would have been somewhere else on Fort Leavenworth's installation, at this exact time. HE could have arranged (for me): to have already run earlier that day; to take a nap or be in the gym (weight room) now; or, caused her to arrive or pass at a different time or on another day, when I was in class or *unavailable* to see or meet her. However, none of those things happened.

For myself, it was imperative that I act (or *flow*) in this situation, based upon how the Spirit of GOD moved (and usually moves), within and through me. Because she was a **senior** or elderly person (regardless of gender) *in distress*, I was already compassionately moved (determined in my spirit) to help her. My *discernment* (keen awareness) of her current dilemma: being *lost*, coupled with her obvious anxiety and distress (fear of seeking assistance) from the residents of that house, which I immediately understood was the result of some personal experiences that she had probably encountered (in her past) with persons partial or loyal to that same *Confederate* flag. Because my own grandparents and parents had also had some of those same experiences, I was even more greatly compelled to go to her aid. If I did not, who else would? And I certainly would have wanted someone to do the same for my mother or aunt, if either of them were in this exact same situation.

As I confidently and purposefully walked across the roadway and over to her car, I said, "*Good evening, ma'am! You look like you need some help. Is there something that I can assist you with.*" She was greatly relieved and a huge, gracious smile *lit up* across her face, as she replied, "*Oh yes;* **Thank you***! It is just so great for me to have a young, African-American man to come to my rescue. You are living proof, that chivalry is not dead in our culture and society (today).*" After we initially introduced ourselves (shared names); then, she informed me that she was a current Professor, visiting from Norfolk State University, who had come to conduct a research study of the inmates at the **United States Disciplinary Barracks** (USDB): our country's *official military* prison at Fort Leavenworth, KS. In order to do this, she was required to interview, evaluate and assess random samples of current **prisoners** over the next ten days. But the first thing that she needed to do was locate (find) the Fort Leavenworth Housing and Billeting Office, so that she could *sign-in* and get her *lodging*.

I told Dr. Annie (Shaw) Barnes that I knew exactly where she needed to go and I would personally get her where she needed to go and **in-processed**.

When Dr. Barnes and I walked into the Billeting Office, I introduced her to the receptionist, while she presented a paper copy of her temporary *assignment **orders*** (sending her to Fort Leavenworth) and her official *picture* ID card.

The sergeant immediately checked the computer system for Dr. Barnes's *reservation* information (and *lodging* location), before informing us that she would be staying in **The Cooke House,** for her entire (10 days) stay. The Cooke House was a (*private*), **prestigious**, *on-Post* cottage that was normally reserved for US Army **Generals**, when they had business at Fort Leavenworth. (Note: This is the same cottage where General Colin Powell stayed (in 1992), two years before Dr. Barnes did (in 1994) to dedicate the **Buffalo Soldiers' Black Militiamen Monument**.)

After in-processing (checking in) Dr. Barnes, the receptionist gave her the keys to the cottage (The Cooke House) and a *strip map* to that military installation. I knew that Dr. Barnes had no previous experience nor been trained to *orient* the map (properly *align* it to the actual terrain) to properly use it. And, she had never been there before. So, I personally offered to take the strip map, drive her over to and carry (move) all of her bags into the cottage. That was a very quick process; for which, Dr. Barnes was extremely grateful and totally amazed that a complete *stranger* would willingly go so far (do so much), just for her personal benefit.

After *moving* her suitcases and personal belongings into that cottage (on Fort Leavenworth), the greatest *tragedy* would have been to (then) leave Dr. Barnes, just before nightfall, without ensuring that she was taken care of for dinner (or *supper*) that night. I ask her if she had already eaten something earlier, during her drive from the Kansas City Airport. Dr. Barnes said, "*No; I have not eaten anything (yet)!*" So I informed her that there were **no** *sit in* restaurants on Fort Leavenworth, except the usual *fast food* places**:** like Burger King, McDonalds or the Bowling Alley's sandwiches or pizza. I also told her that if she ever wanted any healthier meals, the only other couple of restaurants were located ***off-post*** (in the local community), which was downtown and outside of the gates of Fort Leavenworth.

Dr. Annie Barnes (*honestly*) had never even asked or requested anything (of me)! And I (still) had not even showered (myself), after my PT run, earlier (prior to our encounter). However, after witnessing Dr. Barnes's apprehension at the sight of the *Confederate Flag*, flying on the front porch of that house (earlier that evening), I realized that her greatest (current) **anxiety** and ***fear*** was**:** the thought of traveling *off-post* (outside of the gates or into the local community (***alone***), **at** night, to eat dinner (or *supper*). Therefore, I offered to come back to drive (transport) her *off-post* to a restaurant (to eat) and back to her cottage, if she would just call and let me know when she was ready to go. She said, *"Oh, I would greatly appreciated that; however, I just need to catch my breath (rest for a short while) and freshen up (first)."*

That's how **GOD** orchestrated that *Divine connection* and arranged for Dr. Annie (Shaw) Barnes to be my (temporary) ***assignment***, for a period of ten days in 1994, at Fort Leavenworth, Kansas. In order for the connection to occur, HE had me to drive 1,377 miles (in May) from Connecticut to Fort Leavenworth; and, Dr. Barnes had to fly 1,026 miles (in July) from Virginia Beach, VA to Kansas City, KS, before renting a car and driving the final seventeen miles to Fort Leavenworth, KS. There we met along the roadside on that *GOD-appointed* day.

So in accordance with His (GOD's) plan, for the next ten days, I took care of Dr. Barnes, just as I would have (gladly) *personally* **done** (or have wanted someone else to do, in my absence), for my own mother! Although, we had our own separate schedules and work or class assignments each day, I made sure that she was covered every single evening; and she never had to go anywhere (*alone*) **at night** (from the day she arrived until she left Fort Leavenworth). Sometimes, only I transported her. At other times, both myself and Captain Stephen Leeder would escort her (together). Steve was another officer in my CAS3 class (there) and a really good friend of mine; because, we had served (together) in the same unit at Fort Polk, Louisiana, when we were both brand new officers (both 2nd and 1st Lieutenants) in our very first military assignment (in 1986–1989). After Dr. Barnes's temporary job assignment (at Fort Leavenworth) was completed, I drove her back to the Kansas City International Airport in her rental car (for her return flight home to Virginia); while, Steve trailed us in the second car to drive me back to Fort Leavenworth. I never knew or expected that our paths would ever cross again (in our lifetimes). That is how that assignment was completed. Another: **Mission Accomplished!** That's what *combat buddies* (like Steve and I) and *tag teams* **do**!

To express her genuine <u>gratitude</u> and <u>appreciation</u>, for our faithful and willing *service* to her, Dr. Annie Barnes would send *Thank You* and *Christmas* Cards to me (and my family) in Connecticut in 1994 and 1995. She also talked to her husband *daily* (while we were there), about the *favor of GOD* and quality of service she had received, and *constantly* bragged about it (after her return to Virginia).

The very next time that I spoke *directly* to Dr. Barnes was late in May 1996. I called her on the telephone to inform her that I had relocated to a new military assignment and to give her my new mailing address. When she answered the phone I calmly asked, "*Do you know who this is? And guess where I am (now).*" She replied "Yes, I do. Where (are you)?"

When I told her that I was now stationed in Hampton, VA (about forty miles from her home), she screamed with the most jubilant and elated yell that she could muster. Once she could finally contain her excitement (compose herself), she finally said, "*Oh, that's wonderful! Now I can meet your family; and, finally introduce you to my Bennie (my husband). I have to get your family over for Sunday dinner, as soon as possible.*"

My family and I did, eventually, accept her offer for Sunday dinner, about two weeks later. The drive to her house was a *traffic nightmare* (our first experience with Virginia's *horrific summer traffic*, which turned a normal forty (40) minutes trip into a **two and a half hours** grid lock. (During that same travel time, Dr. Barnes worked feverishly to keep all the food properly warmed, without over-cooking it.) However, once we finally arrived, it was a great privilege and pleasure to fellowship with Dr. Barnes and her husband, for hours. After the *great* meal, Dr. Annie Barnes spent a great deal of time giving us a *talking tour* of the photo gallery of her ancestors. She spent absolutely **no** time talking *directly* about her *career* (accomplishments).

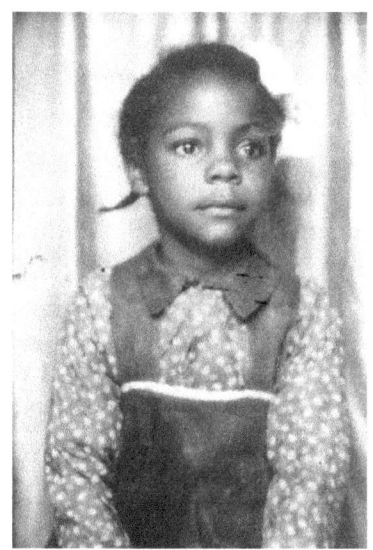

*Annie Lee Shaw* (Dr. Barnes)**, at nine years old**

**Dr. Annie Shaw-Barnes, PhD**
*(Prof. of Anthropology and Sociology, Social Anthropologist, Family Specialist, Author and Lecturer/Speaker)*

Absolutely, Dr. Barnes was one of my special assignments and an absolute ***angel*** that I had the opportunity *to **serve***, if even for such a very short period of only ten days. For those ten days in 1994, I was blessed to be that *stranger*, who was also willing to be the ***good neighbor*** that Dr. Barnes needed (throughout her stay in Kansas).

Since I retired in 2005, I have coincidently spoken to numerous *elderly* citizens in the Hampton Roads area of Virginia, who were *fellow* **educators** and **students** of Dr. Barnes, dating back to 1958, <u>before</u> ***integration***. Therefore, I have met people and learned facts about Dr. Barnes's career from those, whom she had taught and mentored, *two* to *six* decades ago. I would **not** learn (or know) just how much of an angel she had personally been, in the lives of countless others both in the State of Virginia and around the world, until March 2018. That's when I thoroughly researched her, in order to fully honor her in this book. Nevertheless, you (readers) can never image, fully grasp, nor appreciate the ***giant***, that this little *Angel*, has been and is (still) in the **Education** fields of *Anthropology* and *Sociology*, without visiting her inspiring and empowering website at www.annieshawbarnes.com.

(Note: Please See these specific topic sections on her webpage: *About Me*, Photo Gallery, etc.)

## Mrs. Theresa Elizabeth Krosnowski
### (age: 96 years)

In June 2003, I was reassigned and departed from Fort Bliss (in El Paso), TX, on my **final** (military) *permanent change of station* **(PCS) move** to a two-year assignment in New Jersey. I already knew, prior to this move, that this would be my final assignment, leading up to my *Retirement* from a twenty-plus years *Active Duty* Army career. So after spending the couple of weeks (*on leave*), visiting our families in Louisiana, we arrived in New Jersey. This military **move** was GOD's way of bringing me into this widow's life. Moreover, just to prove that GOD does still *work* in ***mysterious*** ways, HE (more specifically) used a particular *house* to bring us together (introduce and *connect* us).

So you ask: **WHO** was Theresa E. Krosnowski? The only (significant) answer, to this question, is that: she was (both) the *Object* (focus) of GOD's attention (in that season and town); and, she was my *new* (GOD-given) **assignment**. Therefore, He used this *military relocation* to **send** me to her (where she lived), for this *critical stage* of her life—and mine. I would later learn that she was (then) 94 years old, a Polish woman living *alone*, who had already been *widowed* for the past twenty-seven years, when I arrived. She had only one child (JoAnn), a fifty-three-year-old daughter, who lived in another town (Perrineville, NJ), about forty-five minutes (drive) away. She also had only one *living*, **best** friend (Mrs. Ann), with whom she had already enjoyed a close (BFF) *friendship*, for more than fifty-five years.

GOD also still uses the *simple things* of the world to confound the *wise*! So here's how He used a mere house to fulfill his **divine connection** (co-joining) of Mrs. Theresa and I. When my family arrived at my new duty station in Edison, New Jersey, there were six of us: my wife (Georgette); three daughters (Aleisha, 17; Karen, 14; Bethany, 7); one son (Joshua, 2) and myself. I immediately sought out real estate agents in the area; before I finally met and decided to *hire* one (Mary Alice Manning) with *ReMaxx* in Westfield, NJ, a town about twenty-two miles (or twenty-five- to thirty-minute drive) away. During my military career, I had already previously served a three and one-half years tour (*four-winters*) of duty, shoveling snow in Connecticut; so, we gave very specific guidelines to the realtor for locating a house for us to rent, including one *non-negotiable* condition (stipulation). The house must have a *Florida Room*, finished *seasonal* room, or a closed-in screen porch, which could serve as a designated *play room* for my two-year-old son. Because I understood that the **winters** would be too harsh for little Josh to play outside, in the open air and yard. If a house did *NOT* have this feature, then, **it could never be considered**, as a suitable residence for us! And time was *of the essence*! Therefore, while the agent was searching in Plainfield and surrounding towns, I was also searching around the townships of Edison, New Brunswick, East Brunswick, and South

River, New Jersey. Fortunately, I was diligently seeking and inquiring, when I came across a flyer, posted on a bulletin board in the Post Office or somewhere. As I read the *details* of the house, on a bulletin board advertisement, I immediately realized that this particular house was exactly <u>what</u> I was looking for. I called my real estate agent and directed that she immediately book an appointment for the next morning. Ironically, this perfect *house* was the *Pastor's Parsonage* (the designated property where only the Pastors normally resided) for the local Methodist Church, in the town of South River, NJ. As GOD had planned and *orchestrated* it, this house was located on Mrs. Theresa Krosnowski's street (*Colfax Street*), exactly two houses down and diagonally across the street from her house. Additionally, GOD ensured that it was *open* (*available*) and accessible for me to rent; because, the current Pastor's family owned their own house, about one hour away; and they were very comfortable and willing to commute back-and-forth. So I was looking to *rent* and the church's trustees were asking the Pastor: what are we going to do with this house? The Pastor said: "<u>*Rent*</u> it out to someone!" Now, Mrs. Theresa did **not** even (personally) know that I existed, and *vice-versa*; still, GOD had to get the two of us together (connected). He knew that if I got onto that street (block) and gained access to and knowledge of Mrs. Theresa, that I would *willingly* take care of and *faithfully serve* her. That's how GOD, in his infinite wisdom, used a <u>house</u> to bring us together; because, if I had not seen or gotten that one particular house, I would have ended up living in *another* (the *wrong*) community or township. As a result, I would have never met or *connected* with my real assignment (Mrs. Theresa), for that season of her life. On her street, at **52** Colfax Street, South River, NJ 08882—I was right where I was <u>supposed</u> to be. I was *in my **assigned** place*!

My initial contact and interactions with Mrs. Theresa, throughout July 2003, were very indirect. Those initial communications consisted solely of: me waving and blowing my car's horn to her, as I drove (passed) by her house, whenever she was outside in her yard. However, I was *immediately* drawn to her, as soon as I saw her. She would be sweeping her sidewalk or street curb; or sometimes, she would be *plucking* (pulling) weeds in her yard. She was a really short, fragile, gray-haired woman, that I immediately estimated to be about eighty-two years old. I saw her outside of her house once or twice each week, during that first month (July). Each time that I saw her, I would say to my wife and/or children: "look at that little lady, it's great that she can still physically move and get around so well." But I also told my wife that I thought that it was *ridiculous* for her to *have to work* outside and try to do so much, at her age. I said that her neighbors, family, or **young** church members should be doing those types of things, for her. GOD placed such a *burden of concern* in my heart for her, that I knew that I had to (***personally***) ***take care of*** her, while I was *there* (on her street).

*Mrs. Teresa Elizabeth krosnowski (a.k.a. "Miss Teresa")*

I will never (ever) forget the very first time that I directly connected with her. It was a day in early September and the wind had started to blow the leaves down around our houses. I passed by her (outside) trying to rake leaves, as I drove to get my daughter (Karen) from school, one afternoon. Upon seeing that, I immediately said to myself: *"Today is the day; I have to take care of her!"* When Karen got into the truck, I asked her if she had any homework and how much. She said that she only had a little bit, that would take about one hour to complete. I told her that was great. So as soon as we arrived back at our house, I told Karen to immediately put her things in her room, get our broom, and come over (with me) to our little neighbor's house. Although I had waved to that widow several times (before), I was still: <u>new</u> on her street, a **stranger** to her, and the only *African-American* man in this neighborhood. So I felt strongly that this was necessary, because I did **not** want the little lady to be frightened or feel threatened, when I went into her yard (approached her), for the very *first* time! I believed that having my daughter (Karen), walk over with me, would provide some comfort and peace of mind for this lady (until she got to **know** me/us). I also had my military (BDU/field) uniform on. As I walked up to her, I immediately introduced myself and my daughter; then, I asked if she would mind if we helped her rake her yard. She replied that she didn't mind doing it herself and I did not need to do it. She (also) said that she used to pay a young *teenage boy* (17 years old), who was a neighbor down the street, to do some yard *chores* in previous years; but, now he was too busy with his new girlfriend.

 I assured and re-assured her that I was **not** looking to *hustle* or make any money. I was an active duty Army officer, and I was well-paid. I said to her that I saw that she could use some help; and, I simply: "**just wanted to be a good neighbor!**" Finally, she said: "OK; if you insist!" And I said, "*Yes ma'am; I insist! Why don't you go inside and rest a bit; while, Karen sweeps your sidewalk; and I'll rake the leaves. Then, Karen can come inside to see if you have anything else that you'd like for her to help you with in the house. We greatly appreciate the opportunity* **to do that**, *just to be good neighbors to you!*" At that point, Mrs. Theresa (finally) told me her name; and said: "Thank you!" She was already panting very hard and I could tell that she welcomed both the *rest* and the <u>help</u>. Karen swept the sidewalk, before ringing the door bell and going inside the house. I could hear the two of them talking, as I raked the yard. Karen walked home (across the street), about thirty minutes later. I finished raking her entire yard and bagging up the leaves in about an hour and ten minutes (total). When I rang her door bell and said, "*Mrs. Theresa, I am finished. You* have a good evening!" She said, "wait; I want to pay you." I said, "no ma'am, I can't take your money. <u>You don't owe me anything</u>. You did <u>not</u> hire me; and, that was **not** a job. Remember, I just volunteered; because, GOD sent me to be a good neighbor to you!" She (sternly) replied (with tears swelling up in her eyes): "Yes; but I used to pay the teenage boy, when he did the work. ***I always pay***. And if you don't let me pay you, then, I will not let you come and do anything else for me, again!" I said, "Yes ma'am; I understand; but, he was a kid who was trying to make a little money doing chores. I am a grown man, with a good job already. Please, I cannot (in good conscious) take your money; what I did was nothing. I am just grateful to have this opportunity to be a blessing (help) to you. Thank you!" (Note: I could both <u>*hear*</u> the anguish in her voice and <u>*see*</u> the pain (of *offence*) on her face. I have learned over the years of ***serving*** elderly people, that the grateful ones are very proud and refuse to relinquish their independence and dignity. They never want to feel *dependent upon* or *indebted* to anyone else. <u>When they start to feel a loss of their **freedom** and/or **self-worth**; then, they feel uncomfortable, afraid and *useless*</u>. They also feel the need (and have a desire) to want to express their gratitude, by giving you something to compensate for your time and effort. So I understood her position. Finally, she said (sternly), *"OK; if you won't take it, I will give it to your daughter to buy herself something for school."* Although I did not want her to do that, I said *"OK; Thank you very much!"* The very next (second) time that I did something for her, we had that same discussion (disagreement) about my receiving *pay*. It was finally resolved, when I said, *"I am okay and <u>don't</u> need anything right now; but, please put it in an envelope or jar somewhere and hold it for me. And when I need it, then, I will come and ask for it."* And a couple of times, after I'd just finished doing the grass or snow, I would be scurrying home (swiftly) back across the street and pre-tending not to hear Mrs. Theresa calling: "Mr. Thomas, Mr. Thomas…" Of course, I never went back to ask <u>*for*</u> what I requested her to hold for me; and, <u>finally she understood that *my heart* was just to **serve** her</u> (and/or GOD). Therefore, she stopped asking me to take anything! As we used to say in Army *air-assault* jargon: **HOOK-UP Complete! Mission Accomplished**!

From that point (in September 2003) until her death in December 2004, it was official. Mrs. Theresa E. Krosnowski was **my assignment**! I never (ever) asked her again, if I could do anything in her yard. I just (faithfully): went over, did *whatever* needed to be done, and left! No questions asked! *Every* single time that I would cut my grass, I pushed my lawnmower across the street and cut her grass, also. Every time that I raked my leaves, I also raked her leaves. Every time that I shoveled snow from my driveway and sidewalks, I also shoveled her porch, sidewalks and driveway. Sometimes, my little son (Joshua) would tag along with his toy lawnmower; while, I would cut our grass and/or Mrs. Theresa's, when he turned three (3) years old.

Mrs. Theresa took the place of a *biological* grandmother for me; and, I began to treat her and care for her, in the same manner that I would have for my own grandmother, if either of them were still alive. So I made it a daily requirement to go over and/or call (by telephone) to check on her every day, just in case she needed something done inside the house, something from the store or pharmacy, to talk to someone, or just get out of the house for a *ride* (through town). This was very important to me and, maybe even *unconsciously*, significant for her; because although, she had been living *alone* (as a *widow*) for the past twenty-seven years, she had **no** operative (*functioning*) radio or television set, nor any other person, living in her house (day or night).

Over time, Mrs. Theresa, wholeheartedly *opened up* to me, more and more, as the *Holy Spirit* revealed to her: who I was and why I was sent to her. In our many personal conversations, she shared her *personal* life's story with me. She was comfortable telling me how she was originally born in Poland (in 1908), where her parents and other poor Polish farmers and peasants were greatly oppressed by the Russians. Her family lived on a farm, out in the countryside, far away from the nearest town. On two different occasions, her parents lost *two* sons to a disease, before she was even born. On both occasions, a son contracted some fatal disease, accompanied by catastrophically high fever, which they could not break nor recover from. Because they lived so far from the doctor, her father loaded his sons (on two separate occasions) in the wagon and drove them to the nearest town to seek doctor's treatment; but, in both situations, the boys each *died* (between the ages of two to four years old), before they ever reached the doctor's home or office (in town). This must have occurred between 1900–1907. Later, Mrs. Theresa (herself) was born on November 18, 1908. During her early childhood, her parents (then) had three living children: her older brother (thirteen years old), her (five years old) and her younger brother (three years old). She remembered that her parents, and all other farmers in Poland (then), were very poor. This compelled her father to come to New Jersey (in the United States), seeking *work* (employment) with some **Polish** *immigrant* family/friends. Each time her dad would *work* for about six or nine months to one year; while saving the money, before returning to Poland. The family lived off this income for about a year or until it ran out. Then, her dad was required to do the same thing all over again. After returning to Poland, from his third *employment* trip to New Jersey, her dad finally had enough money to *relocate* (move) the family over to the United States, permanently. However, his funds (*savings*), at that time, were enough to purchase tickets for only **four** family members, not five.

Her parents made the decision to bring the older son (thirteen years old) and her (Theresa, five years old), along with themselves, over to the United States in 1913. Their plan was to leave her younger brother (Peter?) there in Poland with an uncle, whom he had been named after. Once they settled in New Jersey and had saved enough money to send back to the uncle, her parents planned to have the younger brother shipped overseas, to join them in the United States. However, as things turned out, little Theresa never (ever) saw her younger brother again. Her father worked for many years and the family did very well, eventually settling into a nice affluent *Jewish* community in New Jersey, where she grew up and went to school.

As a young adult, she met and (eventually) married her husband (Frank Krosnowski). To this union, one daughter (Joanne) was born in 1949. Mrs. Theresa's husband was one of eight sons born to an affluent man, who owned a massive Trucking Company. That family's Trucking (Transport) business included two or three very large Truck Yards in Trenton and other areas in New Jersey.

When her father-in-law *passed away*, her husband and his brothers were involved in a bitter dispute; and eventually, they dissolved the family's Trucking (Transport) business. Nevertheless, Mrs. Theresa and their family lived a very comfortable life. This business allowed them to purchase the house, where they raised their daughter Joanne (previously). Mrs. Theresa's husband, unexpectedly, died an *untimely* death, just months before her daughter's (Joanne's) wedding. Joanne and Gary, subsequently, had **no** children. Now, Mrs. Theresa still lived, *alone*, in this same house, during this final *season* of her life.

The most significant thing, that Mrs. Theresa and I (both) had in common, was our **servant's heart and compassion for elderly people**. During one conversation, Mrs. Theresa revealed to me that, when her mother-in-law became ill, they moved the elderly parent into their home, so that she (Mrs. Theresa) could personally *serve* as her mother-in-law's *caregiver*. Mrs. Theresa fulfilled this role, in her own home (this same house), until her mother-in-law (eventually) passed away. Within a year or so later, Mrs. Theresa's own mother also became really ill; therefore, she also *served* as the personal caregiver for her own mother, in this same house, until *her* mother eventually passed away, too. Just imagine, after she had _faithfully_ provided critical, *in-home* care for **both** her biological mother and her mother-in-law in this house, now at ninety-four to ninety-six years old, she needed someone—with the same **servant's heart**—to care for her. Although, she was never afflicted with any *long-term* illness (herself), her age and physical limitations required lots of physical help and routine (daily) assistance. Therefore, her *personal care* required the exact same (genuine) _love_, _compassion_, and faithful _commitment_, with which she had previously demonstrated in her *service* to those elderly **mothers**, who had preceded her.

> "Be not deceived; GOD is not mocked: for whatsoever a man soweth, that shall he also reap. For he that soweth… And let us not grow weary in well doing: for in due season, ye shall also reap, if ye do not faint (or give up)." (GALATIANS 6:7-9 KJV/NIV)

And GOD was faithful, to both Mrs. Theresa and to His own Word, by ensuring that she had exactly what she needed in this *season* of her life, even if that required him to send *strangers*, to be there (just) for her. I believe that this was the reason why GOD had (now) **sent us** (my family and I) to *serve* Mrs. Theresa and to minister to her personal needs. Remember, Mrs. Theresa's only child (Joanne) was born, when she was forty-one years of age. At the time that we resided there (2003–2005), Joanne was fifty-three to fifty-five years of age, lived about forty-five minutes away, and (also) suffered herself, with **Lyme's Disease**. Therefore, this disease (***sometimes***) caused Joanne to be in more anguish, pain and hampered with ill symptoms, *worse* than her mother (Mrs. Theresa) was currently experiencing, at the ages of ninety-four to ninety-six years old.

From the day that I initially approached Mrs. Theresa, up until about three weeks before her death, the biggest challenge she faced was *being motivated and encouraged to continue living*. She would often say: "I am praying the LORD will take me. I don't know why I am still here; because, I am **no** use or good to anyone, any more!" At this point, her self-esteem was very low; and, she did *not* feel or see that she was *valuable* (now). And I would respond by saying, "Oh I believe that you are very ***valuable***, because, you have a great deal of wisdom to share, that others can gain from your life, just by talking to you." So my primary (daily) ***objective*** (and assignment) was to encourage her and demonstrate the ***love of GOD*** to her; while, I also assisted in meeting her physical needs, through certain *routine* (and menial) tasks. My family became so close to her, and I came to know her (and her routines) so well over time, that I knew exactly what she was ***doing*** at a given time, based upon which *light* was on in her house. If her kitchen light was on, around 5:30–6:15 p.m., she was eating her *light* dinner, consisting of a sandwich and soup, boiled egg, etc. If her living room light was on between 7:00–8:30 p.m., then I knew that she was sitting on her sofa, saying her ***Rosaries.*** (Note: This was her *prayers*; as, she was a member of the Catholic church.) If I looked through my front window after 9:30 p.m. and saw the light still on, in her living room, that meant that she had fallen asleep on the sofa. Therefore, we would call her to *wake* her, so that she could go to bed, as opposed to remaining (maybe uncovered and *cold*) on the sofa, for an extended period or throughout the night.

Regrettable, my *biological* mother (Mrs. Virginia Thomas) and Mrs. Theresa never (ever) met, although my mom spent two weeks with us, at our house in New Jersey in (June 2004); because Mrs. Theresa had a viral infection or *flu* bug, during that time. Those two would have (*dearly*) loved each other. **My mother** was a servant of GOD, who **loved people** (in general); and, no matter where (*in the world*) she visited me: she never met anyone that she considered a *stranger*! (She loved and embraced **_EVERYONE_**!)

From the very first time (in 2003) that I told my mother about Mrs. Theresa, whenever my mother (in Louisiana) and I would speak on the telephone, she would do the *roll call* to see how everyone in the family was doing. She would say: "Hello Pete; how are you doing!" (That's my childhood *nickname*, within the family.) How's Gette? (Georgette is my wife's name.) How's Aleisha… Karen… Bethany… Joshua (our children/her grandchildren) doing? She would call each individual child's name (that way). Finally, she would ask: "*How's the little lady across the street (**Mrs. Theresa**) doing*?" This was always the normal *flow* of our conversations, before we got into any other small talk, specific details or topics of discussion. I believe that my mother's inclusion of Mrs. Theresa (like a family member), in her **roll call** was her *special* way of telling me, that **she knew** (herself) and was confirming (to me) that: Mrs. Theresa was definitely *my assignment (responsibility)* in New Jersey. Please understand that my mother wasn't just asking a *hypothetical* question (in reference to: Mrs. Theresa); she actually expected me to know the exact (accurate) answer of Mrs. Theresa's personal status (condition), each time. And while, she (my mother) expected me to fulfill this responsibility, she was very proud: *knowing* that I faithfully and willingly did exactly that!

*Ironically*, while Mrs. Theresa had been praying *to die* and my mother was still enthusiastically and vibrantly **living** her life, it was my mother (Mrs. Virginia Thomas) who suddenly *passed away* (without warning), of **congested heart failure** on November 15, 2004. Therefore, I had to give Mrs. Theresa her birthday present *early*, as a stopped by to wish her a *Happy Birthday* (on November 16), the day before leaving town to travel to Louisiana to bury my mother, at the age of sixty-two years old. Mrs. Theresa turned ninety-six years old on that Thursday (November 18): *her birthday!* We conducted my mother's *Home-going Services* in Patterson, Louisiana on Tuesday (November 23) and her *burial* on Wednesday (November 24): <u>the day before</u> **Thanksgiving** 2004.

As my family and I arrived back in New Jersey on Wednesday (December 1), we were actually (*unknowingly*) returning to experience the final month of Mrs. Theresa's life. Here is how that <u>*final*</u> month transpired.

I had just signed (reported) back into my assigned military unit on Wednesday (December 1, 2004), after returning from *emergency leave*, as a result of the *most devastating personal* experience of my life. I went to work and (also) visited Mrs. Theresa on Thursday, after I had missed her *actual Birthday*, two weeks prior. I believe that was (also) the day, that Joshua (my three-year-old son) made the most astounding statement that I had ever heard from him. He was standing at the stairs in our house, when he looked at me and asked: "*Daddy, did mama Vee go to Heaven?*" I replied: "Yes; she went to Heaven!" Then, he made the **most astounding** statement that I had ever heard from him; he said *sadly*: "*but, she never came to tell us* **good bye***!*" This statement really surprised me (*caught me off-guard*); so I had to ponder my response for several seconds, as I gathered myself (*to hold back tears*). Finally, I responded:

"*Josh, you know when you and mom walk with Bethany to the bus stop in the mornings, and y'all talk and say bye, before she gets on the bus. But after the bus drives away, Bethany can't get back off of the bus to say* **bye** *anymore; because it is too late and they have to go to school. So that's how it was for your MaMa Vee. She wanted to come and tell us* **good-bye***; but, it was* **too late** *and she had to go to be with GOD! So she could not (and did not have time to) come to us.*" I believe that my response actually enabled him to relate (to) and better understand, why he could not see his grandmother again.

On Saturday evening (December 5), I came home from work around 7:30p.m. Our unit was conducting some military drills throughout that weekend. Therefore, I would have to go back in to work again the next morning (Sunday). As I passed Mrs. Theresa's house, I immediately thought that it was quite *strange,* there was **NO** *light* *on* (inside her house), at that time of evening. When I walked into our house, I asked my wife if she had spoken to, or heard from, Mrs. Theresa any, during that day.

She said, "No." I mentioned the fact that her kitchen light was not on. So after about twenty more minutes I went over to knock on her door, but got no answer. I called her telephone number, just in case, she was in the bed and not feeling well. Still, there was no answer. I would have gone into the house myself (then); but, I did not have her key. I tried to call her daughter (Joanne) to see if they had heard from her, or come over and picked her up that day. But I got *no answer* at Joanne's phone number, either. So about *eight* o'clock, I was really worried; because, it was really cold that evening. I continued calling Joanne's phone number, every fifteen minutes, until I finally got an answer (***call back***) from her. When I finally talked to Joanne directly, she said that she had tried calling her mother several times; but, there was no answer. I told her that I believed that she and Gary (her husband) should come right over; and, I would be waiting to meet them there, at her mother's house. It took about forty-five minutes for them to arrive. When they did get there and opened the door, we found Mrs. Theresa *on the floor,* in the living room. She had fallen down and knocked the lamp over, in the process. Therefore, the house was completely *dark* inside; and, Mrs. Theresa had been unable to get up or reach the telephone. We immediately called 911 and the ambulance (paramedics) arrived shortly thereafter. We were able to assess, after getting the lights on and talking to her, that Mrs. Theresa had started on the sofa, doing her *Rosaries.* Later, she really needed to get to the bathroom; but (in her haste), she tripped, fell and knocked out the lamp. So they transported her to the hospital that night. I asked Joanne to please keep me informed; and I would check with them after work (the next day). On Sunday, after medical testing, the doctors determined that Mrs. Theresa had developed a *urinary tract infection*, which would keep her hospitalized for a few days, while being treated. Her daughter provided this information to me, when I called her that same evening.

My wife (Georgette) and I visited Mrs. Theresa, at the hospital, for the very first time on Tuesday afternoon—(December 8). When we walked into her hospital room, she was elated to see us. She was *sitting up* in bed and *eating*. As we entered the room, a huge smile appeared, from ear-to-ear, across her face. Mrs. Theresa's voice was very strong; she seemed to be *in **good** spirit* (very optimistic) and, her daughter (Joanne) and son-in-law (Gary) were also in the room, during this ***initial*** visit. <u>Everything looked so promising</u>! After visiting with her for about an hour or so, we promised that we would come back to visit her (again) on Saturday. However, things were not as they appeared (seemed) to be. When we *optimistically* left Mrs. Theresa's hospital room that evening, we had no idea that this was the best physical and most satisfied condition that we would ever see her in, from that day forward. Everything spiraled, *suddenly*, **downhill** from that point on.

By the time we got back to her on Saturday (December 12, 2004), she was on a ventilator system and could only eat applesauce and drink water. She was hooked up to this machine, that was sucking and pumping congestion, inflammation and phlegm, from her lungs and around her heart, which was collecting (accumulating) in this receptacle (container). On that Saturday afternoon, Georgette (my wife) and I were greeted (met) in her hospital room by Mrs. Ann (Mrs. Theresa's best friend) and Mrs. Ann's daughters (Patty and Gail). Mrs. Ann was the (biological) ***siste*r**, that Mrs. Theresa probably dreamed of, maybe prayed for, but <u>never</u> had! Patty and Gail had been childhood friends of Joanne (Mrs. Theresa's daughter). As the five of us sat, prayed, and talked in Mrs. Theresa's hospital room, we were all quite *puzzled* (both surprised and stunned), by the *declining* turn of events and the stark **contrast** in her medical condition that Saturday afternoon versus the prior Tuesday evening. It was as *opposite* as <u>night</u> and <u>day</u>! On Tuesday, she was just expressing her appreciation and gratitude to be able to *see* all of us. (Now) just four days later, on Saturday, it was very clear that her condition was *dire*; and, she was *fighting for her life!* Within a few days, the doctors did remove the ventilator. As we sat at her bedside (when she was *conscious* and <u>alert</u>), we: talked to her, sang to her, fed her, held her hand, rubbed her forehead, prayed for (with) her, shared stories of, and/or with, her and comforted her—in any ways that we could. When she was *unconscious*, we did **all** of the same things, <u>except</u> the feeding or giving her water. This became our *(daily)* routine for the next fifteen days, which turned out to be Mrs. Theresa's *<u>final</u>* days!

While they (Mrs. Ann, Patty and Gail) had known Mrs. Theresa for decades, and Georgette and I had just begun to know her over the past year and a half, it was *painfully* clear and obvious that we all possessed genuine **love** and **compassion** for her. We all wanted the best for her, wanted to be there for her, and did ***<u>not</u>*** want her to *feel* or be ***alone***, for extended periods of time. If we all met there for four or five hours (together at one time) each day, that would have still left her *alone* for most of every day and night. Therefore, I suggested, and we all agreed, that it would be far better to coordinate and establish different ***shifts***, so that we could ensure that Mrs. Theresa had company and *companionship* for more hours, throughout each day. So Gail agreed to bring her mother (Mrs. Ann) in the mornings and remain about three or four hours from 10:00 a.m.–1:00 or 1:30 p.m. (each day). Patty would visit from 1:00–4:00 or 4:30 p.m. each day, which coincided with Joanne and Gary's (Mrs. Theresa's daughter and son-in-law's) visits. Finally, Georgette and I would visit, after I came home from work, about 5:00–9:00 p.m. (each day). If any of us needed to swap or exchange *shifts* for whatever reason, we would just contact the others (let each other know) and coordinate the *swap*. <u>Everything</u> that was done, we did—out of our love and compassion—for Mrs. Theresa!

Remember that all of this was (now) happening within a month of me burying my *biological* mother. The final ten days of Mrs. Theresa's life were extremely difficult for all of us, who sincerely loved and cared for her; because, no matter how much she asked (*begged*) for food or something to drink, we could **not** give her anything, except little *chips <u>of ice</u>*. Sometimes, she would become so *hungry*; however (at some point) she could ***<u>no longer</u>*** eat or swallow anything.

Some days, Mrs. Theresa would be sleeping comfortable; then, all of a sudden she would begin to groan and moan in extreme pain. Our focus, in these situations, was to comfort her, as much as possible. So one of us would stand on one side of her bed and hold her hand; while, another one stood on the opposite side of her bed, rubbing her forehead and talking or singing to her.

At other times, during her ***transitioning*** process, Mrs. Theresa would be *reminiscing* about events from her childhood. We could identify these occasions, as she would wake out of (break) a peaceful sleep, as if *awakening* in the middle of a dream. And she would make an announcement like: *Ok, everyone, time to go wash our hands. Mother says, it's time to eat our dinner!* Then, later she would say: "*wasn't that a delicious dinner, that mother cooked?*" This reminded me of the times when I visited my biological grandmother (my father's mother), who had developed **Alzheimer's** Disease in the 1990s. So I had learned how to ***just be in the moment*** with the patient, no matter what she says, in order to keep her calm and engaged. So I always tried to lead the others, at Mrs. Theresa's bedside, in *engaging* in these impromptu (unscripted) conversations, even attempting to finish and *fill-in the blanks* to her *reminiscing* statements, as if we were actually in that (previous) <u>time</u> and <u>place</u> with her. Everyone just *stayed in the moment* with Mrs. Theresa, in a way that made her feel: comfortable, satisfied and at peace! Comforting her, in this way, made us feel good to know that she realized that: she was ***<u>not</u>*** alone!

There were lots of *gratifying*, joyful and peaceful moments that I experienced (personally) and that we experienced, as a group, while serving Mrs. Theresa. But one of the most **gratifying** moments that I can personally remember (at her bedside), was when Georgette (my wife) and I were alone with her. It was a couple of days before **CHRISTMAS**; and, she looked directly (*intensely*) into my eyes and she said: **"Thank you. Now I can see clearly; now I understand!"** I believe that, in that very moment, GOD has actually given her the *revelation* of **<u>who</u>** we were and **<u>why</u>** we were there! She both saw and understood why He had sent us to be there and to *serve* her (minister to her *needs*). I also believe, that (both) she and we knew, that she would not be going to her physical house for Christmas (or ever again); instead, she would be going *home*, to be with GOD. She was satisfied and *at peace with* (embraced) that fact, as did we!

About 9:00 a.m. on Sunday morning (December 27, 2004), I received that telephone call from Joanne, notifying me (us) that Mrs. Theresa had passed away (*gone home* to be with The LORD), about 2:30 a.m. that morning. Despite our best intentions, none of us (her *bedside* squad), who loved and cared for her, were actually there at the moment of her final *departure*.

However, GOD was faithful; as Mrs. Theresa went *peacefully*, in her sleep. When He called her name, she just *flew away*.

The final *act of service,* that I graciously rendered to Mrs. Theresa (in this <u>assignment</u>), was to serve as an active *pall bearer* for her final services. It was a great honor and privilege, for me, when I wore my Army uniform and *carried* her (casket) out of her church for that final stroll.

After the final service in honor of her life, my wife and I were invited to participate in the *private* (special) gathering and dinner with Mrs. Theresa's family and closest friends of her family. All of the other attendees (there) shared not <u>only</u> their fondest memories of Mrs. Theresa with us; but, also expressed how grateful they were to meet us. Mrs. Theresa had personally spoken, on the telephone, to some of them repeatedly on a weekly or monthly basis, about my wife and I. She had also talked to others, about my wife and I (both) on various holidays and/or while she was in the hospital. (To a person) they all said, that Mrs. Theresa told them,

> "I have these wonderful **Angels** that have moved onto my street, just for me; and, they (personally) take care of me, as if, I am a member of their very own family." You just have to meet them!

It was both <u>ironic</u> and extremely <u>gratifying</u> to me, that Mrs. Theresa's verbal descriptions (of us) to her closest friends, family and church leaders actually paralleled and reminded them all of the television series: ***Touched By An Angel***; because, Mrs. Theresa did <u>***not***</u> have a television (*TV*). Therefore, she would not have watched that television show; although, this program had aired *weekly* from 1994–2003, starring Roma Downing (as *Monica*) and Della Reese (as Tess), during that timeframe.

Truly, <u>more</u> than an assignment, Mrs. Theresa had become equivalent to a surrogate (or *adopted*) *grandmother* (to me)! After Mrs. Theresa was gone (from January thru June 2005), I continued to take care of her yard and property. Also in tribute to her, for the remainder of that last winter, I repeatedly shoveled snow for her oldest and dearest *friend* (Mrs. Ann). Before I left the state of New Jersey, I recruited a couple of guys (Majors Mercer Hedgeman and Brad Domby), from my lunchtime **Bible study** group, at my military unit, to assist me in *repainting* Mrs. Theresa's entire house; so, that her daughter (Joanne) could put it on the market (to sell).

In July 2005, as we drove away from our South River residence for the last time, there was only <u>one</u> other thing that I would've loved to have accomplished, in my assignment with Mrs. Theresa, but *failed* to succeed in. That was trying to convince her to call me: **<u>Rousell</u>**, instead of *Mr. Thomas*. I can still remember saying to her, on numerous occasions: "Please **don't** call me *Mister* Thomas. Just call me: *Rousell*." And she would, always reply: "Why *not*; you are a <u>man</u>, right?" And your last name is Thomas. Then, I would say: "Yes ma'am." Finally, Mrs. Theresa would look me in the eyes and say, "OK; then, you are **Mister** *Thomas*!"

Departing New Jersey (in July 2005): marked *the end* of a special assignment and relationship; concluded a twenty-plus years *active duty* Army career; and represented a ***defining moment*** and an *Apostolic* (spiritual) ***shift*** in my life. As I proceeded to drive down the Garden State Parkway, heading South toward Virginia, there was one thing that I *definitively* knew—there would be many more *GOD-ordained* **assignments** ahead (in my future).

## James Silas Manley
## (age 53 years)

Consistent with my personal **expectation** for these (future) *GOD-ordained assignments*, I had to keep my heart (spirit) ***focused*** to *discern* (recognize) <u>when</u> GOD would bring specific *opportunities* and/or people (assignments) to me. True to who I have consistently been, in my <u>walk</u> with GOD, He has always led me <u>to</u> *champion* people who are considered the ***under-dogs*** (like elderly, disabled/handicapped, widows, etc.) in society and *life*. Within a year of settling in Virginia, in conjunction with my ***retirement*** from the US Army, I met James Silas Manley. James was a very *active* brother and an usher in the church (Living Waters Christian Fellowship), that GOD led my family to join. James consistently and faithfully *served* in both the Ushers Ministry and the Men's Fellowship Ministry; and participated in every ministry and community service endeavor.

Although, he had *previously* suffered a stroke, about three years earlier (at forty-one years old), which left his speech greatly impaired (limited) and physical challenges with some motor skills. This meant that James walked with a serious *limp*, while dragging one leg; and, he had very limited mobility in one arm, which caused him to *favor* (lean or *depend heavily* on) only <u>one</u> side of his body. Despite these physical conditions, he was one of the *most determined* and ***dedicated*** young men that I have ever met (known). Although James had difficulty walking and did **not** drive, nor, own a car (*daily*) he walked and used the public transit (HRT) bus service to get around our city, as well as, between the seven cities on the Virginia Peninsula area, on his own (*alone*). He was always on his *post* (at one of the church entrances/doors), when he was scheduled to be **on duty**. He participated in <u>every</u> external *Community Outreach* event (opportunity), regardless of its location.

When I initially came to this church in 2006 and connected with James, he was forty-three years old. Despite his *physical limitations*, James was the most willing, enthusiastic and joyful guy that you (readers) have **ever** *met* or <u>not</u> *met*. If you ever *saw* or *could have seen* this brother *hoppling or lumbering,* across our huge church parking lot (toward the church), from the nearby public transit bus stop, you would certainly agree with my previous statement (about James). He always had this beaming expression of *joy* on his face and pride in his (every) step, as if he was approaching the *finish line* as the winning sprinter of an Olympic Championship race. (Note: If you *dis*counted *speed*, Hussain Bolt would **not** have had anything on James Manley!) After offering him a few rides (with my family) to and/or from church services, I later discovered that, although he was <u>near</u> **homeless** (**<u>not</u>** *living on the streets*), James had definitely been and still was living in a *transient* situation. This means that James had been (*temporarily*) living in and <u>moving</u> from **place-to-place** (as opportunities presented themselves). Some of his *short-term* residences (or *temporary*, living arrangements) included: a *boarding room* within a couple of individuals'/families' personal residences, an *unoccupied* room (Law office) inside of a business building, and a local Anglican-Franciscan Missionary (*Living Stone* Monastery) which provided short-term housing for transient people, who met their criteria. I had to move (re-locate) **all** of his personal belongings on two different occasions.

GOD gave me a *season*, from 2006 through 2009, to demonstrate that (indeed)—**I <u>was</u>** (would be) my ***brother's*** (James') ***keeper***! In addition to (regularly) transporting him to and/or from Worship Services and other church activities or Community events, he and I started a partnership workout *routine* of tackling the Nolan Trail (a five-mile long **hiking trek** of rolling hills, with about twelve (12) wooded bridges and four designated *lookout* points, intertwined with and surrounding a huge (Maury) Lake), about **three times/days** per week. Sometimes more urgent things infringed upon this schedule. On Sunday afternoons, following our regular Worship Services, we would bring James back to my house, to have dinner with my family. After dinner, He and I would watch a football game, if he felt *up to it*. However, more often than not, James would fall asleep in my big armchair, in the den, before *half-time* of the football game. Then, I'd wake him up and drive him back to the place where he was currently residing. In the morning of *rainy* school days, after I dropped off my daughter Karen at Warwick High School, I would continue driving (in the opposite direction of my home) to the HRT public transit system's bus stop, nearest to James's place; just in case, James was ***waiting*** *outside in the rain* (for a ride). If he was there, I would drive him to his appointment or errand. I became very proficient in understanding James's *broken* communication (of grunts and gestures); but, just as a *back-up*, I always carried a notepad and/or index cards, that James could write on, while in my truck.

In getting to know James, I learned that he had initially attempted to enlist and serve in the US Marine Corps, and he had papers (documentation) to prove it! However, due to some medical condition or other physical limitations, he was unable to successfully complete all phases of his basic training program and initial enlistment (service obligation). So in order to encourage and motivate James, I habitually referred to him (personally) just as: *Marine*! (Note: As a retired Army Officer (myself), it had always been normal, for me, to refer to other individuals that I interacted with as: *Soldier* (or ***soldiers***).) The more I embraced and supported James, the more I admired his (personal) ***courage***, ***determination***, ***tenacity*** (***perseverance***) and ***grit***. Whenever our church conducted our (annual) ***LWCF*** City-wide 10K or 5K Run/Walk event, Brother James always *participated* and ***completed*** the course. Yes, he was severely hampered or limited in terms of his ***speed*** (*finishing* ***time***); but, no one could ever question or doubt James's endurance and determination. Brother James consistently tried to improve himself and elevate or enhance his current situation, while he tried to ***bless*** (**help**) others that he came into contact with. He always carried personal business cards, as he made efforts to establish a small business of his own.

Here is a positive example or testimony of Brother James's tenacity and perseverance, despite how many times people told him that he could ***not*** do something. In communicating with others who could not understand his communications, as well as I did, James had to carry a notebook to write (scribble) out statements to most people. So I remember when Brother James had began to repeatedly and emphatically (write out) communicate to other people within our church congregation and the community that he intended to enroll in a *Real Estate Certification* Course, in order to get his Real Estate Certification. Eventually, another leader said, that he did not understand why or how Brother James could attempt to get this type of certification. This same individual told James that he could not get a Real Estate Certification or License; because, James could not even **talk** to the people (potential clients). Armed with this added motivation (***fuel***), from someone else's *negativity* or doubt in him, Brother James enrolled in that course and persistently pursued his goal. Sometimes, he rode the bus; on other occasions, I drove him. Yet he went to those classes, despite *adverse* weather conditions or any other opposition (challenges); and, he passed all the written examinations of that course (required by the State of Virginia). Finally, one day when I went to pick-up Brother James from his final course session, his instructor ask me to come inside of the building. When I entered the building, James led me to her office, where she was very excited to share with me, that Brother James had, in fact, successfully completed the course. She (then) presented James's Real Estate Certification to him, in my presence. As you can imagine, James was proudly and ecstatically *beaming* (**glowing**) from ear-to-ear! Brother James had definitely earned and deserved this personal satisfaction and elation, that he experienced on that day; and, deservedly so! I am a *witness* that Brother James **refused** to allow anyone else to determine or dictate what **he** would (or *could not*) accomplish. This was a clear testament to his individual tenaciousness (tenacity) and determination!

In 2008, James became the unfortunate recipient (or victim?) of a ***deceptive* ploy**, by the owner (or staff) of the last property in which he was residing at that time, as a means to get rid of him (as his temporary *living* status had extended beyond their acceptable ***welcome*** period.

At any rate, they called **911**, under the *pretense* that James needed to be hospitalized for some emergency or a possible *mental* breakdown (episode), who sent an ambulance to remove him from their property. A few days later, his older sister was called (by the hospital) from Maryland to Virginia, as his *next-of-kin*, to whom James was (eventually) released into her custody. By the time that I was able to *track* James's movement, through the Monastery staff personnel and the Riverside Hospital, finally, another local *relative* (in Hampton) informed me that James's older sister had already came and taken Brother James back to Maryland, to live with her and her husband. This individual also assisted me, by furnishing James's sister's name and (Maryland) phone number.

After several (*attempted*) phone calls and about three days of talking to a detached and *indifferent answering* **machine**, I finally talked directly to James's brother-in-law and sister. This gave me an opportunity to indirectly introduce myself and assure them of the positive contributions and support, that I (and our ministry) had provided to James's life in Newport News.

I asked them if it would be acceptable (to them), for me to call their home telephone to maintain contact with James; and, if they could make a computer available for James to be able to communicate back to me? They both **thanked** me for *befriending* James, and for my assistance and support to him, both inside and outside of our local ministry. They promised to see what they could do or set-up for him.

Although they vowed to take care of James in Maryland, he seemed to quickly *wear out* his **welcome** (for *living* at his sister's house). It was **not** a situation in which James did anything *wrong*; James simply needed, and was accustomed to having, more ***freedom*** and ***independence***, than what his sister was comfortable or willing to allow him to have in her home.

You see, in Newport News (prior to suffering a major *stroke*), James had previously enjoyed a nice job, owned his own car and enjoyed the freedom of *coming and going* (as he pleased) into his apartment. After suffering that stroke (in 2004), James ***lost*** (nearly) **everything**: his job, his ability to drive and his car, his ability to *comfortably* sustain himself, as well as, his apartment. However, to his own *credit* and a testament to James's tenacity and perseverance, he proved again and again that he would *stand on his own feet*; while, accepting and **overcoming** every obstacle and challenge (physically, emotionally, psychologically) thrown at him. Every time a door ***closed*** to him (in regards to a residence, transportation, and/or finances), James persevered and continued *moving forward* and seeking another solution.

And unbeknownst to his sister, he was able to succeed in doing this for nearly four years, before his sister transported him from Newport News, VA to her home in Maryland. Therefore, James's sister had never been there to (*personally*) **see** (***witness*** for herself) how mentally astute, physically determined and able, or enthusiastically and joyfully he pressed, over every *mountain* and through every *trial* that GOD saw James through.

*Fast-forwarding* to Maryland, James's sister <u>only</u> **knew** that: James was in an *unfamiliar* area; she and her husband were going to work daily; and she required him to **remain (locked) inside the house** each day, while they were at work. But as a grown, forty-five-plus years old man (who had been *free* and *independent*) **on his own** for more than two decades, treating James like a ***latch-key kid*** (who was *home alone*)—that was not going to <u>work</u>! So after coming home to find him outside the house and walking around the area, James was soon placed into a facility called Pleasant View Nursing Home in a town called Mt. Airy, MD. He never had access or the opportunity to establish computer communication with me, while at his sister's house. However, after calling there for him a few more times, I finally learned where he was.

Immediately, I was given a <u>new</u> **objective** in this ***assignment*** (*divine connection* relationship)**:**

I would have to physically go locate and visit James on a regular (routine) basis. So I searched out the place (*Pleasant View Nursing Home*) on the internet, got the directions and planned a *surprise* trip to visit Brother James Manley, on a Saturday morning.

You must understand, that this was a trip of **210 miles** and a **four-hour drive** (<u>one</u> *way*) of *bottle neck* traffic jams, just getting (there) from my home. So I never wanted any expected *hindrances* or unforeseen obstacles, upon arrival. Therefore I always coordinated in advance, about four days before each trip (visit). When I telephoned the facility to make advanced coordination for the very first time, a staff worker (Mr. Vincent Mayengo) was extremely cordial and supportive to ensure that James would be prepared for a local excursion, during my <u>***surprise***</u> (initial) visit, as well as, all subsequent visits. (I thanked GOD for Vincent; he absolutely and **gladly** was the person that I personally *counted on*, from the very beginning, to *genuinely* care for James, even as I did.) The idea and my intent was to go and *sign-out* James, for given afternoons; thus allowing him to *regularly* (routinely) get away from both the facility and its *nursing home* (**confined**) environment for a few hours. This would allow James to feel like he still had some ***freedom*** *of movement*, maintained a source of personal ***enjoyment***, and gave him some <u>hope</u> (something to physically *look forward to*) each month.

As I drove up the hill to the facility, the first impression—that really struck me—was just how <u>isolated</u> and <u>secluded</u> its location was. Upon entering the building, I went to the front desk and asked for Mr. Vincent Mayengo; remember, he was the <u>only</u> one expecting me. He was there, waiting behind the receptionist desk. My initial impression of Vincent and the entire (facility's) <u>staff</u>, to my pleasant surprise, almost *floored* me. As he walked me toward James's room, Vincent pleasantly and willingly shared details about the facility with me, as I intensely observed every staff member's unprecedented level of *genuine* **compassion** that they demonstrated for the patients (*residents*) and the *indisputable* **passion,** with which they ***served*** the people. There were about twelve different staff members that I personally (both) talked to (engaged) and observed in picking up James (that morning) or returning him (that afternoon). Ten of the twelve were originally from African countries (Kenya, Uganda, Senegal, Ethiopia, Congo, etc.). As such, they clearly had a *profoundly* higher level of appreciation, respect and dedication <u>to</u> their patients and <u>for</u> their job responsibilities, that were far above what I have normally encountered in other facilities, where staff members were primarily American born and reared. (Note: I have visited and ministered to elderly people in nursing homes, as well as, rehabilitation centers in several states around this country, for about fifteen years; and, I would absolutely and quickly tell anybody (anywhere), that this was the most compassionate and professional ***staff***, that I (both) had (and <u>still</u> have) ever seen or observed, over more than thirty-five years of ministry and my entire lifetime.

> *"Whatever you do, work at it with all you heart, as working for the Lord, not for human masters… It is the Lord Christ you are serving."* **(COLOSSIANS 3:23-25)**
> *"Serve the Lord with gladness."* **(PSALMS 100:2)**

The very first time, that I visited James, was a great ***surprise*** and a ***joyful*** occasion for him! When he walked out of his assigned room and saw me in the hallway, talking to the staff members (there), he was overjoyed and beamed with his normal **exuberant** personality. Initially, we went to a local restaurant for lunch; afterward, we just hung out at a park to get caught up (talking about the facility, his routine, the staff, etc.) On subsequent trips, we would visit little shops or other nearby places that looked interesting to James. Regardless, every visit was a full *day-long* trip consisting of: four hours of driving there (to Mt. Airy, MD); a four-hour long, local *excursion* (outing with Brother James); and, four to six hours of driving back to Newport News, VA, depending upon (evening) traffic.

I (initially) made this Maryland ***trek*** (or ***visitation*** trip) on two Saturdays per month (every other Saturday). I felt *in my heart* that this was an **assignment** that GOD had given to me. Therefore, I **had** to do this! So it was **not** burdensome to me, nor did I see (view) it as an inconvenience or a bother. At that time (then) Assistant Pastor Charlie Ammons fully supported my *Outreach* ministry with Brother James and authorized me to use one of our LWCF Ministry's vans. I also later discussed (with Pastor Charlie) my *desire* to invite other men (*Brothers* from the ministry) to come along to visit James. This did not stem from any **need** that I had for *help*; but, it was *an opportunity* for Brothers to *rally around* (support) James. Brother James actually <u>needed</u> this; because, he definitely did <u>not</u> belong in (nor did he deserve to be *confined*) to any *nursing home*. Now, he felt <u>betrayed</u> and <u>abandoned</u> by ***family*** members, while (also) being *isolated* and *confined* (with **no** *freedom of movement* or ability to make decisions for himself). This was Brother James's (personal) experience of an ***imprisonment***. Unfortunately, there was no (facility's) ***staff*** that could ***rescue*** (***free***) James from this <u>undesirable</u> reality.

> *"Inasmuch as ye have done it unto one of the least of these my brethren, ye have done it unto me."*
> **(MATTHEWS 25:35-40, 25:45-46 KJV/NIV)**

Eventually, I made these Maryland trips consistently for a period (between) one year to eighteen months. Most of them, I did *with* the Holy Spirit (*alone*). On two or three other occasions, I took my wife and/or son, along with me, to visit James. Deacon (then) Charles Wiggins and I visited Brother James on another occasion. Bro Ernest Hogan went with me, on another trip. Elders Tim Butler and Kevin Wright both accompanied me, on another visit. There was no doubt, that James and I shared a **divine** *(GOD-ordained)* **connection**; and, he knew how *special* our connection was. However, I believed that it was very important for other people to embrace, connect with and visit James, during this season of his life; because I knew that the more **other** people visited him, the more James would feel *loved* and *appreciated* (**valued**), while experiencing (receiving) the **love of GOD**, through them. Thereby, James's **hope**, sense of *freedom*, and his very spirit, purpose (*for living*) and **desire** (*to live*) would be greatly magnified. And James's level of **joy** and exuberance was always greatest (highest), when other people/individuals went (along with me) to visit him.

***Bro. James Silas Manley***

The greatest surprise of James's life probably came on one particular visit, when I was accompanied by the *real-life* (*actual*) Mr. Julius Campbell Jr., #81 from the Titans football team, of the famed <u>movie</u>: **Remember the Titans**! (Note: Julius and I had previously both conversed on a few phone conversations and physically met, when he had invited myself and my guest (Rev. Eric "*Duke*" McCaskill), and I to one of their Annual *1971* **Titans** *Reunion Celebrations*.) A couple of months later, Julius and I were discussing (on the phone) some of our separate <u>community service</u> and <u>ministry</u> endeavors, when I mentioned that I routinely, pass through Julius's area to visit James Manley (my friend and **Brother in Christ**), in a nursing home in Maryland. Upon hearing my **compassion** and **commitment** for visiting James, Julius immediately and enthusiastically said, "*Wow, this guy must really be a (special) "Brother" and a <u>great</u> friend, for you to sacrifice so much! I would love to go along with you to meet (visit) him one day. If you let me know (in advance) when to be ready and swing through to pick me up, I would be willing to visit him, too.*" I quickly replied, "*I certainly will; let's do it*!"

Prior to our conversation, Julius Campbell had never heard of, nor knew that James Manley even existed; yet, the **compassion** of his heart (for people), compelled him to desire to meet and visit James, with me. So that's what we did. I took him with me to visit James, two weeks later. This was amazing; because, James had no reason to expect Julius's visit.

As I went into the facility to get James, Julius waited in the van, to maximize the **surprise**, while, creating a level of **shock and awe** effect. When I introduced Julius to James, and explain exactly <u>who</u> he was, James was ecstatically overwhelmed! James had seen their movie. James's reaction of ***joy*** and ***jubilation***, reached a *ballistic* level, that almost launched (catapulted) James through the roof of the van! I had never seen James so excited before (nor after this visit). As we walked around the park and dined at the local restaurant (that day), Julius showed his championship ring and team photos to James, as he also discussed (shared) some of his experiences and team memories. He also gave James a photocopy of an original photo (of Julius and some of his real teammates and coaches, along with former President

Bill Clinton), for James to hang in his room at the nursing home. Julius Campbell called (referred to) James as *Champ* throughout the day; and James Manley assumed that role, as he proudly *strutted* around that day. As we drove James back to the nursing home on that afternoon, he was the most excited (and happiest) on that particular day, than at any other time that I ever saw him! James's **elation** was the direct result of a <u>stranger's</u> (Julius') demonstration of such <u>genuine</u>**:** love, compassion, concern and regard for James, who was just another human being, whom he had never met or known before.

After he had been in that facility for about ten months, I remember going (there) on one visit and James came *strolling up the hallway* on a two-wheeled and two-pronged *walker*, as if he were an eighty-year-old, ***fall risk*** patient. Initially, I was <u>shocked</u>. So I asked him, "*What are you doing with that thing (walker)? You don't need that!*" James stopped, as he began to gesture and grunt (sound out his normal form of communication). While pointing to the nurse's station, James insisted: "*Yeah, I know; they gave it to me.*" As a response, I told James, "*whenever they offer it to you, tell them:* **No***; thank you. I don't need a walker!*" I encouraged him **not** to use or become *attached to* (or rely on) that walker. As we traveled around on our excursion that day, James left that <u>walker</u> in the van; and he walked around independently, as he had always normally done. After about a year of visits, I noticed and acknowledged that Brother James's spirit was subsiding, as he conformed more and more to his *nursing home* lifestyle; and, the demeanor of his *heart* began to *shrivel up (close)*. Then, James's posture and physical movements slowed and were more deliberate until they (eventually) *diminished*, as he became more and more ***conformed*** to his environment. He even started to *drool* uncontrollably, which I believe was probably an effect of the medication (drugs) that he had been subjected to, while living in the nursing home.

By the time I arrived for what proved (or turned out) to be my *final* visit with James, it was (as if) he had *psychologically* and *emotionally* aged more than twenty years in one and a half years. There were so many obviously noticeable changes in his physical appearance and demeanor. He had a major weight gain, became (both) *less* active and emotionally detached.

He had already **conformed** to and become a *victim* of his environment, or a subdued, lethargic and depressed **shell of** his original self. This final visit was the **saddest** time for both James and I. I remember, as we sat in the local restaurant in the town (that day), James wrote a note on a table napkin to me that read: "*Don't take me back (to the nursing home). Take me back to Newport News with you. You have to find a way to get me out of here. Find a way to get me out*!" (In the words of an old cliché)**:** Brother James's **anguish** and **despair**, at the thought of remaining in that nursing home, were so **obvious** (*thick/heavy*) that you could have *cut it with a knife and fork*. Conversely (*in all sincerity*), it truly **grieved** my spirit and deeply **hurt** me, to have to return James to the **Pleasant View Nursing Home**, unlike anything that I had previously experienced on any other visits. However, I had no other option at that point; because, I was legally obligated to return him to the facility, after signing him out for that day's excursion.

In the months and years that followed, I found myself in an extensive **Transitional** period for myself (personally), as well as, for our Church/Ministry (LWCF). This period brought to me**:** new ministry responsibilities in the areas of Transportation and Evangelism Outreach, as well as, the beginning of *new assignments* (both Bro. Douglas Smith and Mother Nixon, etc.), who were individuals that I was (then) assigned to *serve* from 2008 and beyond. Additionally, I (**simultaneously**) handled Transportation Ministry responsibilities (for eighteen months), for an additional (second/*new*) church that we launched on the Virginia Peninsula; served as Camp Director (of Youth Summer Camps) and aided in facilitating year-around *Christian Retreats* at *Camp Heavenly Waters*; etc. During this same transitional period, Brother James (in the Maryland based nursing home) had **no** computer access, nor did he have any personal computer (there). Consequently, our relationship *connection* was hampered and we eventually lost contact, after I had gone through a series of other **Transitions**, both *personally* (in business, expansion of my individual ministries' and new individuals/assignments like: Pastor Thompson) and *corporately* (our church relocation and transitioning from Living Waters Christian Fellowship (LWCF) to **Restoration Christian Church of Virginia** (RCC-VA).

**Now**, as I was writing this book and desired to thank GOD for my previous *assignment* to **walk with** Brother James, I included this section, as a **tribute** to him. It was about 1:00 a.m. on Thursday, November 16 (2017), that I went on the internet to find some information on James. Initially, there were listings for hundreds of men named *James Manley*. However, I finally remembered that James's middle name was *Silas*; so, upon refining my *search* for James Silas Manley, I (*unexpectedly*) stumbled upon James's **obituary (from 2015)**. Immediately, I was shocked and hurt, to learn that our Brother James had passed away (more than two years earlier), without any warning, notice or previous contact. I definitely was **not** expecting this (now)!

The entire obituary read as follows:

James S. Manley<br>
April 15, 1962-September 2, 2015<br>
Frederick, Maryland

James was born on April 15, 1962 and passed away on Wednesday, September 2, 2015. James was a resident of Frederick, Maryland.

I suddenly went from being *shocked and hurt* to being **offended**, at the lack of *regard (*or *respect)* for and the **lack** of *value* shown toward James or his life, that this two-sentence obituary reflected. It took me (personally) more than a day and a half to **swallow** (and **digest**) what I had read, seen, and did **not**—*see!* Here was a fifty-three-year-old man, who was truly committed to GOD and willingly attempted to help anyone that he could (in the name of *ministry or community service*), regardless of the difficulty of the tasks. However, after he had *lived* more than half of a century, his obituary was written and read as though he were a deceased infant or a young child (toddler), who had briefly *lived*; but, never accomplished anything nor gone anywhere. Additionally, it seemed as though James had **NOT** *(really)* **lived** at all, and had **NO** *known* origin, relatives or *family ties*. WOW! What a *shameful* **travesty!** This was (our *Brother in Christ*) James Silas Manley, not some *mysterious*, unknown *John Doe!* Where was the love for James, from any family or friends? YES; he definitely deserved to have some people to either *mourn his loss* and/or *celebrate his life*.

Finally, I sent a text message at 8:12 p.m. on Friday, November 17 (2017), to notify some of our leaders, who had previously known and embraced Brother James Manley, of his **passing** (more than two years earlier). To a person, everyone was shocked; and remembered James, for that true **servant's spirit** (that he was) and compassionate *heart* that he possessed. Of course, everyone felt that James was a really great guy and a true **servant** of GOD. Just to confirm those sentiments, I have included the following text reply, which I received from Elder Kevin Wright, one of those leaders, who (texted back) said**:**

> *"Wow! Man, that is sad to hear and to see. No notice, but, thanks be unto GOD who always causes us to triumph…and gives us the victory! James's spirit is with Jesus forever. So the tears I shed (now) are for a sweet life (lived). Thanks for letting me know, man of GOD.*

For me (*personally*), this revelation or discovery of James's death marked an untimely **end** (termination) of another special assignment (or *divine connection*) and the **close** to a *valuable* life, that was *profitable* to GOD's Kingdom!

### Brother Douglas Amzie Smith
### (age: 54 years, 11 mos.)

Douglas Amzie Smith was born on April 27, 1954, in Harlem, New York, to his parents (Amzie Smith and Muriel Moore). Douglas was educated in the New York Public School System and graduated from Utica Institute of Technology (New York), where he received his Associate Degree. He worked for the United States Postal Service for thirteen years and was best known as *Smitty*, to his friends. He left Utica in 1997, to be closer to his mother in Virginia. He (then) was employed by the Virginia Department of Transportation, where he was an engineer.

Doug believed in (trusted) GOD for his salvation and was a member of Living Waters Christian Fellowship (LWCF) in Newport News, VA. During that (*fore-mentioned*) **Transitional** period from 2008 and beyond, I was led by the Spirit of GOD, to embrace Brother Doug Smith, who was my next (*new*) assignment. Brother Doug had already been a member of LWCF for a number of years, before we (my family and I) joined that ministry in January 2006. By 2008, Brother Doug's physical health had *declined* from (previously) walking with a cane, to being a *multiple sclerosis* (MS) patient (then) *paralyzed* from the waist-down and *confined* to a wheel-chair, while (simultaneously) undergoing *dialysis* (blood) treatments three days a week (on Tuesdays, Thursdays and Saturdays) for a *kidney* disease.

In 2008, Doug and his mother lived in Yorktown, VA.; but, he could no longer drive his vehicle or get around on his own. After multiple trips back and forth, between short-term hospitalization periods, rehabilitation/physical therapy tenures in the Newport News/Peninsula Nursing Home and their home in Yorktown, Deacon Charles Wiggins and myself were assigned to assist (and spiritually support) Doug and his mother. We made sure that their home was prepared and equipped for Doug's changing physical condition, by ensuring that a handicap ramp (for wheel-chair mobility) was built onto the house. Eventually, Doug became *confined* to *residing* in a local nursing home (Ruxton) in Williamsburg, VA. From the nursing homes, he had access to ambulance service for any emergency situations, as well as, medical transport services for his *routine* dialysis treatments on Tuesdays, Thursday, and Saturdays. However, at that point, Doug and his mother (both) became dependent upon (and **trusted**) me to *personally* transport him around for all of his personal needs and errands.

My GOD-given assignment was to **champion** *this under-dog* (Doug), by undergirding, embracing and supporting him, through three <u>critical</u> phases of his adult life. Those three phases represented (depicted) the **ups and downs** of the *Roller-Coaster* ride, which also proved to be the final three years of Doug's life. Upon meeting Doug, I met him in what I'm calling his **Wilderness** Phase. In this phase of his life, he had **already:** been married (and *divorced*); *lost* connection with his two biological sons; purchased and *lost* (*foreclosed* on) his own home; been diagnosed with a crippling physical disease (MS), which had (subsequently) *robbed* him of both his career and physical **mobility** (been left unable to neither walk nor drive for himself). At that point, he was still a reasonably ***young*** man, who is in a barren, *unfruitful* and broken place or state (phase) of his life; and, he has nothing of his own (**no** *fruit* or visible harvest) for all of his years of labor. There, he was **stuck** or **wandering** (within himself), while constantly being psychologically and emotionally attacked by the enemy's (Satan's) demons, imps, and *minions*. This phase was *reminiscent* of a heavyweight boxer (prize fighter), whose is sliding and ducking along the ropes. He is **trapped** in a corner, where he is **pummeled** (hit with everything that the enemy has). Finally, Doug was **knocked down** and (Satan) the enemy is counting *him out*! It was a phase of great **spiritual warfare**; but, GOD would know (prove) what was in Doug's heart! This phase was *played out* (extensively) in **isolation** between his mother's (Yorktown) home, hospitals, the Newport News/Peninsula Rehabilitation Center and *Ruxton* Nursing Home.

    I can remember occasions when I visited him in that nursing home, when he was literally *battling* (warring) with *demonic* forces. Sometimes, I would just show up (*unexpected* or unannounced), and a facility staff member would say to me: "*he's really angry and literally throwing things at us, when we try to go into his room.*" I would then reply to that individual, "*Ok. Sorry to hear that; I'll go in and talk to him.*" *Upon entering his room, Doug would immediately recognize me and say:* "*Hey T, man I am glad to see you. There are demons all around here. They have us surrounded. Can you see them; how did you get through? Do you think that you can sneak (back) out and get us some reinforcements (Deacon Wiggins or Pastor Charlie or somebody)?*" And there would be plastic cups, a fork and/or a plate cover still lying on the floor, where he had thrown them (at the staff). In these situations, I would reassure him that he had more than enough *fire* power to handle those demons. Then, I would talk (calm) him down; and, we would pray and command (*take authority over*) those demonic forces. After a few minutes, Doug became calm, encouraged, and we'd just talk and have a normal visit. On other (similar) occasions, he actually called (telephoned) me and said, "*Hey T, I need you to come and get me, man. Those demons have me surrounded; do you think you and Deacon Wiggins can get through (quickly)? Hurry!*." First, we would pray for (with) him (over the phone), to get his focus back on the *spiritual* power of the Holy Spirit (_presence_ of GOD) in his current condition, _wherever_ he was (physically) located. Then, I would physically respond to his urgent situation. Doug just wanted (**needed**) to know that somebody was (physically) in his corner; or, that he had a **combat buddy** (someone) assigned and committed to support him (in his warfare). He never wanted to feel that he was in his personal, spiritual *foxhole* **alone**, where the enemy could *over-run* him (in his _immobile_ condition) or *pick him off* from long range (like being shot by a sniper). In our being there for him, our assignment was to keep him encouraged (grounded and anchored) in his Faith in GOD. This phase went on for several months, with various dates on which he might have gone back home to Yorktown, only to result in *setbacks*! However, after the handicap ramp was *built* onto his mother's house, in anticipation of his going home, he never *lived* there (again), nor really got many opportunities to use it. Throughout this phase, Doug **never** lost his faith in GOD! Eventually, Doug was transferred from this *Rehabilitation* Center in Newport News to **Ruxton** *Nursing Home*, a long-term facility in Williamsburg, VA (even farther from home).

This *transfer* to Williamsburg, though <u>not</u> exactly what he wanted (*to go home*), did represent some type of **movement** (progress*?* or just *change*). Whereas, in the previous facility, he was so unhappy and disgruntled with the staff (there), that any change was welcomed. However, this distant *transfer* of about twenty miles actually represented a **shift** into his <u>next</u> phase. It was in this **Overcoming** (or **Conquering**) Phase, where the true *warrior's* spirit (mighty *man of Valor*) was established and appeared in Brother Doug. This phase both required and produced so much more substance, character, vision, fortitude and *fight* in Doug, beyond his current physical *limitations*. This phase was reminiscent of when the *fighter* got up off the canvas (floor), recomposed himself; and fought back with great tenacity and courage. At this point, his foe (the opposing fighter) knew that it would be impossible to *stop* (or knockout) this guy; because his tenacity and *will to win* was too great! He still needed to be medically transported three days a week (every Tuesday, Thursday, and Saturday) to *dialysis* treatments in Newport News. (Note: This required him to commute twenty miles or thirty minutes each way (to and from treatments), with a four to six hours long medical procedure (process) in between.) In addition to those requirements, he would, also, have to prove to be consistently **committed** (***willing***) to travel back-and-forth from Williamsburg to Newport News on Sundays for our Worship Services.

Every Sunday for months (with few exceptions), I would call and coordinate (*in advance*) with Doug on Friday/Saturdays. Then, I would arrive early on Sunday mornings, wheel him out to my personal SUV, lift Doug out of his wheel-chair and place him in the truck. After folding up and loading his wheel-chair into the vehicle, I'd drive him to the church. Upon arrival, I *personally* lifted him from my truck, placed him down (back) into his chair and wheeled him into the church, transporting him into and out of services. At the conclusion of each worship service, I usually took *Brother* Doug Smith to a restaurant (place) of his choice to get lunch (sometimes **take-out** or <u>to go</u>), before taking him back to the Ruxton Nursing Home in Williamsburg (about 2:30 p.m.). Additionally, on the *third* Sunday of every month, the fore-mentioned *routine* became even more deliberate and extensive; because (*in between*) dropping Doug off at the church (earlier or about 8:30 a.m.) and taking him back to Williamsburg (later or about 4:00 p.m.) in my SUV, I would also have to make a round-trip to pick up and return residents from **Rest Haven/Ashewood Nursing Homes** in Hampton, VA., utilizing our ministry's fifteen-passenger van. This means that Doug after having been pick up (earlier), had to wait in our ministry's bookstore/resource center with another member, while I made the additional *round-trip* to (and back from) Hampton, VA to bring another nursing homes' residents (passengers and *visitors*) to our worship service. After service, we would provide an <u>onsite lunch</u> to these visitors before I took them back to the nursing home; because, their lunch period at the nursing home would be over, before I ever got them back to their resident facility (about 2:00 p.m.), in our ministry's van. Meanwhile, Doug waited (back) at our church, until I returned (later about 2:40 p.m.) to switch vehicles and drove him back to his resident facility in Williamsburg (about 3:30–4:00 p.m.), after loading him back into my SUV.

It was Brother Doug's *unrelenting* **faith** and *unwavering* **commitment to GOD** in this process, that (eventually) produced an ***Overcomer's/Conqueror's spirit*** (*within* him), creating increased spiritual determination, fortitude, tenacity and courage (far beyond) his current physical limitations (disabilities). Doug was clearly ***transformed*** by the **renewing** of his mind, during this phase. The spiritually mature, *seasoned* disciple, that he became, was the *fruit* (evidence) of his *personal* transformation/renewal. So in addition, to consistently *pressing his way* to worship services, Doug (also) requested that I regularly transport him to get his haircuts (at Mack's Barber Shop) in Newport News, VA and to visit his mother in Yorktown, VA. However, his focus (**Objective**) *shifted*, from going (back) to live in his mother's house, to finding *a place of his own*. This represented a **renewed** strength, determination and courage to live ***independently*** (on his own) again, as well as, to ***conquer*** the other major challenges in his life. To that end, Doug soon enrolled in a driver's training program for *disabled* drivers, which trained him to begin *driving* himself (again), by utilizing a ***specialized*** vehicle *equipped for disabled drivers*. So I would drive him to these training sessions once or twice a week for eight weeks. Doug had made great strides (progress) in this program and proudly anticipated having his own vehicle converted to this ***specialized equipment*** configuration, with **all hand** controls (including brakes), directly on the steering wheel. Another indicator, of Doug's ***Conqueror's*** *spirit* (***Warrior's*** mentality), was the fact that Doug always (habitually) talked in *military jargon* (using military terminology), in this phase (stage) of his life. For instance, he would say: "*Hey T (man)—I need you to get me a real good laptop computer; so, I can have a nice "base station" set-up, when I get "my own place" (apartment). Then, I'll be better prepared to handle my missions!*" Doug was even talking about starting a personal small business, once he could find a place of his own. Therefore, I had already ordered and received shipment of a new laptop computer (for Doug).

The most significant ***triumph***, of all that Doug **overcame** in this phase (stage) of his life, was his personal <u>*victory*</u> over those *tormenting **demons*** and the ***fear***, which they had previously caused in his life. This was clearly apparent to Doug's mother (Mrs. Muriel), Deacon Charles Wiggins, myself and others who knew and regularly communicated with him. And this fact was best epitomized, through his (renewed) ***courage***, ***tenacity*** and ***boldness*** with which he sought out his next (*personal or private*) residence. He and I drove to and completed applications at several *potential* resident complexes in Newport News and Hampton, that would accommodate residents with partial disabilities. After going through mountains of bureaucratic **red tape**, <u>**no**</u> availability, and several inappropriate or *non-compatible* places (over a period of months), Doug was finally accepted (approved) and moved into a (first floor or ground level) apartment unit at Ashton Green Apartments complex, just around the corner (at that time) from our Church's (LWCF's) ministry complex. All of his dreams were coming true; Doug was *ecstatic*! However, after I physically moved Doug's personal property into that apartment, he actually only spend <u>one</u> single night inside that apartment. Unfortunately, a *mishap* in the middle of the night, while he tried to *transfer* himself (his body) from the bed onto a bedside *toilet-seat*, left Doug sitting on the floor, throughout that *cold* night. Afterward, he was ***unable*** to reach his (cell) telephone, nor move himself across the room or get back (up) onto the bed or the bedside toilet-stool. (That's where the *in-home* aide found him, still sitting on the floor, about 7:30 a.m. the next morning.) As a result, he had to (*temporarily*) go right back into the same resident facility (Ruxton Nursing Home) in Williamsburg, while we sought out an Assisted Living Facility (a Seniors Living/*Resident* Complex with *on-sight* staff), that would better fit his needs. Of course, this was a great psychological and emotional *let-down*; but, I re-assured him that we would go (right back) out to find another suitable residence the next week. And (the next week), he was *raring to go*!

Within a couple of weeks, Doug received the great news, that he had been accepted into ***Morningside*** of Newport News (a *5-star Assisted Living Facility*); however, he would have to <u>**wait**</u> another forty-five days for his designated *residence* to become *available*. Now, Brother Doug was more joyful, enthusiastic, motivated and expectant than I had ever seen him (before). In anticipation of moving into his new residence and regaining his personal independence and satisfaction, you could say that Doug was (then) **<u>on top of the world</u>** or *walking on air*! During this *waiting* period, Doug was still required to complete his dialysis treatments, for which a Medical Transport Service was utilized to transport him from Williamsburg to Newport News.

Everything in this *Conqueror's* phase of Doug's life had already previously whispered, promised, and <u>now</u> (in November 2008), was SCREAMING and depicting: ***victory***, ***conquest***, and ***progress*** toward his ***dream come true***; then, Doug experienced another **shift**!

With all the consistency of the classic *irony* from the darkest ***tragedies***, at the most *unexpected* times, in Edgar Allan Poe's literature (**now**) Brother Doug would face his similar ***macabre*** turn of events. This turn of events, *initially* began when two men—who were loading him (back) into a medical transport (ambulance service) vehicle one afternoon, following one of his *routine* dialysis treatment sessions—physically ***<u>dropped</u>*** Doug, allowing him to fall from the gurney onto the ground (*asphalt* parking lot). Looking around and seeing that no one had actually witnessed the incident, the two men (*professional* medical transport personnel) physically picked Doug up off the asphalt (parking lot), loaded him into the vehicle, drove him back to Ruxton Nursing Home in Williamsburg, put him (under the covers) into his bed, and returned to their company in Richmond, <u>*without telling anyone*</u> (at Ruxton or their own company's office) <u>*about*</u> their accident or ***negligent*** incident. However, this *drop*, subsequently, had a ***life-altering*** (**ending**) affect upon Doug! This particular **shift** started what I have called or referred to as: Doug's **Retreat and Surrender** Phase.

Later that same evening (night), when one of the facility's staff workers (a nurse or patient's aid) came into Doug's room to give him medication and/or check his status, she saw his bare foot protruding (out) from under the covers and very *swollen*. Therefore, she asked Doug: *what happened to your foot or ankle, today*? He informed her that he had been dropped in the parking lot, at which time, he had heard a *pop* (snap), but had never experienced any pain. The next morning, when his ankle was examined (and later *x-rayed*), the doctor determined that his ankle had been broken. (Note: Remember, Doug had MS and was already (previously) paralyzed from the waist down (with **no** *sensitivity* or capability in his lower extremities.) The doctor's initial treatment resulted in Doug wearing an *air-boot* type splint. However, after an extended period of time (about two weeks), the ankle showed no sign of healing. Next, the doctor put Doug's ankle into a traditional (*hard*) cast; but eventually, this also proved to be futile (useless). About thirty days after the incident of Doug's injury, Doug, his mother and I received the most **catastrophic** news, possible. Because Doug's ankle would <u>never</u> *heal*, his leg would have to be **amputated** at the shin (below the knee). The amputation **surgery** was conducted two days later, about eight days prior to his residence *move-in* date. All of this transpired within that (45 days) <u>waiting</u> period, before Doug had the opportunity to move into his anticipated **Morningside** residence (remember that *five-star Assisted Living Facility* in Newport News), from **Ruxton** in Williamsburg, VA.

Doug's amputation (surgery) date was <u>one</u> of the *three most devastating days* of the final phase of his adult life, <u>after</u> being *dropped*. When I entered his **recovery room** (about 8:00 p.m.), on the evening of his leg amputation, he was *propped up* (in a seated position) in his bed. First, he looked at me; then, he glanced down at the wrapped **stump** of his amputated leg and said (to me): "*Tee, look what they did to me, man! Why; why did they have to do* **this** *to me, Tee?*" Doug was thoroughly devastated and had a complete emotional **melt-down**, as he sobbed uncontrollably for about thirty (30) minutes. As hard as I tried, Doug was so distraught, that I *personally* felt wholly **inadequate** to console, comfort or encourage him—in that moment (situation). So after shedding some tears with this brother, I had to *excuse* myself (stepped out into the hallway) to attempt to call a couple of other men of GOD (Pastor Charlie Ammons and Elder Kevin Wright), whom Doug (also) respected, that might be able to speak (via telephone) to and encourage/reassure Doug. Subsequently, I was able to get Elder Kevin (on the phone) to talk to Doug. Upon leaving his hospital room, about an hour later, it was clearly apparent to me that Brother Doug had already begun a negative psychological and emotional **Downward Spiral**.

Brother Doug's second (one), of his *three most devastating days* of that final phase of his adult life, occurred (about ten days later), when Doug and I went back to the ***Morningside*** Assisted Living Facility in reference to his pending residence *move-in* date. This was the day that ***Morningside*** re-assessed and officially *reversed* Doug status, by *disqualifying* him and *declining* his (prior acceptance), based upon his recent amputation and associated *change* in his overall condition/ level of **physical assistance** required for residency. From this day forward, Doug was *doomed* to living the remainder of his days (life) inside of a nursing home, with **no** expectation or further ***hope*** of acquiring his own residence (gaining his independence or sense of *freedom*.) This final decision and **rejection** (by ***Morningside*** Assisted Living Facility) was *the straw that broke the camel's back*!

The culmination of all those devastating events, in a (short) three to six months period of time, epitomized Doug's **Retreat and Surrender** Phase. He began to feel, in a sense, like a *prisoner*, who was confined to serving a life sentence for a crime he never committed. Eventually, Doug was *quickly drained* of all hope, enthusiasm and tenacity. After losing his motivation and *will* to fight, he began to conform and succumb to the *nursing home* **environment** and debilitating **system** in which he (then) lived; but, he (also) **despised** it.

From December 2008 to March 2009, over the last three months of his life, I could see and hear the **Retreat and Surrender** in his: attitude, *voice* (speech), demeanor (body language), etc. While he continued to come to worship services, as much as he could; he no longer sounded, thought, expected or behaved like a *soldier* (*warrior* or man of Valor). The spark, glow or *fire*—(previously) in his eyes— was **gone**! Instead of *continuing* to exemplify his (previous) ferociousness of a lion or having the *eye of a tiger*, Doug had regressed or reverted to depicting a ***whipped*** puppy. He **retreated** (pulled back or moved backward) away from all of his prior ***progress;*** and, he totally **surrendered** (*gave up* on) all of his (former) ***dreams***!

Late one afternoon, in early February 2009, Doug called me on the telephone and *unexpectedly* said a very ***profound*** statement to me. He said, "*Hey Tee, I just wanted to call you (man) and say: <u>thanks for being a true</u> **brother** to me. GOD has already shown me that I only have a very small window of time (left), to make peace with everybody, before I die. So thanks; I love you.* **Bye**!"

And (then), Doug just <u>abruptly</u> hung up, before I could even ask him (anything). Immediately, I became **offended** (annoyed and grieved in my spirit). What was going on; what did Doug mean; what was he talking about? So I frantically and emphatically began dialing and re-dialing his phone number, continuously (for about twenty minutes), with **no** answer (**without** success). Therefore, the more times that I called (without an answer), the greater my level of frustration and/or aggravation became! Eventually, I called Deacon Charles Wiggins and informed him about this (previous) strange and abrupt phone call, that I had received from Doug. Because Doug had not answered any of my subsequent *return calls*, I was determined to immediately go to see him (face-to-face) and get to the bottom of this situation. Within an hour and a half of Doug's original call, I was on my way to the nursing home in Williamsburg, I picked up Deacon Wiggins to accompany me to visit Doug. Enroute to that nursing home, I said (to Deacon Wiggins), "*who does that <u>joker</u> (Doug) think that he was talking to, anyway? He's not going to just call me and say something like that; and (then), abruptly hang up the phone, without answering any questions! And (then) he had the nerve to* **not** <u>answer</u> *the phone for any of my subsequent calls. Really*?!" (<u>Note</u>: Maybe, I just needed to go and *pluck that joker upside his head* ☺, since I was already *steaming from the ears*, by then.)

As we entered Doug's room early that evening, he was sitting (propped up against a wall of pillows) in his bed, just staring at the ceiling lights (as if his mind was *wandering* miles away). My initial comment to Doug was: "*what in the heck is going on (with you), to call me with a statement like that, abruptly hang up (on me), and then ignore (or refuse to answer) about twenty subsequent calls (from me)?*" What has happened? After some <u>apologies</u> and greetings, we *settled down* into the most **profound** conversation of our two-year long ministry (spiritual) **assignment** and personal relationship (between the three of us).

Finally, Doug explained to Deacon Charles Wiggins and I exactly what had happened. In this conversation, Doug revealed to us that, as he was lying in bed (about 2:30 p.m.), while taking a nap, GOD gave him a **vision**, which (suddenly) **awakened** him. He said that he literally saw a huge <u>window</u>. As he peered through this window, Doug vividly saw scenes of his entire life *scrolling down*, like a **movie** playing right before his eyes. As the scenes were *rapidly* scrolling past his eyes, that window (*literally*) shrunk smaller and smaller, as it was continually **closing**. When the (*lowering*) window was only a couple of inches from the (bottom) window sill and almost closed, **suddenly**—the movie disappeared and the window **stopped**! As Doug stared in amazement, he said that the Holy Spirit gave him the <u>revelation</u> that this very *narrow opening*, which remained of that window, represented a very small span of his (remaining) lifetime on this earth. Doug also felt that this (also) meant that his remaining lifetime had been given (afforded) to him to *get his house in order* or <u>make</u> <u>amends</u> <u>with</u> all of the key people (relationships) in his life. One major issue for Doug was the fact that his ex-wife had been, and was still, keeping his sons away from him and their grandmother (Mrs. Muriel), for a few years already (at that point). And all previous attempts by Doug, Mrs. Muriel or Doug's niece (Simon), to re-establish contact/communication with his two young sons, had <u>failed</u> or *gone* **negatively** *or* **not responded to** by the ex-wife; so, Doug had been experiencing that **void** in his life, for about five years. After taking a few minutes to think about and digest what he had just (*supernaturally*) experienced, through that **vision**, Doug said that he had immediately began to make telephone calls to his mother (Mrs. Muriel), his sister (Shelley) in New York, his niece (Simone) in Hampton, VA and myself. After he had previously made that original phone call to me, Doug said that he had just needed to take some time (alone) to process everything. Deacon Charles and I, finally left (Doug) that evening, after about three (3) hours of allowing Doug to share his heart (*confide* in us) and *vent* his frustrations, successes, etc.; and, we (in turn) had the privilege (opportunity) to encourage, minister to and be a blessing to Doug, in his great hour of (*compassionate*) **<u>need</u>**.

Doug's third (and **final** one) of his *three most devastating days* of that final phase of his adult life, occurred (about two weeks later), when the doctors informed Doug's mother in a *private* session that his previously amputated leg (*stump*) was **not** *healing*, either. The doctor said that Doug's leg could never heal, as it currently was. The doctor said that his only other option was to perform another amputation (higher), above the knee of that same leg, ***hoping*** to hit (or *find*) a more viable, *thriving* section of that limb, which might be more susceptible to *heal*. (Note: In term of an analogy, any subsequent procedures would be like watching *a prospector digging and panning for gold* in a canyon, where **NO** gold even ever existed.) However, as much as it *pained* (hurt) her to do so, Mrs. Muriel—(knowing that Doug had ***lost*** his *will* to fight and the *desire* to *live* any longer, in this physical condition)—simply told that doctor**:** "*NO! What's the use of continuing to cut on him, just to keep cutting him (aimlessly doing that), until there is nothing left? If it is NOT going to "heal" or do (him) any good. Just leave him alone!*"

Hearing this latest news from the doctor was devastating enough for Doug; but, it was *most* **devastating** for Mrs. Muriel; because, the sudden **reality** of Doug's prophetic *prediction* of his very small window of (remaining) life had just been *confirmed* (*in her spirit*) and would soon become a *crystal clear* manifestation, in her own life. She had already endured lots of bureaucratic *non-sense* (**red tape**) from this nursing home. For examples, the **Ruxton** facility previously had transferred Bro. Doug, on at least three occasions, to the Sentara Medical Center in Williamsburg, under very questionable circumstances (like Mercer Staph infections, etc.), **without** giving any official ***notification*** to her (his *next-of-kin*/mother). She was only made aware of Doug's location and status in those situations, through my random visits to his room at the nursing home; whereby, I discovered that he was **not** there (where he was supposed to be). Each time, I immediately drove to the hospital, located him and telephoned his mother of his conditions.

On another very memorable occasion, I received a very urgent and disturbing phone call (request), about ***11:00 p.m.*** one night, from Doug's mother. She had been *repeatedly* calling Doug's cell phone all (that) day and night, without getting any answer; while, the staff at the nursing station also failed (refused) to answer her calls. Her level of distress and anxiety was *off the hook* and *through the roof,* but I realized that it was well warranted, based upon both her own personal experiences with and the recent *track record* (reputation) of this nursing home. When she called me, with her voice *cracking* and moving to tears, she simply said: "***please* personally** *drive out to that nursing home and make a visual* **verification** *of Doug's location and medical status, for me. I hate to call at this late hour of the night; but, I am very worried that something has happened to Doug, that those people are hiding (keeping) from me!*"

I ***knew*** that Doug was my current ***assignment*** in that <u>season</u>! So I responded quickly and decisively to her, by simply saying, "*Count it done! Don't worry about it any longer; I'll be on the road in ten minutes!*" However (possibly) for you, or someone else, who may be reading this and thinking that you would not have answered your phone or left your house after 10:30 p.m., I (now) **ask** you (him or her): **What would happen** to vulnerable (or disabled) people (or even *You* and I) in *dire* and/or *life-and-death* situation (between the hours of 10:30 p.m. to 5:00 a.m., if**: JESUS** refused to *hear* prayers and *intercede* (*respond*) on the behalf of *his people* (believers); **GOD** (The Father) refused to *honor* our faith and *dispatch* angels into our situations (on earth); and, the **Holy Spirit** *stopped* or did **not** *lead/empower/work* for and within us—<u>after 10:30 p.m. or during these inconvenient (or inaccessible) hours</u>? *Huhmmm!*

Moving with a sense of <u>*purpose*</u>, I arrived at that nursing home in thirty minutes from Mrs. Muriel's original call. Upon arriving, it was already past <u>normal</u> *visiting* hours and I could see, as I peered through the (sliding) glass door, that **no** one was sitting at the reception station, in view of the front door. However, this was NO normal visit! And I already knew these *jokers*' reputation, routine and procedures down to the letter! So I began to ring the entrance (access) **buzzer** and (*unrelentingly*) continued to ring it over and over and over again, for about fifteen minutes. Finally, an on-duty staff worker realized that I would **not** just *go away*; so, she came to the door to tell me that visiting hours were over. I told her that I was obviously not there for a routine visit, showed her my pictured ID through the glass door, and explained that a patient's (Doug's) eighty years old mother desperately needed to know the status of her son (there) inside this facility. Late tonight, after trying to call his personal cell phone, <u>all</u> day and night with **no** answer, and getting <u>no</u> answer from anyone at your nurses' station this evening, she has sent me to verify his status (condition and location). The staff worker said, "*I am sorry; but, she will have to wait until tomorrow.*" Her statement draw a sharp and immediate response (from me), "*Oh, I beg to differ with you, on that. I have promised this mother, before driving thirty miles to get here, that I will personally verify her son's current location and status; and, I am not leaving here, until I do (exactly) that. So how we proceed from now on is totally up to you!*" Finally, she said, "*if you don't leave the premises right now, I will have to call the police.*" To that staff worker's surprise (amazement), I said, "Don't bother yourself, tying up your line. *I'll do you one better. I will call the police (on my phone)! I am here to accomplish a mission, not to engage in "idle chatter." Whether you let me in* **alone** *or with a police escort is* <u>irrelevant</u> *(does not matter), to me. As long as I leave with the physical verification that I came for, and Mother Muriel has her satisfaction ("peace" of mind)!*" That was my <u>only</u> midnight **Objective**! (Note: Just in case, you are still wondering if I had the personal courage and **resolve** to *follow through*, with the police? You bet? **ABSOLUTELY**! I was already ***dialing***, <u>before</u> I finished my statement (to her).)

When the police officers arrived, I showed them my (retired) military officer's ID and driver's license. As one officer went to *run my ID (name) through the system*, I got mother Muriel on my cell phone to talk to the other officer, to <u>confirm</u> my reason (purpose) for being there. About four minutes after the ***police's*** arrival, we were (again) ringing the access buzzer and banging on the door, to which the staff responded and we entered the nursing home (*unhindered*), as the staff nervously scurried around the hallways. Having been there ***countless*** times (sometimes three or four times a week), I led them directly to Doug's room. When the police and I entered Doug's room, he was surprised to see them, as I woke him. Once in his room, I called his mother and allowed her to speak directly to him (on my phone). We discovered that Doug had *inadvertently* allowed his phone to *die* (go *uncharged* the previous night). Still, his mother should have reasonably been able to get some response (answer) from the staff at the nurse's station, at some point, during that afternoon or evening. As I drove back home (at *nearly 1:00 a.m.*), from the nursing home, the result of my drive to Williamsburg was (another): ***Mission Accomplished; Hook-up Complete***!

So those examples prove the Mrs. Muriel had truly experienced lots of disappointment, aggravation and (eventually) grief with the **Ruxton** Nursing Home. Undeniably, she already knew, that she and Doug could have (*theoretically* and *literally*) filed and won a major lawsuit, against the Medical Transport Company (that *dropped* him and failed to report it), and **Ruxton** Nursing Home (for *failing* to launch a complete investigation into that *negligent* incident, which resulted in the amputation of his leg and the subsequent **down-spiral** toward his death. However (in the face of grave disappointment and deep sorrow), Mrs. Muriel's <u>*heart*</u>, <u>*mind*</u> and <u>*attention*</u> were all focused upon spending any remaining time—*loving* her son (Doug) **versus seeking revenge** or **payback** (rendering *evil-for-evil*). Ultimately, she just wanted her son (Doug) to have, at last, absolute ***peace***!

Doug's *small window* **prophecy** was accurate and true. It only lasted about six weeks; and (then)—he was gone! During that time, I got a small group of the brothers (from the church) to visit him either there at the hospital or at the Ruxton facility. I, even, gave him a small portable cassette tape recorder with a *stand-up* microphone to record any thoughts that he desired to leave. During this final period, Doug did **<u>not</u>** come out to services or get out publicly.

Doug spent this time (alone) in quiet meditation and reflection, as well as, in peaceful visits and conversations with his mother, myself and/or Deacon Charles Wiggins (or some combination thereof). (*Internally*) he was finally ***at peace***; because, he had already *surrendered* (himself) to no longer living a <u>futile</u> ***earthly*** existence, for another season. Instead, he had resolved, within himself, to rather ***go home*** to reside with the LORD (forever). On Saturday, March 21, 2009, our Brother Doug just *flew away* (passed) to be at rest.

In life, Doug told me, that I was the real *brother* to him, since his only *biological* brother had been killed (murdered) some years earlier. His mother (Mrs. Muriel) said that I was Doug's *dearest* friend and the (physically) strongest little man that she had ever met (or seen *in action.*)

In his death, I saluted the *good soldier* of Jesus Christ, that Doug had become. I would just say to you, that: "I was simply the **one**, who had answered GOD's Call and been sent to *walk along side of Doug* (to be both his **keeper** and **combat buddy**)." Doug was my *assignment* in that season. Today, I give **Glory To GOD;** that I never considered my mission (of **service** to Doug) to be *impossible*! Yes! It was sometimes *inconvenient* (sometimes) *uncomfortable* or sacrificially *costly (in time)*; but, it was never **IMPOSSIBLE!**

## Mother Wihemina Nixon
### (age: 87 years, 6 mos.)

I had previously connected with and been planted in my assigned church called *Living Waters Christian Fellowship* in Newport News, Virginia, since January 2006. This is where GOD sent **Mother Nixon** (to me) in February 2009.

Wilhemina Nixon had been born in *Bocas Del Toro*, Panama in 1922. At an early age, she accepted Jesus Christ as her Lord and Savior. She genuinely loved GOD and people! She was also a faithful *prayer warrior*, who loved sharing the Gospel of Jesus with everyone she met.

I believed that GOD had only sent this *widow* to me; because, she was my new *GOD-appointed* **assignment**, in that season. At that time, she was already eighty-six years old, fragile and walked with a *walker*. She had also been *widowed* for about two years. Although I was not expecting (or anticipating) it, GOD used another young lady (Elder Betsy Robinson) in our ministry, to connect Mother Nixon and I. Elder Betsy had been delivering ***Meals-on-Wheels*** (a feeding program through the Peninsula Agency for The Aging) to local elderly residents in our city. And since she had begun delivering to Mother Nixon, as one of the clients (recipients) on her delivery route, she had invited this gracious and loving widow to visit our worship service. As a courtesy to Mother Nixon, Elder Betsy had promised to pick-up and transport her to our church service, for Mother Nixon's initial visit. Mother Nixon's testimony, that she later shared with us, was that she was initially *consumed (overwhelmed) by* the <u>genuine</u> **love of GOD** (warmth of the people and the atmosphere or spiritual climate of our Ministry); and, the Worship experience was phenomenal. She felt that she had arrived: *at home*! Immediately after that first visit, Elder Betsy brought Mother Nixon across the sanctuary and personally introduced her to me, based upon Mother Nixon's own personal request. After meeting her, I (then) had the privilege to drive her back to her residence. From the very first contact (experience), the **divine connection** (and spiritual *relationship*), between Mother Nixon and I, was <u>permanent</u> and <u>sure</u>. The kind of relationship that people refer to, in *cliché*, as *like a marriage made in heaven*. And she had a *sense of humor* that was unbelievably *over the top*! I will never forget the very first time that I was assisting her (up) into the fifteen-passenger van. She said to me (in her distinctive *Panamanian* accent), "wait Deacon; don't lift me up. I can get (climb) up; I don't want you to hurt yourself!" Personally, I was *tickled pink* and rolling with laughter (on the inside); because, I was thinking (to myself): she just doesn't know, that I could probably (*almost*) lift her up and sit her *on the top* of this van.

For the next sixteen (16) months, Mother Nixon was my current *surrogate* (adopted) **Mother**. As such, and being (recently) *widowed*, she grew to greatly depend upon me, throughout the remainder of her life. I believe that this was apparent, welcomed by and very significant to her; because, she only had **one** *biological* daughter (Poncier), whom we affectionately referred to as *Peola*; while, she had **lost all three** of her *biological* (deceased) sons. Those sons had all *died* back in Panama, living *lifestyles* that broke her heart and brought her shame and great pain (grief). During personal conversations with her, Mother Nixon shared a lot of her life's story with me. And after moving, from Matthews County (more than an hour away), into the city of Newport News to be closer to her daughter (Peola), she did <u>*not*</u>

want to over-burden (become too much of a hindrance) or deprive *Peola* of the *freedom to live* her own life. Initially, Mother Nixon had lived with Peola and her husband (Larry); but, eventually, she insisted upon moving into her own apartment, within a local *Senior Living (Community) Facility*, within five miles of her daughter's house.

Mother Nixon physically *moved* and functioned very well; while, living *independently* for a while. However, her health began to decline significantly, as illness and *disease* (eventually) *took its toll* on her body, over the last year. Mother Nixon's daughter (Poncier/ ***Peola***) and one of her granddaughters (***Nikki;*** Peola's local daughter), who had small children of her own, were willing and did **everything** (on a daily basis) to take care of *Mother Nixon*, while also working jobs themselves. It was clear to us (then) why GOD had sent her to me; while, spiritually engrafting me into her family to *serve* her and fill the *void* (gap), that had been created (left behind) by her *biological* sons, from years before. So as I **served** (ministered to) the <u>needs</u> of Mother Nixon, I was (also) able to provide (or afford) some relief, support, stability and respite for the family (Peola, Larry and Nikki), along with Michelle**:** the subsequent *in-home* nurse/aide.

My **assignment** (and our <u>spiritual</u> **Mother-son** *relationship*) was genuine, clear and tangible, from the very beginning. Within the first couple of months, whenever I would take my family to see (visit) her, she would always refer to my children as <u>*her grandchildren*</u>.

When she would see my son (Joshua), she would smile (*from ear-to-ear*) and say: *"Oh, look at me little grandson:* ***Jamesey****. Come and give ye Grandma Mina a kiss!"*

Our relationship grew (astronomically) from providing transportation to worship services; to running errands for her; to accompanying her on medical appointments; to doing things in her residence; to providing fellowship, encouragement, spiritual ministry; and hospice volunteer responsibilities.

She definitely loved our church. Sometimes, as she and I would sit and talk, she proudly announced its name (in her proud ***Panamanian*** *accent*): **"(The) Liv-ing Waters!"** **Bishop Steven Banks and Pastor Charlie!***"* Then she would say, *"That Bishop Steven, him can really preach! But Pastor Charlie (The* **Pretty Boy from Georgia)***, him can preach, too!"*

***Mother Wilhemina Nixon*** *(A Spiritual Mother of our Church)*

During the happier times, she loved *cracking jokes*, and, she gave funny *nicknames* to everybody. I can remember a time in Nov. 2009, when a group of us (Pastor Charlie Ammons, Brother Roger McLain, and myself, along with *Peola*), had gone to serve **Holy Communion** to Mother Nixon at the St. Francis Rehabilitation facility. As we greeted and fellowshipped (talked) with her, Peola or I said to her, "*Mother do you recognize all of these visitors?*" Then, she sat up, smiled and said (in her usual distinctive voice), *"Me know who them is: Deacon Thomas,* me **nineteen years old grandson**, *and* **the Pretty Boy from Georgia:** *(Pastor Charlie)!"* She chuckled loud and proudly; as, we all got a great laugh out of her humorous response. (Note: Roger was actually about thirty years old, at that time, not nineteen!)

During the final year, Mother had a few different hospital stays. Over the final six to eight months, cancer ravaged her body, as she went back and forth, from Riverside and/or Mary Immaculate Hospitals to St. Francis Rehabilitation Center, to home, to *in-home* Hospice care, and finally, to official *Hospice* status in *The Gardens at Warwick Forest (Palliative Care Center)*.

The most special and pleasantly *memorable* day (for her and us), during her final six months, was her **eighty-seventh birthday** (December 23, 2009). Although, she was in the St. Francis Rehabilitation facility, we were able to *reserve* one of the activity rooms (there), and we succeeded in throwing the *grandest (surprise)* birthday party, for her, that's ever been held in that Rehab facility. Her daughter brought in Mother Nixon's favorite and most *glamorous* red dress, which she adorned with all of her jewelry and accessories. Her granddaughter (Nikki) ordered a huge, gorgeous birthday cake, with ice cream and all of the trimmings. The room was especially decorated to match her special favorite colors and *unique* taste. There were guests present from The *Living Waters Christian Fellowship* (Church); family members from her three succeeding generations (daughter, granddaughter, great grandchildren) and her *oldest/dearest* Panamanian friend (Mother Oates); St. Francis's *staff members (who participated in singing Happy Birthday); other facility residents/patients; and, it was a Huge—***Surprise!** Mother Nixon never anticipated or expected it; while, she was (there) in the Rehab facility.

Conversely, one of the worst and most painful nights (for Mother), that I can remember, was the exact (same) evening of our LWCF's Talent Competition and Fashion Show. I had already been *sitting* with Mother for more than three hours. Then, suddenly about 9:00 p.m., Mother became overwhelmed by extremely *agonizing* stomach pains. No matter what I tried, I could not comfort her. And I hated the fact that the pains were persisting, despite all of my prayers and efforts. Finally about 9:40 p.m., I called Pastor Charlie via telephone and asked him to join me at Mother Nixon's house; because I felt like I needed to have *someone* to *partner* with me, in (spiritual warfare) *warring* for her *relief* from pain; comfort and peace (*divine recovery* in her body); as well as, her *peace of mind*. However, I could not just call any *random* person; but, I needed the support of someone who deeply loved her and who she greatly respected and trusted to intercede with me, on her behalf. The *teamwork* of our intercession and (spiritual) warfare, resembled that of a two-man team performing *Cardiopulmonary Resuscitation* (CPR). He sat on the left side of her bed and *prayed*; while, I sat on the right side of her bed—holding her hand, rubbing her forehead, singing to her (calming her spirit) and reducing her anxiety. The synchronization, coordination and fluidity of our effort (operation) were <u>reminiscent</u> of one paramedic providing (blowing) breathes into a victim's mouth; while, another paramedic conducts the *chest compressions*! This operation went on until about midnight. And thank GOD, that we and Mother prevailed! I am sure that (now Apostle) Charlie Ammons, like myself, will never (ever) forget the experience of engaging in spiritual *warfare* (on Mother's behalf) that night, and the deep **bond/connection** that was forged (established) between the three of us, on that night. It was in this personal and intimate setting, with just the three of us, in which Mother asked us to **promise her** (commit to) a special request that she had to ask of us. Mother Nixon said (in her normal *dialect*), "in me country in Panama, **"grave diggers"** and employees of the "undertakers" (funeral homes) steal jewelry from and remove gold teeth out of the mouths of the dead people. Me don't know what them will do to me body, after the family leaves the graveside. Now, ye promise me that you gonna stay there, at the graveside and watch over me, until me buried and me grave has been all covered (closed) up. Don't leave me with them **"grave robbers."** DON'T let them take advantage of me or steal me stuff off of me body. You promise me (now) that you gonna stay there with me, until after the workers have finished and are all *gone*!"

    Myself and Pastor Charlie both promised Mother Nixon, that she could count on us (**rest assured**), that we would stay right there, as she requested, no matter what!

    Initially, for those final three months, her daughter (Peola) did <u>not</u> want to leave Mother Nixon's bedside, attempting to go into the hospital or rehabilitation facility around 9:30 a.m. (to catch the doctors doing their morning patients' *rounds* (visits), and also stay all day and into the nights. However, the Holy Spirit revealed to me that I needed to get her to agree to *pulling* **shifts** (as we had done in New Jersey with Mrs. Theresa). This would allow Peola adequate time to eat, *detox* (release *stress*, vent and relax at home) and get sufficient hours of **sleep** (at night). I also realized that the day would, eventually, come when Peola may become overwhelmed and <u>not</u> be able to continue (at all) in Mother's subsequent **transition** process. And we would have to be ready for that possibility/imminence, as well. Eventually, Peola pulled the *bedside companion* shifts from 9:30 a.m. until 6:30 p.m., with an occasional two-hour break from Nikki or Michelle, between their other jobs/responsibilities (during the *in-home* phase), or from Nikki only (during hospital or rehab facility phases). Then, I relieved Peola (**daily**), by pulling the *night shifts* (from 6:30 p.m. until past midnight). We developed this synchronized routine, in which Peola's shift and mine would *overlap* (both of us there together for thirty minutes to an hour), conducting a *battle hand-off* or *shift change* briefing (between us), to discuss any changes in treatment, appetite, required medicines, etc. So I always knew (coming in) everything that had transpired (that day), as well as, what I needed to expect (or look out for) during each night's shift.

During the earlier stages of Mother Nixon's decline, our **objective** was to ensure that she had the *best quality of life*, for as *long as possible*. As long as she could eat, talk, communicate effectively, watch television, discuss scripture, listen to gospel music *CDs*, etc., we needed to ensure that all of those things were afforded to her. And we wanted her to feel **loved** and know that one or more of us (people) that loved her, and whom she trusted, would always be (there) with her. We never wanted to leave her totally in the hands and *care* of **strangers**. Sometimes on rainy or *bad weather* days, as I walked into her room (in the late evening or night), Peola would say: *"Look Mommie, look "Mina"; look whose here (coming)!" "I told you, Deacon Thomas was coming."* Then, Mother Nixon would glance quickly toward the door, giving me a quick scowl and turn her head away, as if she was angry (at me). Peola would say, *"Yah, Deacon Thomas, she has been pouting and mad; because, she said maybe you wouldn't come, since it was raining."* So I would say, *"OK, sorry she is mad and didn't trust me, I guess I'll just go back home."* Finally, Mother Nixon would turn back toward me (with that huge smile) or sit up and say, "him better come!" (Then, we all laughed and joked about her mood swings' **charade**.)

The last ten days of Mother Nixon's life were extremely difficult for the family, as the doctors could no longer help her. Her eating and communications declined drastically until it stopped. Finally, the <u>only</u> remaining *constant* was the **excruciating** stomach **pain.** Our focus, in these situations, was to comfort her, as much as possible. So one of us would stand on one side of her bed and hold her hand; while, another one stood on the opposite side of her bed, rubbing her forehead, playing gospel music CDs, and talking or singing to her. Initially the doctors released her, to go home to spend her final days, under an *in-home* Hospice program; but, it became too difficult *to manage* her pain, etc. at home. In the end, she was re-located to *The Gardens at Warwick Forests (Palliative Care Center)*. Sometimes, she would become so *hungry*; however (at this point) she could <u>not</u> swallow or eat anything. Some days, Mother Nixon would be sleeping comfortable; then, all of a sudden, she would begin to groan and moan in extreme pain. Peola recognized the signs of the time (as it related to her mother's life); and, she would often say, *"Mommie or Mina is "traveling" (transitioning) now."* We and the family all realized, at about the one-week point, that Mother Nixon was nearing the end of her *transitioning* process. And her *breathing* became more laborious (exhibiting extreme difficulty), during the final three days.

    I was personally working with the US Census Bureau (during those days), conducting the local **2010 Census**, which is normally conducted every ten years. I can vividly remember, on Saturday **(June 5, 2010),** that I had just completed my census *surveys* (interviews) of residents in the *Lincoln Park high-rise* apartments, on LaSalle Ave., in Hampton, VA. I finished my *de-briefing* (required meeting) at about 5:00 p.m., with my Area/Team Coordinator, at the McDonald's restaurant near the intersection of LaSalle Ave and Pembroke Ave. Just before I left that location, I called my wife and informed her that I would be leaving Hampton in about fifteen minutes. I had planned to go home (briefly) for about one hour; then, I would go to sit with Mother Nixon for the evening shift. I started driving on *Interstate 64* **(I-64)**, heading West to go home (*first*); however, the Holy Spirit *blocked*/altered that plan. It was as if I was *unconsciously* driving, with my car on **auto-pilot**; and suddenly, I had already passed the exit to my house and drove directly into the *Warwick Forest* facility's parking lot. **You** must understand that this facility is located about three exits and fifteen minutes past the exit to my house, which I had planned to take. I do **not** even remember making the required turns or *driving* the entire route. That is why I said that, it was as if the car was being driven on *auto-pilot*; because I realize that no one else was in the car with me. So the Holy Spirit had to have *transported* (driven) me directly to that location; due to the **urgency** of the *immediate* situation.

As my car pulled (drove) into the parking lot (about 6:00 p.m.), Peola flew past me, as she was leaving the lot. And although she did not even see me; as she drove (exited) past me, I could see that she was upset and crying. I immediately tried to call her phone a couple of times.

But she (initially) did not answer. Therefore, I rushed into the facility and headed directly to Mother Nixon's room. When I walked into her room, she was breathing in an *extremely slow and exaggerated* or *strained* and *distorted* manner. I stepped back out into the corridor (hallway) to continue trying to call Peola. After about ten minutes, she had already arrived at her house and finally answered the phone. She was crying and **apologizing,** because she had left. She said, *"Deacon Thomas, I left my mother because I could not take it any longer; I could not stand to see her struggling so hard to breathe. So I just had to get out!"* I replied to her, "Peola, don't worry about it. I am already here with Mother. *I pulled in, as you were leaving; and I knew that GOD meant for me to be here to relieve you. Your job is done (responsibility has been fulfilled)! You have gone* **as far as** *you were meant to go. It is my* **assignment** *(now) to be with her, from this point forward.* You just wait at home with Larry; and, I will take care of Mother and keep you guys posted." <u>I promised Mother, that I would be here and stay with her throughout this stage of the process</u>. **GOD BLESS YOU!** *I will call to update you, later (tonight), only as necessary.*

During that day, she had already been given multiple morphine injections (to alleviate the physical <u>pain</u>, associated with her *suffering*), which provided an *artificial* **level of comfort** in her **Hospice** condition (treatment). After I hung up the telephone, Mother Nixon and I shared those <u>final hours</u> of her *earthly journey,* from about **6:30 to exactly 10:55 p.m.** that evening. This was ***not*** your *normal, comfortable, popular,* fun or *glamorous* situation or circumstances, for the average person to be involved in. I knew, without a doubt, that I had been ordained, appointed and anointed for this role. Otherwise, this assignment would have been more than I could have *personally* endured; but, once again, I was in *my assigned place* (right where He had planted me). It proved to be four and one half **(4 1/2) hours** of a ***physical battle for*** <u>***life***</u>, as she fought desperately for each and every (single) *breathe*. The *battle* was so real, that during her desperate struggles to breathe, her face strenuously twisted and contorted into some very abnormal and unpleasant configurations/shapes. Her eyes remained closed for the majority of this time. However, she did open her eyes (temporarily) a <u>few</u> times, during that final period of her *life on earth*. Maybe she was trying to see if it was actually **me** or Peola, who was still (there) at her bedside. I constantly held her hand, rubbed her forehand and stroked her hair (wig), just to make sure that she realized that someone was still there. She was never alone! Each time that her face contorted, she seemed to involuntarily raise (lift) her head and shoulders up from the bed, as if that made it easier for her to breathe (or get air). Like two **soldiers** (**combat buddies**) **sharing a *foxhole***, I made sure that she knew, that she was <u>never</u> *alone*! Although Mother Nixon knew that the *Holy Spirit* was there (in the room) with her; she also knew without a doubt, that her beloved *Deacon Thomas* was still physically with her, as well. Over the entire four and a half (4 1/2) hours period, her *breathing* (breathes) became progressively <u>*slower*</u>, <u>*shorter*</u>, and <u>*farther apart*</u>. The duty nurse came in about three times to check on her (to measure and record her breathing) that evening; however, I was paying very <u>acute</u> attention to the amount of time between her breathes over that last hour, from 10:00 p.m. on.

At about ***10:40 p.m.***, I was holding her left hand (with my left hand) and rubbing her forehead with my right hand, when I suddenly began to sing (*aloud*): ***"Oh, It is Jesus; Yes, it is Jesus; It's Je-sus in my soul. For I have touch the_ hem of his gar-ment, and His blood has ma-ade me whole!"*** I repeatedly sang (just the chorus of) this song over and over and over again. This *anthem* served as a <u>*processional*</u> hymn, for me to **spiritually** escort Mother Nixon up and through her final *transition* right into the presence of GOD, the way that a father would escort a bride up the aisle and into her wedding ceremony. Furthermore, it represented a way for me to (*spiritually*) **give her away** to Jesus, as her ultimate *bridegroom*; even while, I was still <u>*physically*</u> holding her hand. At that time, she opened her eyes and stared directly into my eyes, as **<u>one</u>** (single) *tear* rolled, from the corner of her left eye, and down her cheek. <u>Was she just **trying** to say</u>: "**Thank you**?" Or maybe (*before her departure*), Jesus had just said to her: "**Mother** *behold thy son*"; even as he was saying to me, "*son, behold thy (spiritual) mother.*" As she *saw* **me**, for the last time, and left me (there), <u>she **fully embraced** going to Him</u>! To *reflect* on what we had shared, was (also) indicative and reminiscent of her personal *healing*, from **all** that she had previously suffered or *was deprived of* with her *biological* **sons**. (<u>I</u> <u>don't</u> <u>know!</u>) However, I do know that I squeezed her hand (***firmer***) at that time, so as to reply back (saying to Mother): "**You are Welcome**!" At ***10:47 p.m.***, the nurse on duty, who overheard me *singing*, started to walk in; but, she paused (stopped) just inside of the doorway, respecting what I was doing. I continued to sing, even as I motioned to her that I was *ok*, with her coming in; and that, she was not interrupting what I was doing. The nurse stood next to me for about two minutes (as I sang continuously), then (while looking at Mother) the nurse *quietly* said to me, **"It won't be long, now!"** I paused my song, just long enough to nod my head and reply, "*I know*!" Then I immediately resumed (continued) singing my song; and, the nurse (then) turned and walked out of the room. GOD's absolute, ultimate (Divine) **Peace** now **<u>consumed</u>** Mother. Suddenly, Mother Nixon was no longer *fighting* or struggling to live, as an obvious ***calm*** came over her body and spirit. Mother Nixon's *breathing* (breathes) gradually became more and more <u>*slowly*</u> and <u>fainter</u> (*weaker*). **At 10:55 p.m.** (on Saturday, June 5, 2010), Mother Nixon took her <u>*final*</u> long, *drawn-out* **breath**; and her heart **stopped** all together. Her eyes were closed; but, her mouth remained open. As her *spirit soared* upward, the body was left *motionless* and ***<u>peaceful</u>*** in the bed. I glanced at the clock (on the wall); stopped singing, rubbed her forehead, for the <u>*last*</u> time; and, I smiled *victoriously*. *The storm had (indeed) passed over!* Mother's recent *battle* and *life-long, spiritual* **war**) on earth) were over; but— **WE HAD <u>WON</u>!**

Immediately, I went to notify the nurse, so that the doctor (on duty) or responsible **official** could come into the room and *officially* pronounce her death. I informed her that I had **noted** the time of her <u>final</u> breath, according to the *wall clock* (in her room). It took about ten minutes for the designated individual to come; because, she was in a different wing of the facility. While I waited for her to come, I stepped out into the corridor and phoned Peola's house, where she, Larry, and Nikki (Peola's daughter and Mother's closest granddaughter) were *expectantly* <u>awaiting</u> the call. My second and subsequent calls, at that point, were to inform (then) Pastor Charlie Ammons, my wife (Georgette), and a couple of our other key church/ministry leaders. Pastor Charlie subsequently notified Apostle Steven and Dr. (Pastor) Keira Banks. Like a soldier on *guard duty*, I remained on my assigned ***post*** inside and/or just outside of the doorway to that room, where her body was lying. Poncier (*Peola*) and Larry arrived within fifteen minutes of my phone call. I stepped back (out) into the corridor to give them a few minutes of privacy in Mother Nixon's room. After a few minutes, they called me back into the room and thanked me, for my faithful support. Peola said to me, "*You were a strong **soldier** and a real **trooper**, for my Mother. Thank you for staying with her. You were a true **(spiritual)** <u>son</u> to her, until the very end!*" **Thank you**; because, I could <u>not</u> do it (stay) any longer." Shortly thereafter, one of Peola's best friends (Irma) arrived, at the room (for emotional support); then, we all ***waited*** together, for the funeral home director, who Mother Nixon had previously requested that Peola utilize, from Mother's prior resident area of Matthews County, VA.

I am personally sure, that we, who were in that <u>core</u> ***circle*** (surrounding and supporting) Mother Nixon, were each in our ***assigned places,*** on that particular night. GOD ensured and *orchestrated* that, by working all things together for <u>her</u> ***good***! Everything transpired exactly as: GOD designed and Mother Nixon desired it to be; because, she realized that *her* own time was up (over) and that her daughter (Peola) needed to be released (*relieved*) from the personal cares, *issues of life* and **dis-ease**, associated with Mother's situation, after becoming a *widow* and leading up to her death.

On the day of Mother Nixon's **Home-going Celebration** (June 12, 2010), as we stood in the church before the service began, Elder Betsy Robinson finally ***told*** (revealed to) me, why she had brought Mother Nixon over to me, on her very first visit to our church. She told me that Mother Nixon had actually scanned the entire sanctuary (after that service), until her eyes rested upon me, on the opposite side of the sanctuary. Then Mother Nixon had pointed to me; and with a confidence and assurance that she must have received from GOD (himself), she said to Betsy: *"Take me to that man, over there, in the green suit. Him! GOD said that man is the <u>one</u>; Him will take care of me! Just take me to Him!"* It was very gratifying for me, to receive this **confirmation** (***revelation***) from Elder Betsy, that GOD had (indeed) <u>***sent***</u> Mother Nixon to <u>*me*</u>. I THANK GOD for the opportunity to have (*whole-heartedly*) ***received*** her on that day.

My final ***deeds*** *of service* to Mother Nixon included: being one of four persons (chosen by the family) to give special remarks (reflections) in her honor; serving as a *pall bearer* to carry her body to its final resting place; and, *standing guard* at her gravesite (per her personal request), until her grave was closed (sealed up) and the grave diggers/cemetery workers were gone. In fact, because Peola and the family knew her sentiments and respected her wishes, a large group of the family, Bishop Banks, Pastor Charlie and other *celebration* participants lingered at the cemetery, as her body was being buried. However, I personally ensured that I was the last person standing at her graveside, after everyone else, including the *grave diggers* (cemetery crew), had left. At that point, it was (once again)—just the two of us! That was my final *salute* to her; and the fulfillment of the promise that I had made, in reference to her request. That's how this **GOD-ordained**, ***sixteen-month*** <u>***assignment***</u> transpired and eventually ended (with Mother Nixon) in 2010. Another assignment <u>completed</u>**;** another ***Mission Accomplished***! Another <u>elderly</u> *Saint* ***served***; and, an ***Angel*** promoted (gone home) to Glory!

## Reverend Vernon L. Harris
## (age: 78 years)

This was another very special (divine) connection that manifested as a result of ministering or serving others! I met Reverend Harris, initially, at the **Rest Haven** Rehabilitation and Nursing Home in Hampton, VA in 2006, which later became Ashwood Assisted Living Facility. At that time, he was a resident at this facility; while, I had started ministering there, along with the late Elder Gregory Cherry and his wife (Elder Saundra Cherry) and others leaders from our church. We had a special *partnership* arrangement with this facility and **relationship** with all its residents, wherein, we went there (on the ***first Saturday of every month***) to minister and fellowship with the residents at their facility, through exhortation of Scriptures, singing praise and worship songs, playing games like **Jingo** (a *trivia questions* **board game,** resembling and played like **Bingo**) for prizes, and serving snacks/refreshments to all those participating residents. These were *grand* and *joyous* events/experiences for both the facility's residents and our ministry team, which both **groups** (*partners*) equally looked forward to, loved and were mutually *blessed* by! Sometimes, we even took some of the youth along with us, so that they could also gain the experience of *serving* the elderly and/or disabled residents, by assisting them to locate items on their game boards (score cards) and distributing prizes/snacks to the participants. And from the *residents'* group, Rev. Vernon Harris was *the **life** of the party!*

Wherever our Outreach Fellowship team would arrive and find that Rev. Harris was not already waiting in the dining room (fellowship area), I would immediately ask other residents about him and go to his room to look for (get) him, while our team set-up and prepared for the games. If he was in his room and just *running late* or had dosed off (while waiting), I would personally **assist** him in getting ready and down to the fellowship area. And immediately, a huge buzz and uproar of excitement and counter-claims (protests, cheers and jeers) would *rang out* from other residents (like Roy, Karen, Helen, Harry, and others), as I loudly announced: "*the winner or **Champion** (Rev. Harris) has just arrived*," when he and I entered the game room.

Then, the friendly *bantering* (*trash talking* challenges) would start, and the games kicked into high gear (turned up a notch). There was a group of residents that *teamed up* to always try to preclude or keep Rev. Harris *winless*, that represented a successful (victorious) day for them! If Rev. Harris won (even) one single game early, that room would be *rowdy* (noisy and rocking) throughout the afternoon's fellowship session. On days when Rev. Harris was absent (in the hospital or gone out for an appointment, we all noticed (felt) the difference in the atmosphere or environment, as both our ministry team's members (leaders) and the residents *missed* his presence, which resulted in a more *subdued* party (*fellowship*) environment.

Additionally (from 2007–2012), I drove *one* of our Church's vans to that facility, on the thi**rd Sunday of every month**, as Elder Saundra Cherry and I personally transported residents (to and from Worship Services at our church), who were physically able (on ambulatory status or *mobile* enough), psychologically, medically (and overall *cleared* to leave the facility) to attend services; while, we (also) always took care of their *pre-packaged* lunch and personal needs at our church facility, before returning them back to their resident facility (in Hampton, VA.)

Rev. Harris had already previously suffered a debilitating stroke, that had left him with his hand nearly closed on one arm mostly immobilized and tucked against his waist, while he also walked very slow and laboriously with a cane. It was that stroke that had caused (or resulted in) him becoming a long-term resident of the Rest Haven Nursing Home (later renamed: **Ashwood** Assisted Living Facility). However, he was wide-eyed, quick witted, and had an exceptional and active *sense of humor*. Rev. Harris's mind was very sharp and he loved *volunteering* in the library at (Bethel Temple), a church located in *walking distance*, down the street to his resident facility. People often described him as being *quick or sharp as a whip*! Sometimes, he was a real *jokester*.

Prior to his stroke, he had served some years as Pastor of both **Trinity Baptist Church** and **Wesley Grove United Church of Christ**, both in Newport News, VA. Additionally, he had formerly served as *Interim* Pastor of **World Victory Church and Life Center** of Newport News, VA.

Rev. Vernon Harris loved to serve GOD and His people. As a former pastor, he always felt like a *shepherd* at the resident facility and was a guiding light (spirit) and serious example to the other residents, except when he was in his *heckler* and *jokester* role, during Jingo or Bingo games. This gave him a very special bond and garnered the respect of all the other residents, as well as, with our ministry team and everyone else that he came into contact with (whether inside his resident facility or outside in a public setting (the community)). He was *affectionately* known and loved as *Reverend Harris*! So it was even more imperative, for **me** to: encourage, empower, undergird and serve him, in any way that I possibly could, in order to enhance (extend) **his** ability and opportunities to *serve* others (fulfill his personal ministry).

GOD knows, and I understood, that faithfully **serving** the **elderly** (in general) and/or *disabled seniors* requires: a rare anointing, the genuine love and compassion of CHRIST, extraordinary patience (*for* or toward them), impeccable commitment and dedication (to that *call*/duty), and an unwavering willingness to go above and beyond (what is comfortable and/or convenient), despite all their unparalleled (unique) challenges. For instance, *sometimes* on those third Sunday mornings, I would pull up to the nursing home and the other younger and more capable residents would be waiting outside (on a bench) or come right out as soon as my van arrived; but, Reverend Harris (sometimes) was still inside his room (trying to get ready).

And there were no *male* assistants (or aides) within the facility on Sunday mornings to help him. So I would load those individuals onto the van first; then, I'd go to Rev. Harris's room to personally *assist* him (sometimes *dressing* him, from *head-to-toe*), before we could leave for our *thirty minutes* drive (from Hampton to the Denbigh section of Newport News) to our worship service. Due to Rev. Harris's sincere desire to go and my willingness to help, we were able to accomplish the required feat within a reasonably short period of time; and, I always tried to arrive a little earlier—just in case. Very few individuals are **qualified** to **whole-heartedly serve** this special group of GOD's people. That was the <u>difference</u> in myself picking-up and transporting those residents versus another individual (or a *taxi driver*) arriving for a passenger. (Note: The *taxi driver* or other driver would have only been willing to pull-up (arrive) and blow the horn; but, he/she would **never** have <u>gone inside and assisted the individual in dressing (getting prepared)</u> to be transported (driven) to their destination.) For that reason, I always *personally* covered the nursing home and other *seniors* missions; those were my (*GOD-ordained*) **assignments**. Over the years, our other drivers (Deacon Randy Harris, Brother Ambrose, Bro Ernest Hogan, etc.) were rotated and sent to pick up (transport) college students from Hampton University or younger people from other locations or residences within the city.

Eventually, the **Ashwood Assisted Living** and Nursing Home facility was *permanently closed* (shut-down) by the State of Virginia in 2012. This dissolved a decade-long *partnership* between that facility's residents and our church's Evangelism Outreach Ministry Teams/our Church. The corporate group of residents (from that former facility) were scattered and dispersed throughout several facilities in about four different cities on the Virginia peninsula.

We were still able to maintain some contact and relationship arrangements with some of them at their new facilities. Unfortunately, we totally **lost** contact (communications) with some of those residents.

It was a great blessing for Rev. Harris to be re-located locally (within the city of Hampton) to the **Coliseum Convalescent and Rehabilitation Center**, which was less than five miles from his previous facility's location. That was where Rev. Harris resided (remained) from 2012–2014, the final two years of his life. However, the level of professional and medical care that he received there was greatly enhanced (elevated), over what he had previously received at the former facilities. Also, I was still able to pick-up and transport him to our services on some occasions; however, his attendance and visits to our church became more sporadic and infrequent, as his physical condition *gradually deteriorated* (declined). Still our personal relationship continued to flourish, as I would make personally visits to see and sit with him (in his room or in the dining room) in his new facility, as well as, at other times in the hospitals. Elder Saundra

Cherry also maintained the same type of close personal and ministry relationship with our friend and brother (Rev. Harris).

One of the greatest and most gratifying memories that I have from my relationship with Rev. Harris is when Evangelist Sonya (Gholston) Bradley and I surprised him at his residence (room) for an *unannounced* (personal) **Surprise** Birthday Celebration in 2014. It was on a Sunday, immediately following our church's normal Worship Service. I had just picked-up a half dozen specially decorated cupcakes and a twelve-cup package of individual Vanilla ice cream cups from Walmart. Then, Evangelist Sonya Bradley and I met, at Rev. Harris's room (at his facility) with party hats, cupcakes, ice cream and Holy **Communion** for his personal *Surprise* celebration. To our own *surprise*, Rev. Harris's brother (Edgar C. Harris, called *Gerald*, *visiting* from California) was there in his room, along with a local nephew (from this area). **First things, first!** So (First), we prayed and all took **Communion** together. Then, we passed out the party hats, cupcakes and ice cream, along with forks and spoons. Having his *biological* family members present, whom we had never met before, made it an even more *special* experience for Rev. Harris. Although, this **surprise** Birthday celebration lasted only forty minutes or so (in duration), *fellowshipping* with him and his family members, especially his brother all the way from California, made it a **real** (**special**) party atmosphere for the *Honoree*. We had the privilege to **share** (*with each other*) our stories, experiences and memories (of previous times and experiences that we had with Rev. Harris). Consequently, this was the **first** (and only) time that Evangelist Sonya, myself or any of our ministry team (leaders) would ever get to meet his brother (*Gerald*); and the **last** time that those brothers (Rev. Harris and Edgar (called *Gerald*)) would personally visit and see each other **alive**! That is what I would call a *Divine-appointment* that was orchestrated (arranged) and set-up by GOD! I did not know that Edgar even existed; therefore, I never could have contacted and *invited* him to that party, even if I wanted to.

I only got a ***few*** opportunities to personally visit Rev. Harris again, after that special *once-in-a-lifetime* celebration! Three of the last visits were inside of the facility, while two others were at Sentara

Hospital in Hampton (only about two miles from his resident facility). Every time I located (*found*) him, after he'd already been admitted into the hospital, I would always *jokingly* accuse him of attempting to play **Hide and Seek** with me, just to **t**est me to see if I would go **look** for him and/or how long it would take me to *find* (locate) him, after I had gone to his facility and discovered him **gone** (*missing* in action).

During the summer of 2014, I went back home (*to Louisiana*) to visit my own father and siblings, as well as, my wife's parents and siblings. We stayed about eight or nine days. Upon our return to Virginia, I went to visit Rev. Harris at the facility. As I signed the log-book, at the receptionist desk (of the lobby) there, a middle-aged woman came up the hall corridor and said to me, "*Excuse me, Sir! Are you a Pastor or Minister, etc.?*" My reply (response) was simply, "*Yes, how can I help you?*"

The lady then said, "I just need a minister to pray for (or over) my dad. *Can you come down to pray for my dad (in his room).*" To which I said, "*Sure! I can do that for you. Just lead (show) me to his room.*" As I followed or walked down the hall corridors with her, she made a couple of turns and headed down the same hallway and direction, as Rev. Harris's room. Ironically, we went directly into Rev. Harris's room.

These were *double-occupancy* rooms, with two beds. Rev. Harris had always been in the first bed, right by the door. And the second bed had previously been *unoccupied* for a long time. However, on this particular day, that first (Rev. Harris') bed was *unoccupied* or empty.

Initially, I thought nothing of it and just followed her over to her father in that second bed. I asked the gentleman's name and what his condition was, so that I could specifically focus my prayer to his particular condition (circumstances), etc. After I finished **praying** for him (her father and family), they *thanked* me for ministering (serving) him.

About that same time, one of the nurses walked into the room, that I immediately recognized from my numerous visits with Rev. Harris. As the nurse started to change the sheets (linen) on that bed, I said to her, "*Good afternoon, Ma'am! Do you remember me? I have visited Rev. Harris (here) numerous times in that bed, over the past several months.*" The nurse looked up at me and immediately said, "*Yes; I remember you. I have seen you many times (before).*" Finally, I said to her, "*I have just recently returned from a trip, visiting my family in Louisiana.*

*So where is Rev. Harris? Has he gone back into the hospital or is out for an appointment, today?"* That's when the nurse said something, which **felt** *like*, she had just suddenly **punched me in the nose**. She said, *"No Sir! I'm sorry; but, Rev. Harris is gone! He "passed away" last month."* I somberly responded, by saying: *"Oh no." WOW!* ***Thank you!"***

This was a very stunning **revelation** for me. I really did **not** know this. And no one (from our ministry team) had contacted, me in my absence. I went out into the front lobby and immediately contacted Elder Saundra Cherry and informed her. She loved Rev. Harris and all of those nursing home residents, so much. *Ministering* to them was her heart's ***joy***. So I knew that if she had ***not*** told me about his death, that meant she (also) did **not** know. Suddenly and without any warning, for me (*personally*), another *Divine-connection* and special **assignment** had **ended**. Ironically, Rev. Vernon Harris quietly *flew away*, while I was out-of-the-state (*visiting* my family in Louisiana) in 2014, just as the late Elder Gregory Cherry (Elder Saundra's husband) had previously done (while I was in Louisiana) in 2007. Now, my only **regret** was the fact that, after not being here to say *Good-bye* to Rev. Harris, I also did not have the opportunity (privilege) to attend his **Home-Going Celebration** Service (either). And the only *consolation*, for me, was that I could still reflect back upon my experience with him at his (***last***) *surprise* birthday party (earlier that year).

### Nazea Stephan Twiggs
### (age: 14 days *shy of* 16 years)

Without a doubt, the ***most unique*** and youngest, spiritually **in-tuned** individual that I have ever met, in all my deployments around the world and all my years of ***serving***, was little **Nazea Twiggs**. I have never met or encounter any other child or teen who both: possessed such a profound level of *spiritual* ***acumen*** (*keenness/ depth of discernment*) and willingly demonstrated his **commitment** to *manifest* **GOD**'s *Spirit* in every (daily) activity. I believe this was a result of him truly being *Spiritually* ***Awakened***. However, that is exactly what I witnessed each time that I was in Nazea's presence. So now you are **wondering** (asking): ***WHO*** is or was this person (Nazea)? And <u>what</u> was the ***significance*** of his life?

I am absolutely delighted that you (now) have a ***desire*** to *know* (wonder or *ask*)! People (too often), loosely or *ingenuously*, refer to other human beings as ***angels***. However, Nazea was a <u>genuine</u>, ***angelic*** being, gifted to his parents (Darnella Beale and Stephan Twiggs) on July 15, 1999, at St. Luke Roosevelt Hospital in New York. <u>Real</u> **angels** arrive into the earth realm with immediate, absolute, *supernatural **power*** and (divine) revelation and wisdom; while, they (also) possess the pin-point knowledge of exactly who, what and where their assigned mission is. GOD specifically *selects, instructs (commands)* and *dispatches (sends) angels* to: **deliver** a specific message to a person, family or group of people; **guide** a person or group of people through a particular *season or phase* of their lives (life); or **perform** a special transcending (supernatural) feat, to defeat or conquer evil forces and/or evil influences.

There are **NO** <u>***real***</u> (man-generated) *Super-heroes* in life; because, our human concept of *Super-heroes* focus on and deal in *fantasy, child's play*, and ***make-believe*** (for example: Superman, Wonder-woman, Batman; Captain America; the Hulk; Aqua-Man, Flash, etc.); while, they have no basis (or existence) in our physical ***reality.*** However, *Angels* are *real Spiritual* beings (entities) used or **sent** (sometimes in human/*tangible* or *invisible* forms) by GOD, from the *Spiritual realm*, to impact our physical lives, by interacting, in particular situations, between us (as His human creations) and GOD (Himself). **(Scripture References: GENESIS 18:1-16, GENESIS 19:10-17, DANIEL 10, LUKE 1:5-20, LUKE 1:26-38 KJV/NIV.)**

The <u>length</u> of an ***Angel's*** **visitation** in the earth realm (or their *tours of duty or tenure of assignments*) will vary, based upon each specific purpose and assignment. Nazea's **visitation** lasted for nearly sixteen years. Nazea's mother has told me and others, as she would also tell you that, when this bouncing baby boy came into this world, he had big beaming eyes and the biggest smile.

Nazea's parents and family members began to notice very early that this child had a special (peculiar) ***gift***, which caused people, of all ages, to be absolutely *fascinated* by him. He always possessed a level of wisdom far beyond his years (age). Even as a toddler, he was able to converse and engage in conversations with people of all ages, especially adults. His smile, warmth (positive energy) and awesome spirit just captivated people and drew them in (caused them to gravitate to him). Nazea moved to Virginia in 2008, where he initially attended Epps Elementary School, before subsequently attending both Mary Passage Middle and Denbigh High Schools.

Nazea's assignment in the earth realm was to minister, by sharing his**: love**, **compassion** and a **willingness *to serve* others;** and, to *inspire* and *instill* that same spirit into everyone that he met or came into contact with (on this earth). Every **angel** (*angelic being*) who has been dispatched into the earth realm for a ***special*** assignment (or global *Spiritual* **cause**), like a Dr. Martin Luther King Jr., Mother Teresa (of Calcutta, India), (President) Nelson Mandela, our previous biblical servants, Nazea, etc. **all** must have a peculiar ***process*** (or platform) through which to serve, as he or she carries out (fulfills) their mission. The greater their assignment (cause), the greater and **weightier** (more *agonizing*) their process, which is the individual **burden** (or ***cross***) that he or she has been assigned to bear (in the earth realm). For Nazea, this ***cross*** (process) included bearing the burden of a rare, unrelenting, and ravaging form of cancer, known as O<u>steosarcoma</u>.

Osteosarcoma (OS), also called osteogenic sarcoma (OGS), is the most common type of bone cancer. It affects the large bones in the legs and arms, and it occurs more often in males than females. Osteosarcoma normally occurs in children and teens. Osteosarcoma is the third (third) most common cancer among teens, after lymphomas and brain tumors. This is often a very aggressive cancer, that can spread (metastasize) to the lungs. *Ewing's* sarcoma is more common in children between the ages of four to fifteen years old. It is extremely rare in children before younger than five years old. However, it has also been found in long-term survivors of other cancers, who were treated with radiation therapy.

I (initially) met Nazea for the very first time, at a **Cancer Treatment Fundraiser**, which was conducted in his honor, at a local IHOP restaurant on Saturday (May 31, 2014). The event was a joint *car wash* in the parking lot; while (on the inside), the restaurant was donating twenty percent of all proceeds from ALL customers that ate inside on that day. Missionaries (Pastors Reginald and Deborah "Dee Dee" Freeman) had invited me to this event; because, Nazea was an *official* member of the Freeman's locally owned and sponsored *Pee Wee Football League* team called the **North Peninsula Guardians**. And Nazea Twiggs served as an official ***(Spiritual) Guardian*** of the NP Guardians team's players (his teammates) and coaches; although, he used a wheel-chair and could **not** actually *play* (in their games). At the time of my first encounter (initial meeting) of Nazea, he was still fourteen (14) years old, two months <u>before</u> his *fifteenth* birthday; and, he had <u>already</u> ***undergone*** (and survived) eighteen or nineteen different surgeries, while battling this cancer in his body.

    As I arrived at the IHOP parking lot, for the fundraising event, my attention was immediately drawn to Nazea. There he was sitting in his wheel-chair, behind a table, as he collected donations and personally thanked every individual, who came through to support him on that day. I parked my car in the *waiting* line (for a *wash*), and walked over to his table. As I walked up to Nazea and introduced myself, he greeted me with the biggest smile, stared at me with the brightest, most sincere and penetrating (discerning) glare that I had ever experienced from any other child, and very few adults, ever before. As our eyes directly *locked* (eyeball to eyeball), I immediately recognized the purity, genuineness, *unspeakable* joy and (***divine***) peace <u>within</u> this young ***angelic*** spirit. Then, I gave him a $50 bill, as I said to him**:** "*just give me $20 back, please*!" First, his mouth *dropped* wide open, as if he were shocked. He (subsequently) responded, after glancing down into his hand (as if to *double-check* or verify what I had given him vs. what I requested in change), by saying, "Sir, you don't need to donate that much for a *car wash*!" When I insisted on him taking $30, he expressed the most grateful and heart-felt *Thank You*, that I have <u>ever</u> received **from any *teenager***, in my entire life. Then, I proceeded to ***serve*** as an *active **volunteer***, by helping to wash other vehicles that came into the parking lot.

    Throughout that event, I had the opportunity to ***observe***, interact with, get to know, and fellowship with Nazea. In the heat of the early afternoon, as other youth football players (teammates), and even some adults, began to complain about being *too hot* outside, Nazea insisted on trying to *personally* wash some cars and (later) stood by the road (with a sign) to attract more participants. He also insisted on (*personally*) **thanking** every person, who came onto the parking lot. As Nazea interacted with strangers (*one-on-one*), he constantly sought to encourage, inspire and **give** (*pour into*) all of them. As the day went on, it became transparently *clear* to me, that Nazea did **not live** (his life) for himself, but he *lived* for **others!** (Note: His focus and **outlook** was (and still is) extremely *rare* for a youth or teenager, particularly in our *current 21st Century's* society and world's cultural *environments*.)

For the next fourteen (14) months, I had the distinct privilege and honor of **personally** experiencing some aspects of this **angelic visitation** (a.k.a. Nazea's *physical* life) on earth. And I got opportunities to experience this in different situations and settings. As **volunteers**, Rev. Charles Ralph and I were able to *move* (re-locate) all of Nazea's family's possessions, from one residence to another. Understanding the situation of his family dynamics (at that time), I made a conscious decision to **give** a copy, of a Gospel Music (personal) *Tribute* CD, especially produced *in honor of* my deceased mother, to Nazea and his mother. I knew what a ***blessing*** this musical tribute had been for my siblings and I (over the past twelve years); so, I believed that it would (also) uplift and greatly **bless** the two of them, on their most difficult (painful) days. In terms of ministry and mentoring, I was entrusted by his mother to *personally connect* (fellowship and ***bond***) with Nazea, as I visited him in their home. We just talked, listened to music, or just gave him an *ear*, allowing him to express himself. Sometimes, I visited him *alone*; but, on a couple of occasions, I invited Elder Charles Wiggins to come along with me.

It was in these *closed* or non-public visits and conversation that Nazea's *illuminating* **genius** beamed through; and he made some of his most profound statements, that revealed uncanny *Spiritual* **revelation**. During one of these visits, Nazea asked Elder Wiggins, "*look into that fish tank; would do you see?*" After we stared at the fish tank for about thirty seconds, Elder Wiggins began to respond. "I see two gold fish, and gray rocks, water and a water pump, etc." Basically, he was providing a list of all of the *physical* items, that were present inside the tank. About ten seconds later, Nazea *enthusiastically* and *emphatically* replied, "**Are you kidding, me**?!" Nazea said this with such genuine **passion** and *disbelief*, that we could only **laugh** uncontrollably with (and *at*) him. After the three of us **dried** *our eyes*, from laughing so hard, and stopped laughing, Nazea *seriously* asked, "*Is that all; what else do you see?*" To which both Elder Wiggins and I both began to look again, more intensely, as if he was asking us a *trick* question. Neither of us were looking at the fish tank, in the same way or from *the same perspective*, that Nazea was. After about a minute's pause, Nazea finally said, "*Whenever people look at things like this, they usually see the same things that you guys saw. However, whenever I look at water in a tank or a pond or lake, I will look pass the (obvious) fish, etc.; and my attention is immediately drawn to the point where the "light" (rays) enters the water and (the light) bends, causing me to see other colors in or around the water. I can see the things that are **happening** (occurring) inside of the water.*" So I personally believe that Nazea was trying to show Deacon Wiggins and myself, his secret to living (life), by looking to see and focusing on the **phenomenon** (**wonder**) or **phenomena** (divine *wonders that are beyond one's human control or* supernatural *acts of GOD*). This helps us to realize how GOD uses all physical creations (both inanimate or *lifeless* objects and animals) to display His beauty, splendor, *Glory* and *glorious* **workmanship**, throughout the earth and universe. That was only one example to confirm the fact that Nazea was (always) undeniably, **Spiritually awakened** and absolutely *astute* to the people and things around him.

During that same or a similar conversation, I asked Nazea a personal *question* about himself or his personality, to which he answered, *"On one hand, I am seriously analyzing things. Like, I can see how people just keeping going around in circles, when I can see how they can easily get out of a situation; but, they refuse to change or make the necessary adjustments. However, at other times, I believe that I have this hilarious* **sense of humor***. When I am in Heaven, I (sometimes) think about how weird it will be for me to watch people moving around (on earth), like those fish in a tank or rats on a wheel. Sometimes, I think I will be cracking jokes to try and make GOD laugh."* Whenever Nazea went to any of his required medical appointments and certain other public places (like restaurants, etc.), he liked to wear this *fake*, thick black mustache, along with any one of his many colorful NY Yankees baseball caps. The first time that I saw him with the mustache on, his mother was pushing him (in his wheel-chair) down the sidewalk, in the **City Center** complex (an elaborate complex of shops, restaurants, movie theatre, hotel and residential condominiums. Nazea was looking like a *real* **Steve Harvey <u>mini-me</u>** (or <u>Steve</u> Harvey's ***miniature look-alike***). That's just one example or indicator of Nazea's *sense of humor*, that I personally saw. When I saw him in this persona (disguise), I just nodded my head to him, while chuckling on the inside, as to say: "OK. I see you (player)!"

**Nazea Twiggs** *(15 years old: Cancer patient)*

Although people quickly <u>*noticed*</u> and easily <u>*responded*</u> to his smile, eyes and personality, Nazea's <u>true</u> (genuine) ***gift*** was **not** his *smile*, nor his *eyes* or his *personality*. Clearly, for his parents, myself and everyone else who had the privilege of (directly) communicating with Nazea, those three fore-mentioned features, were just *external (visible)* ***indicators*** that Nazea possessed much greater <u>***internal***</u>

Spiritual *gifts,* as **demonstrated** (proven) and **confirmed** by his sacrifices, decisions, and acts/deeds of *selfless* **service.**

Three of Nazea's true *gifts* that were (personally) revealed to me were: (1) **Spiritual acumen** plus **attunement,** (2) an *unspeakable joy,* and (3) a genuine *love* for people and fulfilling his assigned purpose. And it was the (daily) activation and culmination of these three gifts, *working together* (in him), which empowered Nazea to be an (***Anointed***) ***angel or agent* of Light,** to people of all ages (in his corner of this world).

It was his gift of always being Spiritually *awake* and possessing this profound level of Spiritual ***attunement***, which enabled him to be *present and purposeful in every moment* of his daily activities; while, also ***living*** (life) ***above his circumstances***, physical challenges and personal burdens (*cross*) of **cancer**'s pain, etc. His gift of *unspeakable joy* was ever-present; because, every single time I saw him, no matter when or where it was, he always had this huge, genuine smile on his face, that was **never** erased by pain, disappointment, circumstances nor rain. Although, his body was (usually) experiencing some level of pain, he **never** expressed (personal): anxiety, depression, sadness, frustration, bitterness, or fear to myself or other people. Because the *joy of The LORD* was Nazea's **strength**, that joy always lifted or transformed him above his own situation or himself; and it also caused him to consider others before himself and to seek to meet their needs (before his own).

It was this same **joy (strength)**, **love, wisdom, revelation** (from GOD's Spiritual ***attunement***), ***inner*** *peace* and *faith* that he tried to give to his **mother** (*first*), father and everyone else that he came into contact with, regardless of their ages. He was that personal (*angel of Light*), that I mentioned earlier, to his mother; as well as, her personal example and primary source of joy, faith, and strength, during her own difficult days and personal struggles.

Additionally, it was *imperative* that Nazea serve as the same *angel of Light* (on the sidelines) for his Guardian football teammates, coaches and helpers, despite the fact that his physical condition prohibited him from actually *playing* on the field. Likewise, he served as an active member of the **Peninsula Boys and Girls Club**, where he volunteered (at the reception desk) and mentored the other children (youth). Eventually, Nazea was recognized as the 2015 **Student of The Year**, for the Boy and Girls Club. He (also) always actively strove to have the same *impact* (be that *angel of Light* for others), to include: classmates, other students, teachers, and faculty staff at his schools and, even on the playgrounds/neighborhoods, within his communities. Nazea was the recipient of the **Barack Obama Presidential Award of Excellence**. He was honored by the Mayor of the City of Hampton, VA with the ***James "Poo" Johnson Excellence Award***. He also received an official **Citation** from the City Of New York.

Neil Armstrong, the American astronaut, an aerospace engineer and the very ***first*** man to **walk on the moon** (in 1969), once made the following statement (*verbally* said),

"I believe that every human being has a ***finite*** number of heartbeats. I ***don't*** intend to waste any of mine." (**Neil Alden Armstrong**)

Nazea, had also gained this same **revelation** about the finite tenure (short or limited *temporary* tour of duty), of *every individual* sent into the earth realm to complete his or her specific assignments. Through his life's dedication to **selfless service**; his personal *commitment* to his assignment of ***living*** (his life), **as an angel of Light**, Nazea personally proved to us that he had (*non-verbally*) made that same declaration and taken the same stance (position), as Astronaut Neil Armstrong. Nazea realized that he, too, had a finite number of ***heartbeats***; and, he did **not** intend to waste any of his. Therefore, he refused to allow *Cancer*, nor any other thing or person, to *divert* one breath (away from) or *steal* an opportunity from the fulfillment of his purpose (assignments): ***serving*** *others*, that **GOD** brought Nazea into contact with, during his lifetime.

This *Angel's* (Nazea Stephan Twiggs') **visitation**, although very *brief* (fourteen days *shy* or short of sixteen years), definitely had ***ETERNAL*** Significance, Impacts and Affect; because he was able to ***impact*** and affect current children (youth), coaches, teachers, schools' officials, local city officials and *International* **Missionaries** (who operate in the countries of Uganda and Ethiopia, on the Continent of Africa). Nazea will ***be remembered by*** and continue to ***impact*** (***affect***)—not only this current generation—but (also) <u>**future**</u> generations!

## Pastor Samuel Andrew Thompson
### (age: 82 years)

Samuel A. Thompson was the thirteenth of sixteen children born to his parents, in Prince Edward County, VA on August 27, 1934. After forty-four years of combined *active duty* military (Air Force) service and federal (Civil) service, Pastor T had made plans to retire, and spend his *senior citizen* years, traveling with his wife. However, two years prior to his <u>*final*</u> retirement, GOD changed his plans and gave him a vision to go out and *evangelize* (to witness and share the gospel) with troubled <u>youth</u> *on the streets*. Thus, his ultimate assignment (and Objective) was to establish a Church, where he would serve as the personal **Pastor** to this new *flock* (congregation) of youth. On April 4, 1999, Pastor T became the *Founder* and **Pastor** of Compassion Community Church in Hampton, VA.

You or the average person may have expected GOD to choose a *thirty years* old man to go out into the *gang-infested* streets and *crime-riddled* neighborhoods to *evangelize, gather* and *pastor* a flock of (*former*) renegade, troubled youth. Just the mere fact that Pastor T was sixty-five years old, at the time that GOD sent him out on this type of *assignment*, should tell you just how uniquely anointed, bold and special Pastor Thompson actually was. (He was certainly <u>NOT</u> your *average* pastor!) However, you will never (ever) have the privilege (now) of knowing him or *directly* experiencing the vast <u>**wealth**</u> of <u>**wisdom**</u> and <u>**faith**</u>, that GOD deposited into Pastor Thompson. Although, GOD did send him out to share that same wealth with so many others, including me.

I (personally) met and *immediately* **connected** with Pastor Samuel Thompson in the Summer of 2007, at one of our *week-long* Summer Camps at **Camp Heavenly Waters** Christian Retreat and Youth Camp facilities in Wakefield, VA. At that time, he was already seventy-three years old; while, he and his wife (**Lady Rose Thompson** or *Sister T*) had already been *pastoring* their youth congregation (Church) for over seven years. From the very onset of our *divine connection* (special *GOD-ordained relationship*), it was clearly evident that we were going to be *long-term* ***partners***, in conducting Kingdom ministry. Over the near **decade** (from 2007–2016), ***Pastor T***, as we *affectionately* called him, proved to be an absolute, <u>**walking** **Pillar of Faith**</u>. Together, Pastor T and *Sister T* were a very special and <u>*uniquely*</u> anointed, *married* couple, who were fearfully and wonderfully created (and thoroughly *equipped*) for their GOD-given (Church) *assignment*. Both of them, individually, possessed the <u>purest </u>hearts, full of the most <u>genuine</u> **Love (of GOD)**, for those *most vulnerable* and *at-risk* youth of our society. As our relationship grew over the years, my GOD-given <u>*assignment*</u> and roles constantly evolved, as I was **sent** to (both) <u>stand</u> *alongside and* <u>*walk*</u> with Pastor T, as: an encourager, source of energy and physical strength, provider of needed skills/resources, a trusted *friend*, a spiritual *son* and a *co-laborer* in Christ. Additionally, I was that like-minded, **combat buddy**; with the same *heart* and passion, for sharing the Gospel (*Evangelism*); and compassion for blessing people, through *community Outreach*. Eventually, I became <u>*one*</u> of two faithful **servants** (along with Mr. Tom Tache, Pastor T's next-door neighbor), **called** and **chosen** of GOD, to <u>*undergird*</u> Pastor T and *Sister T*, like extended family members, during their most *dire* times. Like *Aaron* and *Hur* were companions for Moses (in **EXODUS 17:11-13**), so Tom and I also served as those <u>critically</u> <u>needed</u> companions (supporters), *external to their **CCC** congregation*, **who held up the arms** of Pastor T and his wife, in the midst of their most tragic *personal* battles (times of illness/disease, distress, and death), which also *proved* to be their greatest **triumphs**.

From the very time that GOD gave Pastor Thompson the **vision** (in 1998) and mission (<u>*assignment*</u>), that would later become *Compassion Community Church*, he faced constant <u>ridicule</u>, <u>opposi-</u>

tion and _lack of support_. As he tried to share his vision and assignment (to establish a Church, consisting of a new _flock_ of troubled youth from the streets), with his _peers_ and other ministers, they responded by _laughing_ in his face. And asking him questions like: how do you expect to be able to sustain this church, without _tithe paying_ adults; how will you pay your church's bills; while, your members won't have jobs? His hecklers would (then) conclude by saying, _"it will never work!"_ However, while Pastor T lacked a _blueprint_ (plan) and support, he and wife were propelled by great **courage** and impeccable **Faith** _in GOD_. As a result, Pastor Thompson's heart-felt motto (slogan) and **war cry** was establish for both his ministry and the rest of his life: _Where GOD Guides, HE PROVIDES!_ Pastor T and his wife (each), wholeheartedly, stood on and _lived_ by this motto. And both subsequently departed this life, with their personal **testimonies**: that GOD never (ever) failed them, neither in their personal lives, nor in their Church/ministry.

By the time that I met him, he had grown their church to about 110 members, comprised of about ninety-eight youth and only ten to twelve adults. And three of his adults were literally _blind_ men (to include his choir director, guitar player and keyboard player). While Brother Pernell (the choir director) and the other _blind_ musicians had been shunned in other churches, GOD had reserved and ordained their _places_ (and special assignments) in Pastor T's church/ministry. Even in that regard, GOD still faithfully provided everything that they needed. All of the children were from broken and _dysfunctional_ families, with **not** (even) one single _parent_ attending nor participating in the ministry. Every child was being _picked-up_ and transported to the services via their church's two (fifteen-passenger) vans and Pastor T's personal vehicle. On many occasions, Pastor and his wife (_Momma Rose_) had to open up their own home, as a _temporary_ home or shelter, for children _in need_. I am not talking about an _overnight_ or _weekend_ stay; a couple of these situations required them to take a youth (boarder) into their home, for a period of **six to eight months**, at a time. Pastor T and Momma Rose, more often than not, had to serve as a **_surrogate_** father and mother or grandfather and grandmother to most of these youth. As a result of Pastor T's intervention efforts, children who had already been expelled from the public schools, currently attending **alternative** school, or were on the verge of being expelled (eventually), improved to *academically **excel*** in school.

There were occasions when, he went into the schools to meet with the Principal or school officials to initially get students re-instated back into the schools. Pastor T often shared accounts (stories) with me, when he pleaded with those school officials by saying, *"They just need structure and an opportunity. I will serve as a surrogate parent/grandparent to take responsibility for them."* The principal would reply, *"Please, don't waste your time, Pastor. He or she is **no good**. We have already tried everything with him/her."* Pastor T (then) asked, *"Have you tried **Jesus**?"* The school officials (then) replied, *"We don't do Jesus, here in our school!"* Finally, Pastor T replied, *"Then you have NOT tried **everything**!"* Additionally, Pastor T was, also, able to get several of his young congregants (members) to enroll in and to graduate from college. He and his wife would garner support (donations) to provide all of those college students' supplies and required dorm equipment, which they personally transported to the campuses, along with the students. Pastor T enjoyed teaching the Word of GOD to his children (congregation) and stressing the importance of being good (or outstanding) citizens. He always took great satisfaction in knowing that his children were as well taught, in the scriptures, as any others. Pastor T was great at *motivating* (inspiring) his children, through his internal competitions; Report Card checks, along with *grade improvement* incentive rewards; recognition ceremonies; etc. He constantly enrolled his children (students) in City, State, and National Scholarship and *Essay Writing* Contests; and, they often *placed* or *won* something (at every level)!

Although, my initial contact and *partnership* with Pastor T and his congregation (children's Church) started at Summer Camps, it evolved and transformed far beyond just those camp experiences. Pastor T established and consistently maintained five separate **Outreach Ministries** (Programs) in: Hampton and Newport New, VA; Farmsville and Rice, VA; Elizabeth City and Ahoskie, NC; etc. These included donating and distributing everything from clothes/shoes; potatoes and other food supplies; household items (such as portable, *window* air conditioner units, desks, furniture, etc.); and toys to needy families, throughout these areas/regions. This was all, in addition, to providing for the needs of his own Church's congregation/members.

Pastor Thompson had been a real ***champion***, in partnering with and supporting **Camp Heavenly Waters'** Summer Youth Camps every year, since my arrival in 2007. Additionally, he had, previously, participated during other summers (there) from 2001–2006, prior to my arrival. Routinely, every camp basically ran from Monday morning through Thursday afternoon. Pastor T and his church served as one of the *primary*, and sometimes only, external Transportation sources (along with my *Living Waters Christian Fellowship's,* later renamed *Restoration Christian Church of VA* (RCC-VA's) ministry vehicles), by transporting not just his own children, but all campers or participating children from other communities and organizations. Then, his adults and some of his other congregants would visit our camp on Wednesday evening, in support of his children's choir to perform a Mini Choir Concert for all of our campers. Some summer camps, his vans and drivers were, also, used to transport campers to the swimming pool at the Regional 4-H Airfield and Campgrounds facilities on Tuesday or Wednesday. Finally, they were right back out there, late morning on Thursday, to transported the campers (children) back to their Hampton and Newport News (home) destinations.

Without a doubt, the single *most impactful* and unique *Summer Camp* experience that I had with Pastor T was in 2013. That one was (immediately) *life-saving* for one child (**Raheem**), and prayerfully, *life-changing* for many other children and adults at our camp (that year). This particular Summer Camp was uniquely different from the very start; because we normally scheduled the pool for the third day (Wednesday) of our camp cycle. This would allow us an opportunity to get to assess and know the kids that we were dealing with. Additionally, I treated the *pool day* as a privilege only for those, who had demonstrated the proper respect for our Camp Rules; while, repeated *violators* or *non-conformists*, spend that day, sitting on the sidelines (as **spectators**), watching the others kids enjoy the privilege of swimming. Therefore, we had previously never scheduled the pool for the very first day of any camp (before). However, this particular year, Mrs. Pope felt compelled to accept this *opening day* slot for the swimming pool, within only two hours of in-processing all our campers. So she made an exception to our *normal* camp *routine*; because, there would be **no** other available *slot* (at the pool), for the remainder of that week, due to an annual (ongoing) Regional 4-H Jamboree (there), where more than 1,500 *4-H students* had gathered from several states. As a result, Pastor T and both of his van drivers, not only stayed to transport the campers to the *pool*; but also **contrary to the norm**, they all remained at the pool-side, for the entire swimming session. (Note: Normally, they would have already departed, from Heavenly Waters' Youth Camp location, and been enroute back to Newport News, after *dropping off* the children and their personal baggage for *sign-in* at our Camp facility. Required transport vehicles, on the *pool days* for all prior and subsequent years' Summer Camp *cycles*, routinely dropped-off campers and chaperones at the *Regional 4-H Facility's* pool, for a specified period of time. Then, the drivers would return or be called back to the pool (later), whenever we were ready to be picked-up and transported back to our (own) Youth Camp location.)

However, on what would soon prove to be a very ***traumatic*** day, we had arrived at the swimming pool about 11:30 a.m. We had, also, already completed my (personal) *pool requirements and consequences* briefing to our Campers, the *pool-side* (On-duty) *Life-guards' Safety Briefing,* and the **mandatory** (required) **swim tests**, administered by the (On-duty) Lifeguards to determine if any of the *swimmers* were <u>qualified</u> to utilized the **deep end** (eight to ten feet) section (of the public pool), which included a *rock climbing* wall.

By twelve noon the **swimmers** were inside the pool, playing and enjoying this great opportunity. There was one female **counselor/chaperone** (a twenty-year-old college student), *swimming* (inside the pool), with our campers; one *official* **Lifeguard** (also college aged) on the tower/platform; two older (adult) female counselors/chaperones walking around the pool (as monitors) and taking *camp photos*; and, I was engaged in <u>a conversation with Pastor T</u> at pool-side (with my back turned at that moment), while his two van drivers (Deacon Owen and another adult driver) sat at a *pool-side* table.

Suddenly, our conversation was dramatically **severed** by a frantic, *shrieking* **blast** of the Lifeguard's whistle and her *immediate* command, "*Everybody, out of the pool, <u>now</u>! Everybody out!*" As I whirled around (to face back toward the pool), I saw the young *Lifeguard <u>diving</u>* from the tower (into the pool). So without realizing (yet) what had occurred, I immediately **bolted** (ran) around to that edge of the pool, as I began to echo the command, "*Everybody out of the pool. Everybody out!*" Pastor T and his drivers, followed (walking) behind me to that end of the pool. As I arrived at that edge, the young Lifeguard was pulling a boy (Raheem, eight years old) over to the pool's edge. As I helped her to get him up onto the concrete and we rolled him over onto his back, he was ***foaming*** from the mouth. I knew immediately, as an *experienced* (Retired) Army Officer, that this was a **critical** (***dire***) situation. Immediately, the <u>young</u> (female) Lifeguard became *emotional* **overwhelmed**, at the very *sight* of such a young kid in this critical situation. This was probably her very first time dealing with such a small (child) victim. That particular lifeguard was only about twenty-two years old (herself). She began to <u>cry</u> uncontrollably, <u>tremble</u> and <u>panic</u>, as we positioned the child to start **CPR**. I instructed our chaperones to get all of the campers (kids) away from the *pool area* (take them outside of the fence), over to a *near-by* (separate) shelter area of picnic tables, vending machines and bathrooms. Therefore, the other children were **not** allowed to remain at the *pool-side*; otherwise, they may have been *traumatized*, <u>if</u> allowed to watch us *work* (to ***revive***) this child.

I knew that I had to *immediately* get this young Lifeguard **calmed** and *re-focused*, so that we could save this child. So I said to her, "*Listen, take it easy. Calm down and breathe; you can do this! I'm a (Retired) Army Officer; I am (here) with you. I <u>will</u> help you!*"

It was **not** a pretty or *clean* site; and, there was no time to waste, by *trying* to get something to <u>clean</u> his face. Because there was **foam** all over his mouth, which probably made her (*initially*) even more <u>uncomfortable</u>, so I said (to her), "*I will breathe for him, you just do the compression and I'll help you to count.*" (<u>Note</u>: That prompted her to *re-gain* some level of <u>composure</u>; but, I could see that she was (still) quite visibly **shaken**.) After about ten minutes of performing CPR, two more Lifeguards arrived (ran over) from the 4-H Airfield's Headquarters (HQs) Building, nearby. As soon as the initial young Lifeguard saw them, she *lost it* (became ***frantically overwhelmed***) again. One of the new Lifeguards led her away from the *pool-side* scene (took her back to the 4-H's HQs Building), as she was (now) ***sobbing*** uncontrollably. The other (new) Lifeguard, who arrived to the *pool* scene joined in with me, as we continued performing CPR. Finally, a third person chimed into our CPR *operation*. When we (finally) got a *good* pulse (strong enough heartbeat), I began to talk to the child and call his name. After about twenty minutes, the child began to physically respond (with body movements, nodded his head to answer my questions and tried to *open* his eyes. Though *signs* were improved, this child's *fight* (for life) was *far from over*; because he was **not** *out of the wood*, yet.

After about thirty minutes a *ground* ambulance arrived (to this facility), which is located in a rural (country *farming*) area. We turned his medical care over to the *paramedics*, at that point. They continued to monitor and assess him (*on-site*) inside of the ambulance, for another thirty to forty-five minutes, while they waited for an *AIR Medical Evacuation* (**Life Star**) Helicopter to arrive and transport the child to the *emergency room* of an appropriate hospital (in the nearest city). This is the *normal precautionary* measure, in the case of children, who are drowning (or **near drowning**) victims. Otherwise, there may still be water or an *air bubble* in the lung, which could still *potentially* **kill** a child *in his/her sleep* (some hours later or overnight).

As we patiently waited near the ambulance, for the **Life Star** Helicopter to arrive (first) we **prayed** and **Thanked GOD** for *giving life back to that child*. Secondly, we recognize that this gave us (Pastor T, the chaperones, his drivers and myself) a perfect opportunity for a **teachable moment** for our campers (on the consequences of *playing and trying foolish tricks in the water*. The manifested *revelation* (here) was just how quickly **life** can be ***stolen or taken away*** from them, when they allow themselves to be deceived or distracted by any *evil influences*, for just a split second. The lesson was undeniably *crystal clear*, amid the gravity, severity and reality of what had just happened *right before their very eyes*. What they saw (witnessed) that day, at the pool, **validated** everything we had previously (consistently) told them, on that subject. Prayerfully, the images (pictures) that *re-play* (in their minds), from that day's experience, will ***always*** be more valuable than *thousands of words*!

Only GOD knew (in advance), what would transpire at that swimming pool on that day. And HE placed *every* adult (there) for a particular assignment or *function*, once the **crisis** (incident) occurred. Pastor Thompson (Pastor T) said to me, "*Man, anybody who saw you "in action," at the pool, could tell that you were military-trained. Your training clearly showed; because, you <u>never</u> panicked, bolted right into action, took charge of the situation (with the situation of the initial Lifeguard, made the right assessment/decisions, asked the right questions (to have the requisite information to pass to the paramedics and hospital). You were the ultimate professional.*" My reply back to Pastor T was simply: ***I just THANK GOD;*** because, **<u>HE had placed (pre-positioned) everybody</u>** required (**needed**) *right (there) on-site*. Initially, the Lifeguard was there for the *swimmers*. At the point that she became overwhelmed, due to her youth and lack of experience *under fire*, GOD used me (and my experience/training *under fire*) to aide and ***cov**er* that Lifeguard. Then, GOD used Pastor T and his deacons (there) to cover me, by conducting spiritual warfare and interceding for the child's life, as they immediately ***prayed*** for both the child's life and for those of us who were <u>working</u> to **revive** him. The female chaperones were, also, used to gather, comfort and manage the other swimmers (campers) in a *holding area*, away from *drama* (at the pool-side).

Eventually, other Lifeguards came to both relieve and (evacuate) the young one, who was *overwhelmed*; they took her back to the HQs, where the supervisor gave her some time off.

Finally an ambulance arrive to monitor and/or further treat the victim, until he could be *air-lifted* to the nearest hospital for **emergency** *follow-up* by doctors.

Eventually, the emergency room doctors called and spoke to me (via telephone) at our Camp Heavenly Water facility, later that evening. First, they wanted to speak directly to someone, who had actually participated in performing CPR *at the pool-side scene*, to both ***commend*** us for an outstanding job, which actually save this child's life. The doctors also needed to get as much *real-time* data (as possibly available) in terms of: how long was he in the pool (before the incident); how long was he under water; <u>how</u> <u>long</u> did we *work* (administer CPR), before he had a good (strong) pulse; how long before the ambulance arrived; did the child *regurgitate* (or expel) any water (before, during, or after conducting CPR)? Before hanging up with the doctor (on duty), I asked him, "so, what is his (current) status; how soon or long before he can be released (to go home; etc.?" The doctor said, "*Thanks to you guys, he's doing great! And barring any <u>unforeseen</u> issues, the boy should be going home either tonight or tomorrow.*"

> *"And we know that all things work together for the good of them that love GOD, to them who are the called according to his purpose."* (**ROMANS 8:28 KJV/NIV**)

> *"Therefore, my beloved brethren, be ye steadfast, unmovable, always abounding in the work of the Lord, forasmuch as ye know that your labor is not in vain in the Lord."* (**1 CORINTHIANS 15:58 KJV/NIV**)

*Pastor Samuel Andrew Thompson (a.k.a. "Pastor T")*

As we ministered (*served*), collaborated, planned, bonded and **co-labored** (together) for nearly **ten years**, Pastor T and I shared many great experiences, conversations, and military memories (*war stories*). Sometimes, we just sat and talked about childhood memories**:** his days on the farm with his father in Farmville, VA; and, my childhood experiences in Louisiana, with my grandfather (born in 1887). We shared our *personal* experiences in **segregated schools:** his *participation* in the earliest (in-school) boycott with Barbara Rose Johns's *Moton Students Strike* (1951) at Robert Russa Moton High School; and, I shared my initial elementary years of segregation's transition into the inaugural years of integrated schools in Louisiana. We discussed his twenty years active duty Air Force career (1954–1974), tours of duty and his family's travels; as well as, my twenty years active duty army career (1985–2005), and its associated tours of duty and family's travels. He shared with me stories of his family (parents and ancestors) and his only son (Samuel A. Thompson Jr.), who was an acclaimed *Boy Genius* at only five years old, before he died (of a childhood *disease*) at the age of twelve years old. And we discussed our lives of **service to GOD**, HIS *Calling* and the developmental processes for each of our lives. He grew to trust, confide in and love me, like a ***son***; while, he always respected and treated me like a *peer* leader in the area of Kingdom *ministry*.[However, I (*respectfully*) could not consider myself to be his *peer* (equal).] I will *forever* consider *Pastor T* one of my most valued *Spiritual* **mentors**. Whenever I called the Thompson's home phone, and they saw my (732) *New Jersey area code*, cell phone number displayed on their phone, they grew to automatically recognize, *who* was calling. If Momma Rose answered the phone (initially), Pastor T would ask her, "*Who is that?*" She replied, "*it's New Jersey.*" Then, Pastor T would tell her, "*Oh, that's the Bishop.*" Then he would get on the telephone and say to me: "Hello, Bishop!" From that time forward, whenever I called, Momma Rose just looked at the caller ID and said, "*Sam, it's the Bishop!*" Pastor T greatly **appreciated** and **respected** my input, fellowship, friendship and our **bond** (a **Divinely-connected** relationship), as much as, I did his. There was *nothing* that he could not discuss with me, without hesitation or apprehension; because, he knew that I had his back. I was *assigned* to be there (only) to **_bless_** him, in every situation. He often said to me (as we sat and talked), *"Elder or Bishop, man you're a real soldier. Man, you just have so much energy. But what I love most about you, is the fact that, you don't just "talk the talk"; you go out and **_do_ (live) the Gospel**."* Then, Pastor T would look me in the eyes and say, *"I love you, man. You are the only brother (friend) in Ministry, that I have who will just come, sit down and talk (fellowship) with me. I have been a **_lonely_** Pastor, most of the time. Just because my Church is a congregation of children (_not_ a _traditional_ church congregation), other Pastors seem to **_shun_** my "church" (children). Whenever I have invited or **_invite_** other Pastors to fellowship with us (in our services), not only do they _not_ come, but, they _don't_ even bother to answer or respond to my correspondence (invitation letters)."*

It was this obvious **sense of _rejection_**, which Pastor T experienced, felt and (often) expressed, that bothered me, more than anything else. I, personally, believe that it was a *travesty* and a *disgrace* that **both** the *more seasoned* (longer-tenured) Pastors and younger (junior) Pastors, acquainted with him, all **_failed_** to: recognize, appreciate (value), embrace and support him in his **_vital_** ministry (of *shepherding* his flock of **Youth** (young *lambs*). Therefore, they also **_failed_** to recognize and honor the great **_gift_**, faithful **_servant leader_** and **_model of wisdom and faith_**, that he was both for and to the entire Body of Christ (*Kingdom* of GOD). While Pastor T's *reality* (**experiences** in this situation) did *bother (or annoy)* me, it never *shocked* me; because, I knew (and know) that, even **Jesus**, himself was also _rejected_ by men (_some_ **people**).

My personal annoyance and frustration was so great, at the *rejection* and isolation of Pastor Thompson and his ministry, that it grieved my spirit. While Pastor T loved the Spirit of GOD that he connected with in me; I (like Christ) thought it not robbery to introduce and bring him into *divine connection* (relationship) with my Spiritual leaders, under whose *covering* I was serving. Therefore, I was compelled, by the Holy Spirit, and resolved within my heart, that I must bring Pastors and other *5-Fold* Ministry **_gifts_** (Men and Women of GOD) to **_connect_** with him, beginning with my own. And GOD ensured that _every_ single person that I personally introduced (connected) to Pastor T **were immediately:** of the _same_ heart and spirit; drawn to his _wisdom and faith_; connected to and loved him; _under-girded_, stood (fellowshipped) with; interceded for and spiritually embraced (Pastor T, _Lady T_ or Momma Rose, and their CCC Ministry)—with their whole hearts! As a result, Pastor Ryan Brown (of the Salvation Army in Hampton, VA.), Evangelist Denise James and myself _partnered_ together with Pastor Samuel Thompson, in forming our _Evangelism Outreach Coalition_ (EOC). Additionally, Apostle Charlie B. Ammons, Senior Pastor Vikki Ammons and Pastor Chuck Lee came to <u>know</u> and <u>love</u> (our) _Pastor T_; as we all experienced and enjoyed our **divine connections** and **covenant relationships (fellowship)** with them, so (all) this was—and could only have been—<u>_ordained_</u> and <u>_orchestrated_</u> by GOD (Himself). My (personal) _covenant connection_ (to) and GOD-given **assignment** (with) Pastor T was so genuine and profoundly <u>**sure**</u>, that (without any hesitation or _mental_ reservation), he automatically called (leaned) upon and confided in me, for sharing (_<u>bearing</u>_) his most significant personal challenges and personal concerns. This included required _shifts_ and obstacles in executing his ministry, writing appeals to the Veterans Administration (VA) for medical claims, etc.

Like me, the vast majority of adult Americans (over the age of twenty-five) can probably tell you exactly _where_ they were and _what_ they were doing on the (Tuesday) morning of **September 11, 2001** (also referred to as **911**). Most Americans, who are over sixty years old—and <u>not</u> suffering from _Alzheimer's Disease or Dementia_—can probably provide the same facts, in reference to the days on which President John F. Kennedy or Dr. Martin Luther King Jr. were assassinated. However, I can also tell you exactly where I was and what I was doing, when Pastor Samuel A. Thompson (_Pastor T_) personally telephoned and informed me of his **Cancer** diagnosis. While this situation did not have the exact same impact on the United States (as a Nation), it had a very similar, if not the same, significance for **me** (_personally_); because of its impact on the **Kingdom of GOD** and how it immediately thrust me into <u>both</u> the associated **spiritual warfare** and Pastor T's (physical) **battle for Life**, which lasted for _nineteen_ months (more than a year and a half).

It was about 12:30 pm on a sunny, Tuesday afternoon (**March 10, 2015**). I had just finished delivering meals to in-home clients, on my assigned *Meals On Wheels* route; and, I was (simultaneously) listening to a Gospel *Sermon* on a compact disc (CD), while driving my truck in Hampton, VA. Suddenly, my cell phone rang; and, it was Pastor T. His initial words to me were: "*Hello Bishop; how are you?*" After I responded by saying: "*Hi Pastor T. I am fine; I just finished delivering my "Meals On Wheels." How are you doing?*" Then Pastor Thompson said, "*I have just gotten some very bad news, today, Bishop.*" I responded by saying, "*Oh no, I am sorry to hear that. What's up?*" Finally, Pastor Thompson said: "*My doctor says that I have a rare form of "skin cancer"; and, that the form or type that I have is the* **worst** *(kind) he has ever seen.*" I (then) asked where he was (at home or the hospital). He said that he was at his house; so, I said, "*I am heading over to your house, right now. And I have something ("a Word") that you need to hear,* **right now***! I will be there in fifteen (15) minutes.*" As I drove to his house, it became immediately clear to me, why I was listening to this particular sermon, entitled: *Even Now!* This was a *sermon* message (on CD) that had been preached at our church in March 2008, but I had unpacked (pulled it out) and began **re-listening** to it, over and over (while driving) for the past two weeks, prior to Pastor T's latest phone call. So after listening and *meditating* upon this message for a couple of weeks, it was *freshly* **in my spirit**. And now I definitely realized (knew) why; because (now) Pastor Thompson needed to **hear** it! After just (recently) hearing what the medical doctor had told him, now—he needed to hear what the *Spirit* of GOD wanted to say to him, through this sermon.

When I arrived at his house about 12:45 p.m., he was sitting in his Study. I could sense that his spirit was very low. Initially, I only asked him if he had already shared this news with any of his adult leaders (*Deacons*). He said that only about three of his adults knew; but, he was uncertain about how and when he would break this news to his Youth congregation (children). First, I prayed for (with) him, before I asked him to just sit and listen to the **sermon** message entitled: *Even Now* (on CD), with me. About five minutes into the CD sermon, Pastor T's spirit had been **rejuvenated** and his strength had been **renewed**, as he sat upright on the edge of his seat and a great big smile *lit up*, across his face. Hearing this *Word* from GOD, caused his faith to soar. By the end of the CD sermon, Pastor Thompson was beaming with excitement and enthusiasm, as he said to me: "*Bishop, man you are alright! You have been **a breath of fresh air** to me (today)—as usual. You don't even realize what a great Blessing you (and this visit) have been to me.* Now, I want you to see something." Finally, he told me to pull out the keyboard tray on his computer desk and read what was on his monitor screen. I could see that he had started a sermon message for his upcoming Sunday morning service; however, he had gotten *bogged down* and couldn't proceed. When I finished reading that initial page, he said to me: "*Now, I must scrap that draft and start all over again; because, GOD has given me a new message theme (focus) and an approach for how I must* reveal—my diagnosis and (pending "battle")—to my congregation (children). From that initial day of his diagnosis (**March 10, 2015**), until what would eventually be Pastor T's final day (Saturday, **October 22, 2016**), I had the honor and privilege of witnessing, receiving from and ***being blessed*** by Pastor T's wealth of: faith, wisdom, courage and faithfulness, even in the midst of a (personal) ***fiery furnace*** of the most *excruciating* and *agonizing* physical suffering; some of his greatest *challenges*; and his deepest earthly *sorrow*.

For the first fourteen months (over a year), after his initial diagnosis, Pastor T ***fought*** *against cancer* with such faith, grace, anointing and vigor that no one could ever see any indicators (or affects) that he even had any medical condition or disease. Had he not personally told me, I would never have even suspected its existence. That is how graciously, faithfully and loyally, he executed (carried out) his **Kingdom** assignments and responsibilities for his church, and throughout his Outreach areas/communities, as well as his personal matters at home.

During this time (*season*) of his life, he was relentless and there was **NO** signs of doubt, slowing down, nor retreating (*giving up*) in his spirit (*heart*) or in his mind. Despite his condition, he seamlessly and steadfastly continued to preach, as he gallantly *led* his *flock of youth* (church congregation). He and his wife also traveled and conducted Evangelism and *Outreach* ministry activities within their *assigned* regions of Virginia and North Carolina, while blessing several hundreds of people (outside of their own congregation). As his local doctors, as well as, cancer specialists at Duke University's Medical Center struggled with what to do or how to proceed with his treatments' process, he went on *each* day/week/month with his same: **TRUST GOD and business as usual** approach. True to form, Pastor T's focus and attention were consistently on *the needs of others*; while, his care and concern for the plight of others always took priority (outweighed) that of his own situation (or himself).

Miraculously, it was (also) in this *season's storm* (Winter's *blizzard*) of their livers, that **GOD's Love and Faithfulness** were clearly more *visible* to Pastor T and Momma Rose, than ever before. (Note: I used the description above to depict this *last (final)* season, which was also the *coldest, harshest,* most *isolated* and *bleakest* conditions of their (physical) lives.) Now, they were (*divinely*) surrounded and undergirded by a *GOD-sent* group of (us) Spiritual warriors, intercessors and *angelic* supporters (manifested in human bodies), who were sent to them (the Thompsons) to fulfill all of their needs, accomplish their desires and secure their *Spiritual legacy*. We were the current *manifestation* (evidence or *representation*) of **all** GOD's promises: ***flowing* into their lives (coming to them)**! And ironically, every single time that any one or a group of us visited Pastor T to: encourage, *cheer up* or just sit and chat (***fellowship***) with him, regardless of how *feeble* or low he was feeling (before our arrival), his spirit (attitude), energy and posture *automatically* **soared** into *MENTOR* **Over-drive**. Suddenly and enthusiastically, Pastor T would transform, reminiscent of *Clark Kent* to **Superman**, as he imparted his personal wisdom, faith and *warring* spirit into each of us. To a person, every one of us have shared (and often attests) that each time we left an encounter (visit) with him, we always felt like Pastor T had blessed (uplifted and encouraged) us—even more than we could have ever done for him. He never failed! We always felt like we had **received more** (*from visiting* him) than we were ever able to **give** to him. While our objective (intent) was to encourage and strengthen him, he greatly encouraged and strengthened us! Without a doubt, those *spiritual* **treasures**—

that he *imparted* into us—will serve as *fuel* to propel and carry us, through the rest of our natural lives!

About one year into Pastor T's *battle* with cancer, his wife Lady T or *Momma Rose* had (now) grown accustomed to driving him around and handling a greater *load*, as the cancer was progressing and his *chemotherapy* treatments increased. Suddenly, after a few short months of this, Lady T had a minor car accident; so, doctors insisted that she stop driving. Of course, this *gentle* kitten, became a roaring (aggravated) **lioness**, at the idea of someone trying to take away her driving privileges. Still, Momma Rose was a real *warrior* Queen; and, she continued to take on (handle) as much of the *load* (with its associated *stress*), as her huge heart and *little* body could handle. (However, no one really knew (**yet**) what was *brewing* inside of *Lady T*!) After a few incidents (beginning in late April 2016), in which Pastor T had awakened to find his wife sitting alone and crying in a separate, darkened room of the house, we became greatly concerned that she was starting to become depressed. At this point, our focus shifted to surrounding Lady T with other ladies to personally under-gird, spiritually support and encourage her. I thank GOD that Elder Edna Jones, Mother Louise Grimes, Sis Lisa DeBeauville and Evangelist Denise James (all from our RCC-VA's Ministry) were, more than willing, to fulfill these requirements (through both physical visits and phone calls), in addition to Rev. Doris Hamilton and Deacon Brenda Owens (from Pastor T's own church), Pastor and Lady T's own daughter and grand-daughter (Cynthia and Nicole), neighbor (Cathy Tache), as well as, *Caregivers* (Berverly Douglas and Rita Meckley).

This is how and when Pastor T's and Momma Rose's *final* six months began to transpire. Pastor T's and Lady T's last time attending a Worship Service (*together*), at their beloved *Compassion Community Church* (CCC), was on **Resurrection** *(Easter)* **Sunday** morning. After Pastor T's condition deteriorated too much for him to physically attend services (personally), Lady T continued to attended services, as Reverend Doris Hamilton (his Assistant Pastor) faithfully led the ministry, along with *Momma Rose*, in Pastor T's absence. He continued to lead (*guide*) his flock from his home, by holding meetings (there) with Rev. Hamilton and his key leaders.

He never stopped *living for* and **serving GOD** (through his church congregation, community, and Outreach Ministries).

**Lady Rosella Johnson Thompson** (a.k.a. "*Lady T*" or "*Momma pose*")

They celebrated Momma Rose's eightieth birthday on Saturday, May 14, 2016. One week later, on May 21, she was rushed to the hospital emergency room for: what we <u>believed</u> was clearly symptoms of **depression**, resulting from Pastor Thompson's *deteriorating* health condition and her (stated) **inability** *to walk*. Or was this a **stroke**? Within a week, Momma Rose was going through *physical therapy* at Sentara Rehabilitation Center in Hampton, VA.

Although, we had already *previously* begun to rearrange and make adjustments in their home; as, we cleared and de-cluttered his study and lower level library/office areas. Pastor T had also begun preparations to officially disclose his *plan for his successor* (<u>next</u> *Pastor* of his church), by letter to his congregation; and, he had already taken other necessary steps, along with: Rev. Doris Hamilton and his senior deacons (Deacons Ben and Brenda Owens) and other key supporters, to **<u>transition</u>** the CCC Ministry, in the direction and way that the Spirit of GOD had instructed (and was still *instructing* him) to.

Friday (May 27) was the *pivotal* date, on which Pastor T underwent surgery to replace or exchange his *old* pacemaker; on that same day, the doctor *officially **diagnosed*** that Momma Rose was actually suffering from **stage 4 cancer** on the **brain** and in her ***stomach***. The doctor also made it very clear that when she returned home, Lady T would require constant in-home care for all of her daily functions like eating, bathing, etc. Now, Pastor Thompson's focus and attention shifted solely to the welfare, care and comfort of his beloved and devoted wife (Lady T). He asked me to personally prepare the house for *wheel chair* accessibility (spacing) and operations, throughout the house. This required me to: *dis-assemble* and *store* her regular bed in the outside shed; remove *non-essential* items of furniture/etc., from her room. Additionally, one of their *original* neighbors (from 1974) personally, built (added) a **wheel-stair** *accessible* ramp onto the house; and, a hospital bed was delivered and set-up in Momma Rose's bedroom.

That *period of separation* (from May 21 through June 23, 2016), between Pastor T and Lady T, was more than either of them would have welcomed or *voluntarily signed up* for; yet, they were stuck with it, under the current circumstances. It finally ended, when Momma Rose finally returned home, in a *wheel chair* on Thursday, June 23. Pastor T and I were awaiting her *arrival*, as their daughter (Cynthia) and Rita drove her home from Sentara Rehabilitation facility. When I rolled her up the ramp (in a wheel chair) and into her home, to be *re-united* with Pastor T, I was actually witnessed the most *dramatic* and *final* **shift** (redirection or turn) of their *personal* (*physical*) and *spiritual* lives. This also marked *the beginning of the end*: **the last two months** of both sixty-one years of marriage (together) and their physical lives (together). Before Momma Rose became *immediately* stricken with stage 4 brain cancer, Pastor T had courageously fought his (personal) ***war*** against skin *cancer*, with the most focused faith, determination and resiliency. I believe that the **tenacity** with which he had been *fighting* was probably more to survive (to be here) for *Lady T*, than for himself. However, since Momma Rose's diagnosis (in May), Pastor T (now) had to **simultaneously** *fight* **two** *separate **wars*** on two *different* ***fronts:*** both his and hers.

The current situation for Lady T was extremely difficult. As her physical **motor skills** rapidly and drastically *deteriorated* (declined), the challenge was to keep her motivated, inspired and engaged; because her *mobility* and *independence* were gone (lost). After a few weeks, she lost her appetite; until eventually, she refused to eat anything. Doctors officially placed Momma Rose (Lady T) on *Hospice* care status on Wednesday, August 17. To all of us that were there to *love* and support her, she went very quickly. Even as their only daughter (Cynthia) mentally adjusted to her mother's eventual *transition* and began to verbalize her acceptance and need to start preparing for the associated requirements, she said, *"I think I need to sit down soon to write an obituary, while I still have the strength (emotional stability) to do it."*

However, Pastor T, in all of his *infinite* (endless) **Faith** in GOD and **Love** of GOD *for* his wife, said: *"NO! We are not going to talk about or do that, yet; because, GOD has **not** said that to me. I am going to wait **to hear from GOD**, about this!"* He was still continuing to **fight both wars** on **both** *fronts*, *with all his might* (with everything that was within him: faith, love, tenacity, courage, etc.)

During that same week, Sis Lisa DeBeauville and I had gone over to visit and pray with both Pastor T and Momma Rose (Lady T). After *initially* speaking to Pastor T, in the living room, we both proceeded into Lady T's bedroom. Although, she did not open her eyes and appeared to be resting peacefully, we began to speak to her (the Word of GOD) and prayed over her, while holding her hand and rubbing her forehead. After about ten minutes, we went back into the living room to encourage and pray with Pastor T. First, we talked to him for about fifteen minutes or so.

I will never forget that day; because as I placed my hand on his head and prayed (aloud) for him, Sis Lisa began to initially rub his hand and (later) appeared to begin to be *continuously* pulling something away from (or off of) Pastor T's body. After we had ministered to him, for about twenty-five or thirty minutes, we left him (resting on his sofa). Once we were outside (near our cars), Sis Lisa began to share with me that, as I was praying for him, she had a (spiritual) **vision**, wherein, she saw a number of black **ravens** (birds) that were landing on Pastor T and attacking (or *eating* at his body/

*flesh*). Therefore, she had begun to pull and throw them off of him. As we continued to pray and minister, she said the birds (*in her vision*) retreated and flew away from him. The revelation that we received, from this experience (encounter), was that Pastor T had been suffering great **agony** (torment) before we arrived; but, he had gained **great relief** *(been spiritually rescued)* and blessed by our visit! As we both glanced upward, before getting into our cars, we actually saw the telephone line (wire across the entire span/width of Pastor Thompsons property), was *physically* full of **ravens** (large black birds) just sitting there (*lined up* on that wire) over his house and yard. (The actual (*visual*) picture of this scene reminded me of a scene from the old movie: *The Birds* (in which massive flocks of *enraged* birds would accumulate in towns and then launch *attacks* on and kill the people).) This was an immediate and direct confirmation for me, of Sister Lisa's *vision*, which she had just shared with me!

    Eventually, GOD spoke to Pastor T's *heart* (spirit), and gave him the grace, peace and confirmation to *release* Lady T (as GOD's decision was to *promote* her to Glory)! Momma Rose *passed away* (**went home to be with the Lord**) about 2:38 p.m. on Friday, August 26, 2016.

    Pastor T's *final* months and days on this earth, without his *beloved* Rose (Lady T), were—(by far)—the absolute **loneliest** of his entire life. He had already (previously) endured and survived so much: racism, segregation and initial *integration*; the **death** (loss) of his <u>only</u> son, who was only twelve years old; a **twenty years, active duty** (US Air Force) career and its associated deployments, hardships, war, etc.; establishing (founding) a church organization to **pastor troubled teens and youth off the streets (for more than seventeen years)**; personally having suffered a **heart attack**, also undergoing and recovering from **twelve major surgeries** (while *flat lining* (himself) and being **resuscitated** (revived) on the operating table.

Now, having just received his *improved* (*replacement*) **pacemaker** and in the midst of his own **(personal) war, with a rare form of skin cancer** (for more than eighteen months), he has just experienced **the death (loss) of his beloved wife** (of a proven **sixty-one-years marriage**). Still, he refused to *mope*, indulge in *self-pity* or focus on his own problems or circumstances. As a testament to and proof of that fact, when I told him (in his hospital room), on Tuesday evening (Sep. 27, 2016), that I needed to go dial-in to *open* our weekly **PRAYER (Conference) CALL** *telephone line*, so myself and other *prayer partners* could pray and intercede for our list of people (or even for strangers, who might *call-in* to request that we pray for them), Pastor T immediately said: *"I would also like to participate on that call line and to pray for some folks!"* So after dialing-in, I introduced him (over the phone to the other members), and he actively PRAYED (on our call) *for other people,* including his children (youth of his church) and adult leaders of his ministry, other patients in the hospitals/nursing homes, and *homeless* folks on the streets.

This was huge for all of us! For Pastor T, to have an **opportunity** to fulfill this Christian *duty* (praying or *interceding* for others) was like an *infusion* of oxygen (or a surge of **renewed** life) into his own *physical* body and spirit. For my prayer team members (Evangelist Hattie Holloway and Minister Senitha Phelps), this represented a **blessing** from GOD, for them to be able to personally hear this awesome vessel of GOD pray (into their hearing and personal contact) on the telephone line; because they had been personally praying (<u>for</u> <u>him</u>) for months. And now they actually got to participate and minister both to and along with him; although, they would never get to meet him (*face-to-face*) in their (earthly) lifetime.

That previous requirement (*burden*), for Pastor T to *simultaneously fight* **two** separate wars, on **two** different fronts, ended (went away) with the passing of Lady T. Unfortunately, his *desire, motivation and inspiration* to *fight* his own (personal) war, also, **ended** (was **gone**), as well. And while he still **maintained** his Faith and Trust in GOD, Pastor T <u>no</u> <u>longer</u> felt a desire or *need* to continue (physically) **fighting**, for himself! I believe this sudden **absence,** of Pastor T's <u>internal</u> **fight (tenacity)**, was the reason why his own (*physical*) life *ended* **less than two months**, after his eighty-second birthday and Lady T's (Momma Rose's) *passing* in August.

Thereafter, he spent his last two months (on earth), the same as he had (previously) spent most of his lifetime: ***encouraging*** and ***imparting* (*pouring into*) others**! (The previous and current ***recipients*** of his *outpouring* (Ministry) included**:** <u>strangers</u> *on the streets*, residents in nursing homes, patients in hospitals, youth *congregants* (whom he had all but adopted), fellow *laborers in Christ* (ministers), fellow travelers, family members, *needy (Outreach)* recipients, summer campers (kids), his/Lady T's *care givers*, hospital staff (doctors/nurses), military veterans, other (*cancer treatment*) *patients*, etc.)

Some of my fondest and *most valued* memories, from my friendship and covenant connection with Pastor T, consisted of enjoying the opportunities to *serve* him in some of the *simplest* (daily) activities like: being asked to mix and bring his favorite drink (a mixture of one-half glass each of orange and apple juices) from his refrigerator; go to *fill* and pick-up his medicine prescriptions from Langley AFB or other pharmacy; *rub on* (apply) his *anti-itch* skin cream (treatment); change his clothes; transferring him into and out of his bed; as well as (obviously) discussing scriptures and *partnering* (participating) in Evangelism Outreach endeavors (*opportunities*) *together*.

However, one of the most gratifying events for me, occurred on Thursday morning (October 20), when the Veterans Administration (VA) held a very special *Veteran's* **Recognition Ceremony** to *officially* **honor** Pastor Samuel Andrew Thompson's twenty (20) years of *active duty* (Air Force) military service, as well as, his additional twenty-four (24) years of *civil service* (between the Hampton, VA *Dept. of Veteran Affairs* and Fort Eustis). Although, Pastor Thompson was (then) already in *Hospice* status, his Dept. of Veteran Affairs (VA) Palliative Care room was filled (by special invitation only) with those (*available*) people, who genuinely loved and whole-heartedly supported him. It was an honor for me to personally witness Pastor T being **honored** for his life of service and his decades-long *labor* of love for mankind, as the **Chaplain** *(of the Dept of Veterans Affairs),* presented the special recognition *mementos* to him in a special ceremony, with Cynthia receiving (and responding) on behalf of her father. Those in attendance included: his daughter and only living child (Cynthia); his Assistant Pastor of CCC and his *designated* (chosen) successor (Reverend Doris Hamilton); his most *senior* Deacons (Ben and Brenda Owens); his personal Hospice *Caregivers*; his beloved and *loving* next-door neighbor and close friend (Tom Tache); a spiritual connection and *co-laborer* in Christ (Evangelist Denise James); a divine spiritual connection and special *confidant* (myself: Elder Rousell Thomas); and VA's *Hospice* Staff/personnel. Upon completion of the military formalities, the gathering quickly *shifted* into an unforgettable, spiritual experience for everyone present, including Pastor T. I can still feel the peace and love that saturated that room, as we shared special memories/stories. While Evangelist Denise James spent several precious minutes *comforting* Pastor T, I simultaneously began to sing (aloud) a favorite hymn: "**Oh, I Want To See Him** *(To Look Upon His Face)*," to which the entire gathering (group) began to sing and rejoice. He was very peaceful. Immediately, we all knew (and agreed) that it was **good** *for us to be there*!

    Pastor Thompson never *second guessed* or questioned GOD's decisions nor their subsequent results, which occurred in the **twilight** of his life. However, there were multiple occasions in that last month, when he personally said (to me): "*Bishop, I don't know* **why** *GOD changed His plan (for me/my life); but, he did.*" I believe that this statement was made in reference to the time (*timing*) of Lady T's and his *departures* (*Home-going*).

    In the final week of his life, Pastor T began to talk about his **vision** of constantly seeing the presence of: two little (black) hands or feet that were visibly hovering or rising up toward heaven. Whenever he was conscious (alert), during this week, he would say to me (or others in the room), that these little black *hands or feet* were <u>not</u> there to *harm* us; but, they were sent (there) by Jesus, only **to *help*** us. These conversations allowed us to anticipate his pending or *imminent departure* (death). However, there were some days and hours (periods) of **excruciating** (torturous, tormenting and violent) ***pain***.

As peaceful as Pastor T was on Thursday morning (Oct. 20), during and after that special Recognition Ceremony, the Holy Spirit led me to go and sit with Pastor Thompson about 11:00 p.m. that same night. When I walked into his room, I immediately saw that he needed me to be there to pray and engage in spiritual *warfare* on his behalf; because, he was experiencing great agony and pain. At some point, I also summoned the nurse on duty to give him some *morphine* (medication) to aide in relieving his level of pain and discomfort. For myself, to *personally* have had the privilege and honor to *serve*, under-gird, and *walk with* (support) Pastor Thompson, through this *critical* stage of his life, was equivalent to (personally) *witnessing* and <u>accompanying</u> **JOB** and/or the ***Apostle* PAUL** (*in 2015–2016*). And I can personally testify that, after all of his afflictions, sufferings, and hardships—Pastor T **never (ever):** <u>abandoned</u> his process, <u>falsely accused</u>, <u>walked away from</u> or **rebelled** (or turned) against **GOD**! And like Job, ***Pastor T*** didn't *delight* in the fore-mentioned *hardships*; yet, he **honored GOD**, *through* **heart-wrenching** *circumstances* and continuously **responded by trusting the LORD**, *throughout his* **suffering(s) and afflictions**.

Those were just a few of those **Divine Connections** or *GOD-ordained assignments* that I was **called** and **sent** to (personally) **serve** <u>for</u> <u>a</u> <u>season</u> of their lives. However, there were **others** individuals like: the late Deacon Fred Grimes (77 years old); the late Mr. Grainger Browning Sr. (99 years old), who I simply referred to as *Pop*, along with his late wife (Mrs. Esther Browning); and Mr. William "Bill" Nelson Sr. (85 years old), *Pop Nelson* to me. Then, there's a great group of <u>adopted</u> **Mothers** in our Church, consisting of widows and/or other elderly women with serious chronic health challenges or extreme personal tragedies, like: Mother (Evangelist) Ozzie Gray, 92 years and counting; Mother (Minister) Sallie Carter, Mother Helen Page, Mother Irene Pressey, battling Lupus every day (for over twenty-seven years); Mother Gwen Carlisle; Mother Elaine Little; Mother Cynthia Armistead; Mother Louise Grimes; as well as, many others within the *Seniors' Ministry* of our church. Elder Edna Jones is the Ministry Head and primary coordinator for our Seniors' Ministry care and activities. Additionally, she (too) is a *widow* since both her husband and only son **passed away** within an eleven-month span after she'd already personally been revived from the threshold of death's door just a few years before. In this particular season of her life, GOD has **sent** me to *undergird* (support) *Prophet* Edna Jones. Additionally, there was (*initially*) an *over-burdened* group of four elderly women and Brother Leon Brown, that I was **sent** (in 2007) to **undergird** (come alongside of, support, reinforce and strengthen) at ***Camp Heavenly Waters Christian Retreat and Youth Camp*** facility for the past thirteen years. Two (Mrs. Maggie Counts and Mrs. Marie Rogers) of those original four were already *widows* (in 2007). In recent years, illnesses and death have reduced that group to only two (Mrs. Queen Pope and Sister Barbara Wallace) of those original *(year-round)* **volunteers**, who were tasked and taxed with the burdens and challenges of operating and sustaining the facilities on this 163-acre property.

    Although, I had originally been asked by Rev Eric "Duke" McCaskill to go to Camp Heavenly Waters to *run* or conduct one (single), *week-long* **Summer Camp** for the children of his *Children of Absentee Parents' Project* (**CAPP**) *Program* in 2007. Rev. *Duke* had recruited me to conduct this camp for him, due to my twenty-plus years of active duty military experience. Therefore, he sought to *tap into* my experience and expertise to instill structure and discipline into the camp experience of these *inner-city*, disenfranchised or *under-privileged* children, who **all** had *incarcerated* parents (in jail), at that time. By that week's end, after witnessing how I mentored, disciplined and demanded high standards (in terms of manners, respect, etc.) from them toward all adults, Mrs. Queen (Pope) said to me, "*Mr. Thomas, would you (please) come back in three weeks to run our (church's) annual "summer camp," for me?*" (Note: That was another individual request for one more (single) camp.) Because she was one year older than my own mother would have been (if she were still alive) and I am called to help (*serve*) the <u>elderly</u>, I said: "**OK! Yes ma'am; I will do tha**t (for you)!"

And (now) I have been there (at Camp Heavenly Waters) for thirteen years, **serving** and taking care of seniors and elderly citizens, while they provide and serve the love of GOD to visitors of all ages, that come *year-round*, through the property's facilities. Camp Heavenly Waters has been a GOD-sent (*Respite* or *Safe Haven*); and more specifically, Mrs. Queen Pope (and Bishop Lawrence Lewis, its original founder and *Visionary*) have been *Angels* in the lives of thousands of people in the Body of Christ (for the Kingdom of GOD) in the earth realm, over the last twenty-three (23) years, since Heavenly Waters began operations in 1997. Meanwhile, she (**Mrs. Queen Pope, seventy-nine years and counting**) has been another ***Divine Appointment*** (*assignment*) for me, personally. Suffice it to say, it has been a very unique and monumental <u>***spiritual***</u> (*Mother-son* relationship). The proof of that was verbalized, after Pastor Thompson (*Pastor T*) had passed away, when Mrs. Queen said to me, "*I hope that you are still around (here) when I am near "my end." If so, I want you to look out for me, just like you did for Pastor T.*" To adequately shed *light* on this season of *serving* (at and through Camp Heavenly Waters), would require an additional (whole) book to be written about **Mrs. Queen Pope's** <u>***own***</u>**:** *service*, *loyalty*, *dedication* and *commitment* to Bishop Lewis's original **Vision** (and her ***faithful*** service to GOD). If she or I were to write *that* (potential) book, I could imagine its title being something like: <u>**BEARING A GIANT'S VISION**</u>, or <u>**BEARING (The Weight of) A GIANT'S VISION.**</u> However, that book would ***not*** even *breach* an introduction or *glimpse* into her (***own***) personal childhood or thirty-nine year career of continuous *government/civil service* (from 1962–2001). Those specific periods of Mrs. Queen Pope's life of *exceptional **service*** would warrant a second book.

Ironically, while her personal career began (in 1962) at the *National Aeronautical and Space Agency* (NASA), at the exact time that Mrs. Catherine Johnson (featured in the movie ***Hidden Figures***) also worked there, Mrs. Pope's career eventually ended with *retirement*, after decades of service at the *Headquarters* of the *United States Army's Training and Doctrine Command (HQs, TRADOC)* in 2001.

Finally, there have been an <u>unrecorded</u> number of other *widows*, elderly, disabled and/or homeless people from neighborhoods, in communities or other churches, as well as, in public forums (whether convention centers, supermarkets, hospitals, nursing homes or rehabilitation centers, parking lots, etc.) that GOD has also blessed me to have the honor and privilege *to serve* in various capacities (over the years). Some of them I have connected with, known and walked closely with, through a *critical* season of their lives (like the late: Pop "Bill" Nelson, Dr. Grainger Browning Sr., Deacon Fred Grimes; and others, etc.) Some of whom I had only met and helped *in passing* (while traveling around the world, even overseas); and, I will never ever know their names.

You will not find any pictures of myself (in this book), while doing any of the personal **services, demonstrations** of GOD's love nor **acts of kindness**, for even one of the **countless** individuals that I have highlighted in this book. Nor do I have any such pictures at my house. I have *never* taken any myself, nor had anyone else take any pictures of me (while ***doing*** those assignments). None of those were ever done: to draw attention or create publicity for myself; to build a resume (portfolio) or generate income. Instead, **serving GOD,** through the fulfillment of my assignments to <u>serve</u> and <u>bless</u> his special children—(elderly citizens, widows, others who were *disabled*, *homeless* or had been *forsaken*, or the *lost*)—has always been ***for the Glory of GOD (alone)***! It has always been and will always be about *delivering* the **Gospel of Jesus Christ** and **GOD's love** (to His people), as He provides me the daily (*personal*) **opportunities** to do that. You *see*, GOD has actually given each of us (literally) "***millions of opportunities***," during our lifetime. As HE allows us to encounter, interact with, sow or pour into, affect and serve others (everyday) for HIS Glory. We each get these opportunities to ***choose*** *to serve HIM*, <u>through</u> them (the opportunities and the people)!

## THE SERMON (MESSAGE)

On Wednesday night (September 7, 2016), our team of ***Evangelists*** (from our *Evangelism Ministry* Team at RCC-VA) were tasked to minister to our church congregation on this topic of: ***Freedom In Servitude.*** The five speakers for this assignment consisted of all our ***Evangelists***: Hattie Holloway, Charlette Terry, Denise James, Sonya Bradley and myself (Rousell Thomas), *except* (minus) Mother Ozzie Gray (our *eldest* and *most seasoned* Evangelist), who was traveling (*out-of-state*) at that time. ***Each*** speaker was tasked to speak (or *preach*) for about **twelve minutes** *in succession* (following one behind the other, without interruption or intermission) on this assigned topic. In preparation for our assignment, we were instructed to study the life of **Joseph** in the BIBLE's *Old Testament* Book of ***Genesis*** (focusing on **GENESIS 39:19-23**). Our five messages were *individually* prepared; therefore, we had **no** discussions or *collaboration* in our study or preparations period. We all *gathered* with our senior leadership (***Pastors***) for prayer and final instructions, about twenty minutes prior to proceeding out into the main sanctuary, to preach. We were **not** even told (and did **NOT** know) the sequence or *order* of the delivery of our message(s) until the minute to *line up and procession* (march out into the sanctuary). So everything was done (conducted), by the ***leading*** of the *Holy Spirit* (***Spirit of GOD***), at the moment of the mission's ***execution***. In actuality, our five messages were really separate *pieces* or **sections** of **One** (*Unified*) Message. It was like a *jigsaw* puzzle; and only Holy Spirit knew who had (or where) each piece was. Therefore, it could only fit (or come together) as GOD Himself had designed and orchestrated (through His Spirit) for its precise delivery. As the Spirit would have (and so ***ordered***), I was the third of the five speakers, assigned to deliver the *middle* (climax) of the Sermon message. The collective (unified), message had the perfect start; (then) built or rose to a *resounding crescendo* climax; before, finally *receding to an expected end*, concluding the whole matter. As we (our *procession*) *marched* into the sanctuary (in GOD's *divine* **order** or sequence), it was the emanation of (represented the actual ***entrance***, appearing and *flow* of the aura) of GOD's Spirit entering that sanctuary (room). In the end, those congregants and participants in attendance, ALL witnessed, and a great percentage of them (also) verbalized how the entire (***Unified***) Message: formed or *painted* a vividly clear picture of Joseph's attitude, heart, willingness and faithfulness in ***Serving***; and denoted complete (inner) **FREEDOM**, despite where he was or what his predicament (conditions) were at any given point in time!

I (now) share the same message with you (readers), that I shared with the congregation/people present on that evening (Sept. 7, 2016).

As a *lead-in* to my segment of the sermon, I shared a testimony, with the congregation, that as I was driving alone in my truck (in 2013), GOD gave me a *clear **Vision*** and deposited (within my spirit) just the title for a book: ***<u>Always A Servant; Never A Slave</u>***! I didn't understand (at that moment in 2013) exactly when, nor under what circumstances, I would eventually write this book; but, I knew that I would (eventually) have to do it.

As I said earlier in chapter 1 of this book, it was absolutely essential to recognize and distinguish the <u>difference</u> between a willing ***servant*** and a ***slave***, based upon the irrefutable ***difference in the spirit/attitude*** that each possesses, as well as, their ***conditions/circumstances*** (reality) in which each serves. These two are NOT the same.

What you and I must realize is that there is a **profound** difference in *being a servant* versus being a *slave*, as different as *night* and *day*! They are not the *same*! Now, you and I have NOT *personally* experienced the *cruel* reality (experience) of officially <u>being a slave</u>; but, all of us have served in some positions, roles, or jobs, where we have been under someone else's authority (or supervision) to perform some tasks or responsibilities: *servitude* to some extent. The servant possesses this <u>different</u> spirit (attitude); because he knows **who** and **whose** he is, which makes him/her—(*first*) <u>*willing*</u>, and (secondly), <u>*obedient*</u>! Those two attributes must go together or <u>both</u> be present. **So when you are in a position to *serve*: You** can, **either,** serve as a (***willing) servant*** or you will (***grudgingly***) serve ***as a slave***!

<u>*Always A Servant; Never A Slave*</u>! That's another way of saying: **Freedom In Servitude!**

Yes; You <u>can</u> be *FREE*, while in servitude—if you maintain the <u>*right*</u> spirit (attitude) in the midst of the situation. What GOD revealed to me (about Joseph), was that Joseph was **always the servant,** and never the *slave*! So I will ask you: Whose servant was Joseph? And you will probably say: **<u>when</u>**? When (1) he was put *in the pit* by his brothers—whose servant was he? When (2) he was sold to and *in the hands of the Merchantmen* (traders)—whose servant was he? When (3) he was *in Potiphar's* house—whose servant was he? When (4) he was *in prison*—whose servant was he? And finally, when (5) he ends up *in Pharaoh's palace* (his destiny)—whose servant was he? In order to get and understand the answers to all of these questions (above), you will have to read, not just the small portion of **GENESIS 39:19-23** that was referenced; but, you must read and research <u>*ALL*</u> of **chapters 37, 39, and 40-45**. In ALL of these situations and circumstances above, <u>Only</u> **GOD** *owned* Joseph, in every situation. In every situation: the LORD *was with him*; the LORD showed him *mercy*; and the LORD gave him *favor* with everyone that had authority/jurisdiction/control over him **(GENESIS 39:21).**

While serving in Potiphar's house, Joseph had to *distinguish* himself and *demonstrate* his **different spirit** (*exemplary or excellent attitude*) consistently over a prolonged period of time. This is why Potiphar came to trust him so completely; and, why Potiphar's wife fell madly in love with him, to the point that she could not take *no,* for an answer. (Look very closely at **GENESIS 39:1-11**.)

Although there is a saying (cliché) that says: <u>*possession is (equals) nine-tenths of the law*</u>; whereby, people or a person have been **granted ownership of property or something, just because, it was in their possession.** However, Joseph proves to us that (no matter): **where** I am located or situated (at a given time), **whose possession** I am in, or **whose *control or jurisdiction*** I am under, that **does <u>not</u> determine** (*Ownership* of me)—**or determine who I** *belong* **to!** I have got to <u>**settle that, within myself!**</u> (I <u>*can't*</u> let somebody else determine or decide: who owns me or who I belong to!) Neither can **YOU** allow someone else to decide that for you: *who owns you and who you belong to.*

The fact of the matter is, while *in servitude* or just living our (daily) lives, that our **FREEDOM** <u>must</u> be a reality that *exists* **within** *us* in three (3) distinct areas. First: My *Freedom* must be a reality that exists *in my mind*. I knew (and continue to know) that I am *free*, even when I was working for the government, commanding a US Army (military) unit, in a foreign country or wherever. Although I had to take (obey) some *orders* sometimes, I had to know (in all situations) that I was <u>always</u> *free* **to:** <u>*be me (myself)*</u> and to <u>***do the right thing,***</u> in every situation. So in every situation, Joseph (also) <u>knew</u> who he was and <u>held</u> onto his dreams (GOD-given *Vision and destiny* for his life).

NO matter where I am (or you are), *every* **situation** or **encounter** represents (provides) two different **opportunities**. Here are a couple of *Biblical* examples.

When Joseph found himself constantly pursued and eventually entrapped by Potiphar's persistentwife: he had opportunities to *succumb* (give in) to her sexual advances; instead, he chose to *flee* the situation. Brother Joseph *flew the coop!* (**GENESIS 39:12**).

Pastor Wilburforce said, when David came upon Saul (his pursuer/*hunter* stalking him) asleep on the battlefield, and David's men were encouraging (enticing) him to *cut off* Saul's head, David chose to *spare* King Saul's life (let him go *unharmed*). David told his men: don't touch Saul (GOD's anointed servant). David's decision was driven by his respect and honor for GOD's *anointing* on King Saul's life, despite the fact that Saul was seeking to kill him—(and would have killed David, if the *tables were turned*) (**1 SAMUEL 24:4-12**).

David's men said to him, this was the <u>*perfect*</u> *opportunity* to cut-off Saul's head; and, they were *right*. It was the perfect opportunity to kill David's pursuer/stalker. At the same time (conversely), it was also the <u>*perfect*</u> *opportunity* to **do what GOD required** and prove that, he could have (see) that opportunity to *do evil* and **say: "no"** *(not yield)* to the temptation.

The Samaritan man (referred to as *the* **good** *Samaritan*), when he came upon the man that had been beaten, robbed and *left for dead* (by thieves) along the roadside, he saw an opportunity to help this stranger, whom he did not know (not one of his own people); but, whom he realized was in distress and *dire* physical condition. Therefore, he chose to: *show compassion*, tend to his wounds (then) transport the wounded stranger to the inn. The Priest, Levite (others) who *passed by*, on the other side of the road, thought this is the *perfect opportunity* to leave this (him) alone; because, they each had something else that they desired or preferred to do. The **good** Samaritan (also) could have passed by and *left him for dead*, laying on the side of the road (**LUKE 10:30-36**).

NO matter where I am (or you are), *every* **situation** or **encounter** represents (provides) two different **opportunities**. There's the opportunity to *do what's right* (the **good** that GOD would have you to do); and conversely, there is also the opportunity to *do what your flesh says to do (what feeds your lust* or what you feel like doing). And **you have to see them BOTH**! So when **you** get the **opportunities**, **which one(s)** are you going to do?

In every situation, there are whole lots of *expectations*. People have expectations of you. Joseph faced expectations, in every situation. GOD had expectations for Joseph every day. **GOD** also has expectations, for you and I, *every* day and in every situation. But (then), **you** have some expectations for yourself. And finally, the **people** *around you* have expectations—the **boss (supervisor)**, your **spouse**, the **children**, the *co-workers*, the *whoevers*, the **people we evangelize to** *on the streets*, **everybody** (you meet) has some *expectations*—**FOR YOU!** And **YOU** have to know which expectations **take priority**!

So when you talk about your *freedom* being a reality **in your Mind**, it's not just what you *think*. It starts with you thinking right and your thoughts; but you have to (also) stay *on top of* and (remain) consistent in: *who* you are and *what* you **know and believe**. As a child, Joseph had *dreams* (**visions**) from GOD. For his older brothers, the *interpretations* of Joseph's dreams/visions meant that they were to reverence, honor and *bow down* to him (in the future). "Oh, you think you're special, huh?" the brothers said, They recognized that he was **special**. That's what the brothers did *not* like about him. They also realized that Joseph was their father's *favorite* son, which led their father to give Joseph a special **coat** *of many colors*. Therefore, Joseph's brothers *hated* him. And Joseph had to deal with and accept this *reality*.

In all of the situations (phases) of his life: moving *from the **pit**—* to the *hands of the traders*—to *Potiphar's house*—to the *prison*—to the King's *Palace*, and in all of these places, Joseph (still) never lost **the dream**. The dream, inside of him, never ***died***!

The envy, malice and hatred that the brothers developed for Joseph was an ongoing *issue*, at that time, which GOD allowed and used to ***move*** (re-locate) Joseph to Egypt (**GENESIS 37:28**).

About thirteen years later (in **Genesis 41-43, 44-46**), Joseph has been promoted by Pharaoh and is serving as *Governor* over the Pharaoh's whole Kingdom of Egypt. However, if GOD did not move him (earlier) to Egypt, then he would ***not*** have been there to do this (fulfilling his GOD-ordained *destiny*), as promised in his childhood *dream* (***vision***).

Sometimes, people may think that if they just *lie* on you or me (in a given situation) or try to *hinder* our progress (then) they can *sabotage* our (future) destiny or *kill our dream*.

[Note: That is what Potiphar's wife thought; and, what she attempted to do to Joseph.] (**GENESIS 39:11-20.**) Right here, where Potiphar's wife ***lies*** on Joseph, it's like those shows you guys are watching on television (now in 2017 and beyond). How many of you are watching: *The Haves and The Have-Nots*; *If Loving You Is Wrong*; and *Empire*; etc.? You know they only run (show) about eight episodes; then suddenly, it's already the *season finale*. The television show's producers (intentionally) *leave you hanging*. Why? Just because, they want to leave you *craving* for more (like a *pregnant* woman—*craves* for pickles and ice cream or something). Of course, there's more coming—but you have to wait until—**next season**! So Potiphar's wife ***lying*** on Joseph, is just the *uhhmph* (*climax* or *cliffhanger* scene) for this season, of the *drama* playing out in Joseph's (life) *transition*: from one of GOD's casting *extra* members to His *Leading Man* role in Egypt's Kingdom saga. Just *stick with (ride with)* Joseph, through the *process*; because, in the next seasons: **JOSEPH** is the Man, *running everything at the Top* (as ***Governor*** *over All of Egypt*)**,** in the subsequent **chapters (GENESIS 41-49)!**

So Joseph's ***freedom*** was **in his mind**. No matter where he was located (whether: in the pit, in prison, etc.), his *freedom* was—

(**_First_**)—in his mind! However, it was not **only** in his mind; but, his freedom was (also, secondly) **in his spirit**. When it's in your **_spirit_**, it's where? It is (then) in your **heart**. I don't mean in the _physical (heart) muscle_ that pumps your blood; but, in the **_core of your being_: the center (or _essence_) of who you are**. That's your real _heart_ (of your spiritual _self_). When something _good_ (positive) or _evil_ (negative) gets into your heart, then it is already _rooted_ (embedded) into your _core_ being and _essence_ (fabric/fiber) of you and your true DNA). Once _freedom_ is in your spirit, nothing or no one can _take it out_! They said, "if you go to school and _learn_ how to read; then, no one can take that from you." This is what we were told, as little children going from the segregated school system over to the newly _integrated_ schools. So if **_freedom_** or any other _positive_ attribute or character trait is or gets into your spirit, and _you hold onto it_, you should never let anyone take it away or anything erode it away, under any circumstances (regardless of the situation).

Joseph's _freedom_ (then), was _in his mind_; it was _in his spirit_; third or _lastly_, it was **in his character** (was **_demonstrated_** and **_visibly_ evident** in his **lifestyle/behavior**. You could clearly **see** it, as he: **_served_** GOD; **_discharged_** his assigned duties; and **_performed his services_** to all those to whom he was obligated to _serve_. Everyone **saw** it! He did not _tell_ anyone; but, they all saw it (in the manifested results); they _discerned_ his **_anointing_** and realized (perceived) that GOD was with Joseph. They all saw that _it_ was in his mind; in his spirit (heart)…in his character; and, they saw that EVERYTHING Joseph was responsible for or put in charge of: **_prospered_**! Everyone (around him) _acknowledged_ this fact, and said that: "GOD is with him!"

Everyone (owners, other _slaves_, guards, other _prisoners_, King/Pharaoh, etc.) recognized and appreciated Joseph's spirit, anointing, GOD-given grace, favor, _gifting_, and his _Blessings_ to them**, except his brothers**. In his (childhood) home and _in the pit_, where Joseph's brothers put him, they could **_NOT_** appreciate or _understand_**:** who he was; what he had or did; nor, how he operated.

**I am _comfortable_** _doing what GOD has ordained and assigned (for) me to do_, even if or when people don't understand. They might _figure it out_ (realize) later; they might not.

Hey, **I am *comfortable*** doing: *what I am suppose to be doing*, whether you or others are comfortable with it or not. Joseph was also comfortable doing what GOD required him to do. He was always comfortable with that! And you have to get to the point, where you are *comfortable* (in your life) with that, too. Amen!

So that's how Joseph *served*. His ***Freedom*** was clearly there: in his **Mind**; in his **Heart (spirit)**; and in his **Character (*visibly poured out*** through his service/lifestyle/behavior)!

> *"He whom **the Son** (Lord Jesus) makes "free"*
> *is **Free** (Indeed)!"* (**JOHN 8:36 NIV**)

JOSEPH, in every situation, was **always FREE** *Indeed*! He was always *free indeed*; because, he was always *free* in his **spirit (heart)** and no one could take that from him. I encourage you to look back over this passage of scripture, that we just covered (**Genesis 39**), as well as, studying Joseph's life through the entire chapters of **Genesis 37, 40-49, and 50.** By doing so, you will discover (clearly see) that, historically, Joseph was always *free*, no matter what situation or circumstances he was thrown into. Therefore, your *FREEDOM* has to be ***internal***, so that no one can take that away from you. However, you must (*first*) ***know*** that you are **free**! Additionally, you have to **be *comfortable*,** when other folks don't: understand ***how*** you operate and ***what*** you do!

Therefore, we can look back (historically) at Joseph; but, I can also look (back) over my own life and see this. That's why I said: **"*Always* A Servant; Never A Slave!"**

I never (ever) felt like I had to do what I was doing (*in service* to **GOD**), because I expected anyone to pay me anything for doing it; nor because I feared that *not doing it* would stop me from achieving something or prevent me from getting something later on. No one was *paying* me anything; nor did I ever feel: *trapped*, stuck, intimidated (threatened) or coerced! Nor was any of it (ever) a part of my employment requirements, associated with any of my military career positions or other employment opportunities. But I was compelled to do these things (solely) because, that's what **GOD** had given me *to do*, at that particular time and in those specific assignments/locations. That's **when** and **why** you or I **have to** do it!

Joseph **had to** *operate* (*live, serve, function* and *respond*), exactly as he did; and, he knew it. Do you want to know how I know, that Joseph knew (realized) this? Because of the question that he posed to his eventual *accuser* (Potiphar's wife) in verse 9 (**GENESIS 39:9**), where he asked this woman: "how (then) can I do this *wickedness*, and *sin* **against GOD**?"

He did *not* say**:** how can I do this wickedness, and sin against *your husband* (Potiphar), who has trusted me. So Joseph was *free* of worrying about, and beyond serving *the husband*. This tells me that, Joseph's **loyalty** was ultimately **to GOD** (alone); and, that's <u>*who*</u> he was determined *not* to fail, disappoint or betray. Even if a friend, co-laborer, a relative or this *temptress* wanted him to disappoint GOD, Joseph consistently refused to do *it* (or to give into her demands)! Joseph remained focused; and, maintained his *freedom* **in serving GOD!**

**GENESIS 39:1-18** represented a *drama* series that played out *day-after-day*, over and over again, for about *ten* years. During which time, Potiphar's wife aggressively and tirelessly *stalked* and pursued Joseph; while she schemed, plotted and sought *opportunities* to **seduce** him. After Joseph had repeatedly refused all of her seductive offers and sexual advances, it is quite *ironic* that she would accuse Joseph of trying to rape her. When, in fact, she actually was attempting to (seduce) and *rape* him, in the midst of his refusing and resisting her *aggression* upon him. Her false accusation and outright *lie* (a blatant willingness to frame an *innocent* man) was her *response* to Joseph's final *rejection* of her. Yet (in all situations), Joseph was always *free* **to:** <u>*be*</u> **himself** and to <u>***do* the *right thing,***</u> in every situation.

[Note: We know, for sure, that this period lasted **about ten years**; because, Joseph was only seventeen years old, when he arrived at Potiphar's house (**GENESIS 37:2,14,28,36**). However, he was nearly twenty-eight years old, when he was thrown into prison (**GENESIS 39:17-20**); and, after two full years in prison, Joseph was thirty years old, when he (later) stood before Pharaoh (**GENESIS 41:1,46**).]

In order to *be Free in Servitude* or <u>be</u> *free while serving*, your *freedom* must be **internal** (inside); you must **know** it; and you must **stand on** it! I can even see *Freedom In Servitude* in my current *assignment*, as I am **serving** (assisting) Pastor Samuel A. Thompson. This man, a faithful servant of GOD, who is eighty-two years old. He turned eighty-two on (Saturday) August 27, 2016, exactly one day after his wife of sixty-one years, *went home to be with the Lord* (passed away). One day before his eighty-second birthday, his wife (*Lady T* or Momma Rose Thompson), with whom he had shared sixty-one years of marriage, *passed away* on Friday, August 26. *Lady T* went suddenly, as she had just been recently diagnosed in late May, with **stage 4 cancer** in her **brain and stomach**, shortly after her eightieth birthday. *Pastor T* himself, at this point, had already been *battling* his *own* rare form of **skin cancer**, for the past sixteen months or so. Now, his wife is gone! After a short *three months* **battle** (beyond her initial diagnosis), she **succumbed** to brain cancer. Pastor T, Momma Rose and I had originally met and (previously) began our ministry *partnership* about nine years earlier (in 2007) at *Camp Heavenly Waters*, a Christian Retreat and Youth Summer Camp in Wakefield, VA. During those nine years, they transported their youth and others from many different neighborhoods/communities to the Summer Camps each year, where I served in the capacities of *Camp Director* and *Senior Mentor* for male *campers* (attendees). However, my current assignment (with him) had taken on a far greater and more *personal* role over the last three years. In addition to *co-laboring* (together) in various **Evangelism Outreach** and Community Service activities, such as: mass *Potato Give-Aways*; Food and Clothing (Distributions); Volunteering at *Toys For Tots* Warehouse (Distributions of Toys to children of *Incarcerated* Parents, as well as other *disadvantaged/needy* children);

This was the **most devastating** ***blow*** that he could be hit with, at this point; because, he had already endured twelve major surgeries over the last seventeen years. Those included suffering a heart attack (on one occasion) and *flat-lining* (being lost on the operating table), and (then) being resuscitated (revived) on a couple of occasions.

Tuesday (*September 6, 2016*) was the first time, I saw **cancer face-to-face**. I mean I saw him <u>uncovered</u>, while assisting the nurse, as we had to change his clothes. And I could see the **cancer** on the outside of his body. If you ever see… We are not talking about *his head being* **bald**; I mean that I saw the *legions* (spots on his body) that were: rectangular, *red and* **raw** lumps like pieces of beef meat, just *sitting* on the outside of his body, on his chest (torso). Two of these *legions* were very large, each about *three inches wide by five inches long* (3x5), or about the size of an index card. Additionally, the skin on his *back*, from the armpit on one side to the armpit on the other side, had a very *rough* and thick, *wrinkled*, *black* and *crusty* surface, that resembled **burnt bark** on a tree's trunk (after a forest fire). Yesterday I saw that. And he said to me: *"Bishop, man—I just want to thank you; because, you just come. And you're willing to do this and do that. You* **demonstrate** *the* **love of GOD**; *you don't just talk about it. You show the action!* **I thank you**; *and,* **I love you***!"*

I responded to him (Pastor T)**:** *"No Sir, you do* **not** *have to thank me. There is no other place where I am supposed to be (right now). I am (here) in my* **assigned place***. So I am not here for you to* **thank** *me."*

I concluded my sermon (message) with two final statements. When you are *in your assigned place*, then, you have **Freedom (on the inside)**. Your *freedom* is *(internal) on the inside*, when you are: *in your assigned place*!

## PERSONAL REFLECTIONS

**Who I am; how I think; and what's my focus, motivation, and work ethic** can best be summed up in this poem that I'll share (below) with you. It's the very same poem that I shared with my soldiers on March 21, 1991 (or 21 Mar 91) in my initial **Change-of-Command Ceremony** speech, as their (new) *Incoming* Battery Commander in Kaiserslautern, Germany. I had, previously, been praying about (and meditating upon) exactly *what I needed to say* to my soldiers (in this speech), when I would address them for the very first time, as their new commander. About ten days before my pending ceremony and initial speech, I heard this poem, for the first time, in a church service and I thought that this poem accurately described Jesus's approach to life. I knew, as soon as I heard it, that this was

GOD's answer to my prayers: for the focus of my speech; because I had (consciously or unconsciously) already adopted and would continue to live according to this same perspective (outlook) for my entire life. It had been supernaturally deposited (imparted) into my spirit and character. So based upon my *past* experiences growing up in the *legally segregated* school system in Louisiana, and faced with the *reality* of the obvious challenges of life (yet to come), I had certainly adopted this perspective/approach to my job, life and the daily *personal* challenges that I knew I would still (later) encounter. After quoting the poem below (and acknowledging its author), I told my soldiers that I had just shared it with them for two reasons. First, so that they could understand how **I** would approach my **job** and LIFE every day; and secondly, so that they would, also, know how I would expect (demand) **them** to approach their jobs each day, as well.

Now, I share this same poem and ***outlook*** (on LIFE) with you, to encourage you to be determined to **always *give your best effort*** so that you can **make a positive impact or *make a difference.*** And like the Lord **JESUS** CHRIST**, don't** *limit your efforts* or *measure* your *success* by: **the awards** or **recognition** that you may or may not receive; **nor the crowds**, who may or may not follow. Instead, measure your (own) success, based upon: *you* always **doing *your best*** and your *personal **sacrifices**,* your ***serving*** *(others)* and your ***giving!***

## GIVE THE WORLD THE BEST YOU'VE GOT
(by African Bishop Montoye)

People can often be unreasonable, illogical, and self-centered.
<u>***LOVE***</u> **THEM**—ANYWAY!

If you do good, people will accuse you of selfish, ulterior motives.
<u>**DO *GOOD***</u>—ANYWAY!

If you are successful, you will win *false* friends and true enemies.
<u>***SUCCEED***</u>—ANYWAY!

The good you do today, will be forgotten tomorrow.
**DO <u>GOOD</u>—ANYWAY!**

Honesty and frankness make you vulnerable.
**<u>BE HONEST</u> and <u>FRANK</u>—ANYWAY!**

The biggest persons with the biggest ideas can be shot down by the smallest persons with small minds.
**THINK <u>BIG</u>—ANYWAY!**

People favor *Under-dogs*, but Follow only *Top Dogs*.
**YOU <u>FIGHT FOR</u> SOME <u>UNDER-DOGS</u>—ANYWAY!**

What you spend years building, may be destroyed overnight.
**<u>BUILD</u>—ANYWAY!**

People really <u>need</u> help, but may attack you if you help them.
**<u>HELP</u> THEM—ANYWAY!**

Give the world the best you've got, and you'll get kicked in the teeth—BUT
**<u>GIVE THE WORLD THE BEST YOU'VE GOT</u>—ANYWAY!**

Here is **the moral of this poem.**
Regardless of your circumstances, no matter what situation you find yourself in or where you are in *life's **struggles**—give it your **best*** and make a ***positive*** impact, while ***blessing others*** to *Glorify* God. Like Christ, be motivated to live your life from this perspective; **not** because, **you expect** it to be *easy*, *fun*, and full of *popularity* and *recognition*. Do this (instead), because, this will enable you to fulfill **GOD's *purpose*** for your life.

Eventually, I asked my soldiers (as I now ask you) to remember two things from me. First, remember that ***attitudes are contagious!*** <u>Each day</u>, ask yourself: *Is <u>Yours</u> Worth Catching?* Secondly, remember that as a ***servant***, you and I must realize—after I have **done *everything that I'm required to do*** (in service): **I am an *unworthy* ser-**

vant (**not** *worthy* of any rewards or accolades)—**because,** I have *only* done my *duty*! **(LUKE 17:7-10) PERSONAL REFLECTIONS (Continued)** I have never been or claimed to be **perfect** (in life) before; nor, am I *perfect **now***! However, there is an old (familiar) Gospel song entitled: *I Have Decided To Make JESUS My Choice*, that we (children) sang in our children's (Youth) choirs in our churches, during my childhood. I sincerely and *whole-heartedly* made that *personal* **decision** (or ***choice***), for myself, at the age of *six* or *seven* years old. At that age, I already knew that I (both) wanted to and would *live my life, for the Lord* and **serve** GOD for the rest of my natural life. Because that decision was whole-hearted and *non-negotiable,* I have never **regretted, waivered in** or thought about **reconsidering** my decision (***choice***). For the past fifty-two years (since that decision), regardless of: where I was, who I was with, what the situations (circumstances) were, what I had or did **not** have, where I was or how I got there, *I always realized (knew)—**WHOSE servant** I was*!

Oh, Trust me; I have *personally* experienced *my* **own** *pits and prisons* (like **Joseph** in the Bible), or *fires and storms* (in my own life)! As a young *negro* child, entering those old *segregated* schools (to *actualize* **integration** in 1969-1971) in Louisiana, I knew whose servant I was. While playing in our yards, neighborhoods or housing areas, as well as, walking to and from school, I knew whose servant I was. While playing sports, as a pre-teen and teenager (high school student), in city and school leagues, I knew whose servant I was. As a college student, faced with **opportunities** *to* **prove** *my loyalty*, in the midst of the *minefield* of **temptations** and **snares** (evil *vices* and traps set-up by Satan/the enemy of our souls), I knew whose servant I was.

When I was a college student and an adult, traveling across multiple Southern states (Louisiana, Mississippi, Texas) playing in softball tournaments (1981–87), I knew whose servant I was. As an *active duty* Army officer (*soldier* from 1985–2005), traveling around the world and working with some commanders and *"higher ranking"* (senior) officers, who *sometimes* inferred, tried to *coax* or directly requested that I do something unethical or alter some statistics/records for their benefit—I knew whose servant I was. During the past *nearly* fifteen years (since my retirement in 2005), there have been ***countless*** other opportunities, situations and circumstances to *change* my mind (decision) or to make a different choice. However, there is <u>*no*</u> *turning back*, for me! GOD has always (continuously) been, and still **is:** in every situation (<u>*with*</u> me), faithful and caused me *to triumph*; despite any buffeting, turbulence, or *backlash*. And <u>HE</u> continuously **does** that (over and over again) in my life, **not <u>*because*</u>** of me; but, He does it, despite or in spite of me (or my *imperfections*)! Therefore, I (still) know—whose servant I am.

# CHAPTER 5

# Whose Servant Are *You*?

"*I have always been a **servant**; but, I have **never** been a **slave**!*" (Rousell Thomas Jr.)

"***No man can serve two masters:*** *for either he will hate one, and love the other; or else, he will hold to the one, and despise the other. Ye cannot serve (both) GOD and Mammon.*" **(MATTHEWS 6:24** KJV)

"*Know ye not, that to whom ye yield yourselves **servants** to obey, his servants ye are to whom ye obey; whether of sin unto death, or of obedience unto righteousness?*" **(ROMANS 6:16** KJV)

"*For when ye were the servants of sin, ye were free from righteousness. But now being made free from sin, and become servants to GOD, ye have your fruit unto holiness, and the end—everlasting life.*" **(ROMANS 6:20, 22** KJV)

*Y*ielding yourself, as a servant to someone is a matter of the heart. When you submit yourself in this way, in order for that submission to be *genuine* (real), you must do it ***willingly,*** based upon your (personal) **permission and consent**! To be *forced*, coerced or placed in such a position or situation, by any other means is **never: *valid*, *legal*, *acceptable***—nor **binding**. *Remember*, as I have said before, **you** must determine or resolve within yourself: (1) **Who** you are; and (2) **Who** you **belong** to!" (Never allow someone else to determine or dictate this to you, or make this decision for you!) Additionally, I said that in every *situation or encounter*, you <u>always</u> have *two choices*; but you have to <u>see</u> them **both**! In the end, **Who: *you*** (<u>*whole-heartedly*</u>) submit to *as (your) master*, or pledge your loyalty to—will ultimately be the overwhelming factor in determining the decisions and choices you make. [Note: This is an individual **obligation** (*requirement*) for *personal* **resolution,** over and above the amount (or *lack*) of money, risk, consequences, etc., involved in the situation or the very *opportunity* (itself). To that end, GOD allows each person to demonstrate *freedom of* **choice**, as indicated by the previous scripture references.

Although you and I can choose <u>*Who*</u> we yield ourselves to **serve**, we do **not** get to choose <u>the</u> *processes*, that we must *go through*. Our *processes*, yours and mine, were and <u>are</u> *GOD-ordained*. Through the storms and fires, that have shaped and developed me, over the past fifty-eight years, I have been able to (both) submit and remain true to GOD's **process** for my life. In order to know, attempt to *visualize* or relate to, and understand my (*individual*) process, you would have to read another book, that I have written, entitled: **Emerged From Fires and Storms.** Suffice it to say, GOD used the accumulation of all those **forging** (*purifying*) and *consuming* **fires**, as well as, the **catastrophic** and *devastating* **storms**, which I faced and endured, before the age of ten years old (and ever *since*), along with the wisdom and influences of *positive* role models, to effectively lead me to profoundly **resolve** (within myself), that I would live my life **in service to GOD**. I didn't know exactly *how*, *where* or *what* all that would entail (yet at ten years old); but, the **who** and **whose** *servant I was (and still* **am** *today)* was already **resolved** (solidified *within me*), as a very young boy. And because my **decision** was *whole-hearted* (and settled in my spirit and heart, as well as in my mind), it has <u>*NOT*</u> vacillated, wavered or changed, over the years, from season-to-season, or situation to situation.

When I was an **eight-year** old elementary school student, *actively* participating in the ***integration*** of the public school system in Louisiana, I already knew: **who I was** and ***whose servant* I was**. So I *refused to buy into or accept* the ***racist*** labels and stereotypes that ignorant people tried to *shackle* or snare me with; but, I (also) *personally **refused*** to become a racist (myself) or to ***generalize*** (believe or think that ALL *Caucasian* or other people, who do **not** look like me, must be **dishonest**, **bigots** or ***worse***). Nor did I succumb to or allow any of the other challenges, injustices, or disappointments (in life) to separate me from GOD.

The biblical *Model **Servants***, that I referenced (earlier) in chapter 2 of this book, each faced his/her own, individual developmental *process* in life. **Joseph** faced and endured: the jealousy, hatred (resentment) and betrayal of his *brothers* (family); slavery (*physical bondage—twice*), *false* rape charges against him, *unjustified imprisonment*; to the King's Palace, etc. Yet this was his developmental **process**, through which these same <u>obstacles</u>, became the *building blocks*, that facilitated his *rise* to the climax of his ***service to GOD***. Thus, he was successful in accomplishing *GOD's* Plan and Purpose for his life, because he never rejected or aborted that *process*. **Joshua** faced and endured: the years of wandering in the wilderness (as a boy and young man); tests and challenges from the people (as their new *leader*); constant *wars and opposition* from the inhabitants/nations in order to occupy (take possession of) the Promised Land, etc.

**David** (both) faced and endured: the early responsibilities of keeping his father's herds; being sent back (kept) in his *shepherd's* role, after he had been *anointed* for ***Kingship***; the attacks from, and his conquering of, the lion and the bear, to recover his father's sheep; the challenge from and conquering of the giant *Goliath*; jealousy, resentment, pursuit and attempts (by King Saul) to murder him. **Ruth** had to face and endure: the loss of her husband (widowed) at a very young age; homelessness; loss of her own country and identity; entrusting herself and *whole-heartedly* committing her very life to her mother-in-law (Naomi; also *widowed* and without substance); acceptance of her mother-in-law's lifestyle, culture and GOD (**all** as her <u>own</u>); her submission to all of the counsel and instructions of Naomi. However, in so doing, she (Ruth) gained acceptance and favor of

Boaz; and (eventually), she also became *Boaz's wife*, birth *mother* to a son (Obed), *grandmother* of Jesse, *great grandmother* of David, and an *ancestor* in the lineage of Jesus (Christ). **Paul** (the *Apostle*) had to face and endure his *former* **lifestyle** of, and **choices** as, Saul of Tarsus (chief **persecutor** of JESUS'S *disciples* and the Gospel message); his *encounter* with The Lord (on the road to Damascus), and his subsequent *blindness* and *conversion*; initial mistrust and rejection of the other **Apostles** (JESUS'S original disciples); *persecution*, shipwrecks, hunger, *beatings*, afflictions, a personal *stoning* and *imprisonment* (all for the *Gospel's* sake). His genuine embracing of his *calling* and wholehearted *commitment* to the Gospel of Jesus Christ, propelled the Apostle Paul to successfully *evangelize* the **Gentiles** and to become the primary (foremost) writer of the New Testament scriptures commonly referred to as The **Epistles** or ((**Letters**) to the seven churches that he had established at Rome, Corinth, Galatia, Ephesus, Philippi, Colossae, Thessalonica, as well as, to other *servants* (of Jesus Christ) like: Timothy, Titus, and Philemon).

    Just as GOD had a specific Purpose, Plan and *Process* for each of them, so too, HE has for each of you (*readers*) and I. With that *absolute* **truth** (*certainty*) in mind, I did **not** write this book to put a **spot-light** on my own life or assignments, but, merely to cause or encourage each of you (readers) to ponder **your** own (GOD-given) *opportunities*, *assignments*, and (personal) *choices* in life as you **do** (that), just realize that the assignments, which GOD **assigns or calls you to,** are **not** *assignments of convenience* or *comfort*; **nor** *assignments of entertainment or pleasure*; and, they certainly will **not** be *choice, selective assignments of your own choosing* (like some **Dream** assignments that a celebrity, actor/actress or politician might graciously request or truly desire). In fact (initially), your assignments **will** even seem (or appear) to be: *unattractive, undesirable, unbearable, over-burdening* and/or *unacceptable* to you.

    However, you must be absolutely **certain** (*rest assured*) that these *GOD-appointed* assignments (*opportunities* **to serve**) have *eternal* significance; because each and **every** one of them has **embedded** (*built-in*) Power to trigger or *release* **Eternal** impacts and affects, as well as (**Eternal**) consequences for *multitudes or masses* of people. Even <u>unborn</u> (future) generations can be positively impacted (blessed)—through you; or, they may be *negatively* impacted (cursed or in bondage), as a result of your <u>current</u> choices/decisions.

> "*The question is <u>not</u>, if I stop and help this (needy) man, what will **happen to me**; the question is, if I **do not**—stop and help—<u>what will happen to **him**</u>*!" (Dr. Martin Luther King Jr.)

Therein lies the *significance* of <u>your</u> **decisions** and choices, of <u>**who**</u> and <u>**how**</u> you *choose to serve*: their ***potential to reach far beyond yourself** or just your immediate family*. This is why JESUS urged his disciples to **weigh the costs**!

That quote (above from Dr. MLK Jr.) was one of the most profound statements, though overlooked or lost in the magnitude and grand scheme (and not normally quoted), from his final speech on the eve (night) before his assassination.

In the end, it all *boils down to* two questions:

(1) Are <u>YOU</u> a *servant* or a *slave*? And,
(2) If a *servant*, Whose servant are you?

Remember, this is a personal ***resolution/decision*** (within your *core* being: *spirit* and *heart*, as well as, your *mind*) that each individual must make for himself or herself. Based upon the ***brevity** of life* (an awareness and appreciation for just how <u>short</u> and *uncertain* one's lifetime may be), *the **sooner (earlier)** this decision is **whole-heartedly made—the Better*** (for each individual). The three scriptures, that I referenced in the beginning of this chapter, also clearly ***reveals*** the connection (correlation) between: *who we yield ourselves **servant** to, the choices we make, and the things we are willing to do*. Therefore, another way to ask this critical question may be to ask: <u>*Who*</u> is your *spiritual **Father***? Or, as some *die-hard* New York Yankees fans might say: (*spiritually*) "*Who's Your Daddy?*" That's what they asked Pedro Martinez (in a *certain* span of *seasons*, during his Major League Baseball career). However, Pedro would play long enough to (eventually) get his days *to shine* (and *the last laugh* at), against those same *Yankees'* fans.

Unlike your *biological* father, whom you *could* **not**, nor *did **not*** **choose,** this <u>one</u> is totally**:** *up to you!* It **is** <u>your</u> choice; ***You*** **make the call (Decision)**! I know **Whose** servant I am.

***Whose servant*** *are* <u>*YOU*</u>*?*

# ABOUT THE AUTHOR

The author was born and reared in southern Louisiana, where he attended (both) the legally segregated (*Negro or colored*) school and the newly **integrated** school system of the Deep South in 1968–1971.

Since childhood, Rousell Thomas Jr. has continuously and consistently lived a *life of service* including: volunteerism, military service, ministry and community service. He graduated early from high school (in three years).

In conjunction with his graduation from college, he was simultaneously commissioned, as an *active duty* US Army Officer (2nd Lieutenant) in 1985. He was married to his wife (Georgette Clark Thomas) in September 1985, eight days before they reported to Fort Bliss, TX for his Officer's Basic Course. During a twenty-year *active duty* army career, the couple had four children (three daughters and one son). All their children are successful, college-educated adults now. Rousell and Georgette also have one granddaughter. Since his retirement from active military service in November 2005, the author has been continuing his *life of service* through active ministry and volunteerism (outreach and community service). Additionally, this author has been driven by a GOD-given passion and assignment for *serving* elderly and disabled citizens, around the world, since the age of eight. In ministry, he has sang in choirs; taught Sunday schools and Bible study groups, all over the world, since the age of thirteen years old. Additionally, he has preached in churches and served (ministered) on the streets, in hospitals and nursing homes/rehabilitation centers, around the world. Today, he is an **Elder** (in

Restoration Christian Church of Virginia or RCC-VA) and a functioning ***Evangelist*** (to the ***Body of Christ***) *globally.* Now, he has officially added the title of *AUTHOR* to his life's work, assignments, ministry and legacy.

CPSIA information can be obtained
at www.ICGtesting.com
Printed in the USA
BVHW032014181121
621821BV00002B/6